Enterprise Interoperability

Enterprise Interoperability

Research and Applications in the Service-oriented Ecosystem

Proceedings of the 5th International IFIP Working Conference IWEI 2013

Edited by
Martin Zelm, Marten van Sinderen
Luis Ferraira Pires, Guy Doumeingts

WILEY

First published 2013 in Great Britain and the United States by ISTE Ltd and John Wiley & Sons, Inc.

ISTE Ltd
27-37 St George's Road
London SW19 4EU
UK

www.iste.co.uk

John Wiley & Sons, Inc.
111 River Street
Hoboken, NJ 07030
USA

www.wiley.com

British Library Cataloguing-in-Publication Data
A CIP record for this book is available from the British Library
ISBN: 978-1-84821-662-4

Table of Contents

Foreword

IWEI 2013 Workshops
on Enterprise Interoperability

These proceedings contain the results of five workshops, which were held in conjunction with the 5th International IFIP Working Conference on Enterprise Interoperability (IWEI 2013) in Enschede, The Netherlands.

IWEI is a series of meetings targeting academics and practitioners interested in Enterprise Interoperability. The goal of the meetings is to accomplish information exchange and stimulate discussions on the latest developments, breakthroughs, ideas and challenges in this dynamic field. IWEI started as a spin-off of the IFIP Working Group on Enterprise Interoperability, WG5.8, with support from INTEROP-VLab. The first edition was in 2008, in Munich, Germany, in the form of a modest workshop. The following edition in 2009 took place in Valencia, Spain, again as a workshop, but with more participants. The third edition, in 2011, had the working conference status, granted by IFIP, and was organized in Stockholm, Sweden. During this edition it was for the first time that IWEI also comprised satellite workshops. In 2012, IWEI went outside Europe to Harbin, China, as a working conference without workshops. This year's edition therefore has been the second time that the IFIP Working Conference was organized together with satellite workshops.

The workshops took place on March 26, 2013, preceding the working conference held on March 27-28, 2013. The workshops were designed to address specific challenges and new issues within the scope of Enterprise Interoperability, and to provide ample opportunity for debating the content and consequences of presented ideas. Typically, the workshops solicited concrete intermediate or final results of current research projects and case studies that may guide future work. Specific areas of interest of the call were:

- Enterprise Interoperability in the service domain;

- Standardization for Enterprise Interoperability;

- Interoperability to support business-IT alignment;

- Case studies and experience reports on interoperability solutions;

- Selected applications and methods for Enterprise Interoperability.

The results contained in these proceedings include the papers presented at the respective workshops as well as short accounts of discussions and outcomes of each of the workshops. Overall, one can conclude that the workshops were successful in bringing forward and discussing current issues and approaches for which the working conference had less space. They also reconfirm the importance of Enterprise Interoperability in various application domains, where due to global competition and increased focus on core values, collaboration has to be more intense, more diverse and more dynamic. Moreover, such business level demands have to be aligned with proper support from information technology (IT) systems. Continuous developments at both the business and IT levels make the best choice of yesterday not necessarily the best choice of today. Generic and stable solutions should be standardized, and adoption of standards should be promoted to foster better interoperability. Change is however inherent to both business and technology. Standards thus provide only a partial solution; extending their scope too much would lead to overly complex or too rigid systems. Case studies and industrial experiences may provide useful information on how to cope with trade-offs in practical situations.

I would like to take this opportunity to thank all those who contributed to the five workshops of IWEI 2013. I am grateful to the Workshop Chair and the Workshop Organizers for launching the workshops, managing their contents, and ensuring their quality. I like to thank the authors for submitting content, which resulted in valuable information exchange and enriching discussions during the workshops. The participants of the workshops initiated the discussions, leading to interesting perspectives and useful feedback to the presenters. Finally, I like to acknowledge IFIP WG5.8 and INTEROP-VLab for their continuous support of Enterprise Interoperability research, and the University of Twente for hosting the workshops.

Marten van Sinderen
Associate Professor at University of Twente
IWEI 2013 Conference Program Chair
September 2013

Preface

IWEI 2013 Workshops
on Enterprise Interoperability

In the fast changing world of global economy governed by Enterprise Services and the Future Internet, enterprises will self-organize in distributed, interoperable, non-hierarchical ecosystems where the issues of Enterprise Interoperability need to be solved in a greater multi-view context throughout Enterprise Network.

This book contains the papers and summary reports of five workshops held on March 26, 2013, co-located with the Fifth International IFIP Working Conference on Enterprise Interoperability, IWEI 2013, organized at the University of Twente, Enschede, The Netherlands. IWEI is the International IFIP working Conference covering all aspects of Enterprise Interoperability with the goal to achieve cross organisational collaboration through integrated support of at business and technical levels

Complementing the conference, five Workshops explored new issues and innovative solutions of enterprise interoperability focusing on Service Engineering and particularly in the Manufacturing Service Ecosystem, with industrial case studies, applications and standards for interoperability. The workshops have been carried out discussing ongoing research to identify new solutions and research directions.

Workshop 1: Model Driven Services Engineering Architecture (MDSEA): a result of MSEE project. The goal of the workshop has been to present initial results of the MSEE (Manufacturing SErvice Ecosystem) project in the domain of the Servitisation. Starting from the selling of a product, enterprises are evolving towards the selling of services round the product. The MSEE project has developed models, methods and IT tools and case studies to support this transition. These results were presented during the workshop with the participation of industrial key persons who develop the service round the product using IT tools to support the transition

Workshop 2: Interoperability to support Business – IT Alignment. This workshop aimed at discussing the main research and industry challenges in Interoperability to support Business-IT alignment, including the role of new, innovative business models such as SaaS, Cloud, mobility and its European enterprises both in large enterprises and in SMEs.

Workshop 3: Standardisation for interoperability in the service oriented enterprise. The objective of this workshop has been to disseminate standardisation activities of the European project MSEE (Manufacturing Services Ecosystem) and to increase awareness of standards development in the frame of other European projects with focus on the service oriented enterprise. The workshop has addressed selected standardization topics in the field of Service Modelling languages, Service Life cycle Management and reference ontologies for the manufacturing enterprise.

Workshop 4: Case studies on enterprise interoperability – How It managers profit from EI research. The objective of this workshop has been to develop a first version of an industry-oriented and standardized use-case template. This template aims to bring together theoretical and practical views of enterprise interoperability. Interested IT managers respectively strategic decisions-makers should be provided with the latest scientific approaches and latest industrial experiences of Enterprise Interoperability. Practitioners should be enabled for a better evaluation of scientific approaches in Enterprise Interoperability by a collection of industrial use cases.

Workshop 5: Selected applications and methods for Enterprise Interoperability. Enterprise interoperability is a critical success factor for a sustainable economy and society, and as such it has to be handled in different application domains. In this workshop we discuss approaches to enterprise interoperability in a couple of domains - logistics, collaboration in the cloud and flexible staffing - aiming at identifying generic methods and best practices.

Martin Zelm
IWEI 2013 Workshop Chair
Coordinator Standardisation Group
INTEROP-VLab
September 2013

Workshop 1

Model Driven Services Engineering Architecture (MDSEA): A Result of MSEE Project

An Architecture for Service Modelling in Servitization Context: MDSEA[1]

Yves Ducq

IMS, UMR 5218, University of Bordeaux
351 Cours de la libération, 33405 Talence Cedex, France
yves.ducq@ims-bordeaux.fr

ABSTRACT: *Currently, manufacturing enterprises are progressively migrating from traditional product-centric business to product-based service-oriented virtual enterprise. This paper aims at presenting the service modelling architecture that is proposed in the frame of a FP7 project: MSEE. The proposed Model Driven Service Engineering (MDSE) architecture is adapted from MDA developed by OMG and from MDI model developed in INTEROP Network of Excellence. This architecture defines the various modelling levels and the related constructs to model based on servitization principles. The proposed modelling languages to represent these constructs at each level of MDSE will be presented at the same time. Templates to describe each concept will be also illustrated in example. Conclusions and perspectives are given in the end of the paper.*

KEYWORDS: *service system modelling, enterprise modelling, MDI/MDA approaches*

---

1. This paper is elaborated on the basis of MSEE deliverable D12.1: Service concepts, models and method: Model Driven Service Engineering – second version, WP1.1, MSEE consortium, 2013.

1. Introduction

In the economic context moving continuously, manufacturing enterprise, including SME's, are progressively migrating from traditional product-centric business to product-based service-oriented virtual enterprise and ecosystems [1]. In this sense, traditional companies have to cooperate in one or several virtual enterprises, considered as service systems dedicated to support the service design, development, and implementation. In order to facilitate this migration process, service system that will provide desired services around the product will have to be modelled, designed, implemented, tested and managed along its entire lifecycle in order to ensure the correct migration of the company.

This paper presents a second version of a model driven architecture with associated modelling formalisms which are the results of a research work performed in the frame of the FP7 MSEE Integrated Project [2]. Particularly, the goal of this work is to develop service system modelling language to support service system engineering and implementation. The approach adopted is to use Enterprise Modelling techniques as a basis under the Model Driven Service Engineering Architecture extended from Model Driven Architecture developed by OMG and Model Driven Interoperability approach developed in INTEROP Network of Excellence [3].

So, in a first part, the servitization process and the definition of what a service system is will be developed as well principles of system modelling. Then, the Model Driven Service Engineering Architecture will be presented insisting on its interest for the implementation of a coherent and complete virtual enterprise based on business models and on the description of each modelling level. The various levels of the architecture will be detailed as well as the required constructs to represent at each level based on the previous servitization principles. Then, enterprise modelling languages will be proposed to represent the constructs at each level. Finally, the perspectives of this work will be proposed.

2. Servitization and virtual organization as a service system

The studies and researches in the domain of Service have been mostly devoted to support tertiary sector domains (e.g. banking & finance, tourism, trade, public administration), with an obvious focus on ICT. At the end of the nineties, the concept of Service in Manufacturing appeared and the evolution from an economy of products towards an economy of services round the products becomes more and more important in manufacturing: this evolution is called *Product Service System (PSS)* or *Servitization*.

According to Wikipedia "a service is to make available a technical or intellectual capacity" or "to supply a work which will be useful for the user without material transformation".

Most of the time a service is opposed to a good. The following list characterizes a service [4]:

- A service is not owned, but there is a restricted access.

- Services have intangible results.

- Customers are involved in the service production process.

- Other persons than the customers can be involved in the service process as stakeholders, sub-contractors, etc.

- Quality in service is difficult to control while increasing productivity and also difficult to apprehend

- Service cannot be stored.

- Service delivery delay is crucial.

- Service delivery integrates physical and electronic way.

Since a decade, new research thinking has been emerging, trying to systematize the multi-disciplinary knowledge involved in service systems. On their web page, IBM describes service science as "a growing multi-disciplinary research and academic effort that integrates aspects of established fields like computer science, operations research, engineering, management sciences, business strategy, social and cognitive sciences, and legal sciences" [5].

In the computer science domain, Service Oriented Architectures (SOA), have revolutionized information systems, by providing software engineers with powerful methodologies and tools for decomposing complex systems into autonomous components. The final aim of such evolution is to support enterprise vital processes and workflows, by simple orchestrations and compositions in the hand of business specialists.

Clearly the servitization of manufacturing companies covers different levels of service provision and consequently different stages can be followed to evolve.

In servitization, the product is considered as the core element of the service to deliver to customers and subsequently we follow a manufacturing approach taking into account the market pressure that oblige to create new models in order to meet the servitization challenge. An appropriate concept to link products, product related services and the needs of the users is the "Extended Product" (EP) [6].

The Extended Product concept belongs to the category of Product-Service System. The Extended Product-Service is characterized by a layer model based on manufacturing product and defining the process extensions. The Extended Product is a complex result of tangible and intangible components.

The Core Product is the physical product that is offered to the market; while the Product Shell describes the tangible "packaging" of the product (e.g. one enterprise sells machine-tools and will add the maintenance which can be done by another company). Supporting Services are intangible additions, which facilitate the use of the product (e.g. maintenance plans or mobility guarantees). Differentiating Services provide individualization of the Extended Product on the market.

Then product extensions are described by the tangible and intangible aspects of a "utility package" to satisfy the customers' needs. They can be used to gain competitive advantage by offering added value to the customer. While in the past production costs, marketing, quality and reliability or time to market have been key success factors, nowadays innovation is the decisive characteristic [7].

The resulting Extended Product would be the specific solution satisfying the customers demand. As the solution can become very complex, several business partners may be collaborating for the provision of the EP in the frame of an Ecosystem.

Customers are looking for solutions and benefits (not only to acquire products) or even more they are requesting intangibles like leadership on the market, success, fame, etc. Manufacturers need to package their core products with additional services to make them more attractive.

The different stages of service provision are shown in Figure 1.

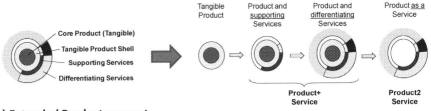

a) Extended Product concept

b) Servitization process

Figure 1. *From extended product concept to servitization process*

The first stage is the selling of a product (e.g. a machine tool).

The second stage which initializes the servitization process and the evolution toward Product+Service, start by adding a simple service (Product and supporting service) (e.g. the company will add a device on the machine-tool allowing to check continuously the running of the machine etc.).

The third stage (Product and differentiating service) is an evolution of the previous one. The service is more elaborated and increases the differentiation (e.g. the company can propose to sell the machine plus a service which guaranties a high percentage of availability of this machine).

The fourth stage, Product2Service scenarios are in contrast sharply decoupling manufacturing of goods and selling of services, where in most cases physical goods remain the property of the manufacturer and are considered as investment, while revenues come uniquely from the services (e.g. the company does not sell the machine-tools but sells hours of running of the machine-tool).

However, in this context, this is difficult for most of the companies to work alone in the Product2Service scenario but need to be associated to other companies all along the service life cycle. Working together in design and production networks results in an extension of companies' "ability to reach" e.g. wider markets and knowledge spheres, a higher level of the companies agility, as well as the possibility to share risks and resources. An industrial model for collaboration to exploit the various opportunities is a Virtual Manufacturing Enterprise (VME) (figure 2).

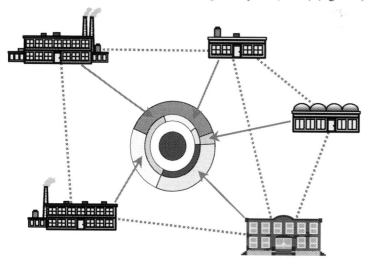

Figure 2. *Virtual Manufacturing Enterprise*

A virtual manufacturing enterprise (VME) is an enterprise that marshals more resources than it currently has on its own, using collaborations both inside and outside of its boundaries, presenting itself to the customer as one unit. It is a set of (legally) independent organizations that share resources and skills to achieve a mission/goal.

However, such a virtual organization must be implemented differently in the different phases of a service life cycle in order to support the service system as shown in figure 3 below.

So from a common Ecosystem (Service Manufacturing Ecosystem) composed of several kinds of companies as research centres, SME's, large companies, consultants..., it is possible to select the companies which will be virtualized for each stage of the life cycle.

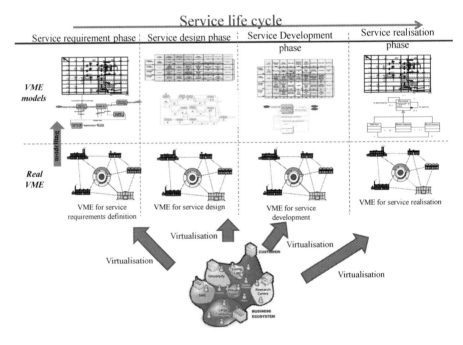

Figure 3. *Virtualisation of enterprises and modelling for each phase the service life cycle*

Then, the implementation of each VME must be done with agility and without spending too much cost, reaching an interoperable organisation. In order to do so, modelling of each VME will be done through a set of modelling languages used in the frame of a common model driven architecture. In this sense, the next part will present the proposed architecture, describing in detail each modelling level and the required constructs to represent based on the servitization principles.

3. Model Driven Service Engineering Architecture

The main interest of model driven approaches is to separate the different preoccupations from the business view of the product-service system to the technical preoccupations.

The proposed Model Driven Service Engineering (MDSE) Architecture is elaborated as an adaptation and an extension of MDA/MDI [8],[9] for the engineering of product related services in virtual enterprise environment.

The Model Driven Architecture (MDA) was defined and adopted by the Object Management Group (OMG) in 2001, and is designed to promote the use of models and their transformations to consider and implement different systems. It is based on an architecture defining four levels, which goes from general considerations to specific ones.

- CIM Level (Computation Independent Model) is focusing on the whole system and its environment. It is also named "domain model", it describes all work field models (functional, organisational, decisional, process…) of the system with an independent vision from implementation.

- PIM Level (Platform Independent Model): model the sub-set of the system that will be implemented.

- PSM Level (Platform Specific Model): that takes into account the specificities related to the development platform.

- Coding Level The last level consists in coding or more generally enterprise applications (ESA: Enterprise Software Application).

To complete this description, a Platform Description Model used for the transformation between PIM level and PSM level is added to these four kinds of models corresponding to four abstraction levels.

The "Model Driven Interoperability" (MDI) consists in the early consideration of interoperability between enterprises models. Then it guides keeping the models interoperable regardless of their abstraction level rather than only facing that problem at the coding step as it is frequently done in IT domain.

The MDI works were realised in the frame of the Task Group 2 (TG2) of INTEROP-NoE dedicated to define an approach inspired from OMG MDA. The goal is to tackle the interoperability problem at each abstraction level defined in MDA and to use models transformations techniques to link vertically the different levels of abstraction or horizontally to ensure interoperability of models at each level. The main goal of this methodology, based on model transformation, is to allow a complete follow-up from expressing requirements to coding of a solution and also a greater flexibility thanks to the automation of these transformations.

These architectures are presented in figure 4 below.

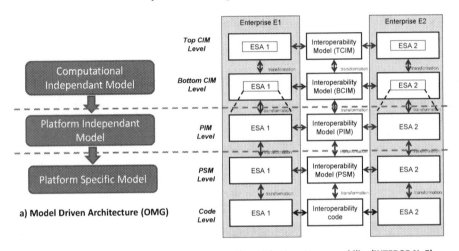

Figure 4. *MDA (a) and MDI (b) developed architectures*

Although MDA/MDI approached are more focused on IT system deployment, MDSE architecture aims to allow supporting the needs of modelling the three types of service system components (IT, Human and Physical Means). The main benefits of this model driven approach is to allow a continuum in the modelling from the business to the realisational level and to specify and implement a set of component coherent with the chosen strategy of collaboration in the virtual enterprise.

The adapted MDSE architecture is shown in figure 5.

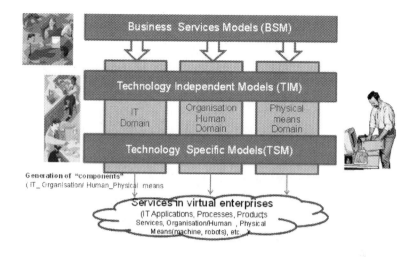

Figure 5. *MDSE architecture*

Similar to MDA/MDI, the proposed MDSE defines a framework for service system modelling around three abstraction levels: Business Service Modelling, Technology Independent Modelling and Technology Specific Modelling.

3.1. *The Business Service Modelling level and related constructs and languages*

The Business Service Modelling (BSM) aims to model the service system, at the global level, describing the running of the virtual enterprise, i.e. the running of the collaboration between the considered enterprises. The models at the BSM level must be independent to the future technologies that will be used for the various resources. In this sense, it's useful, not only as an aid to understand a problem, but also it plays an important role in bridging the gap between domain experts and the development experts that will build the service system (adapted [9]). In fact we develop the BSM in two sub-levels: the Top BSM and the Bottom BSM. The Top BSM sub level models the enterprise and its environment at a global level in order to analyse the possibilities to develop the System Service. The Bottom BSM will allow to model in details the domain concerned by the servitization process (we can use the languages defined by the local modeling). Based on this first analysis, the service system will be decomposed in the various components domains (IT, Organisation/Human and Physical Means) with a detailed description. For instance, at the BSM level (top and bottom), the decisions are listed but not the related decision makers are related decision support systems. Similarly, the type of resources doing the activities is listed but not the precise name or location of these resources. The concepts identified on the basis of the principles of servitization and virtual organization as presented previously are listed below:

o   Service

o   Product

o   Value

o   Customer

o   Partner

o   Stakeholder (provider, intermediary, designer,…)

o   Functionality

o   Resource (Human type, Physical mean type, IT type)

o   Process (business)

o   Organization (responsibility, authority)

o   Decision

o   Decision structure

o   Performance indicator

This list of concepts is considered as a list of core concepts.

Based on these concepts, several modelling languages can be used to represent the virtual organization at the BSM level as indicated in the figure 6 below:

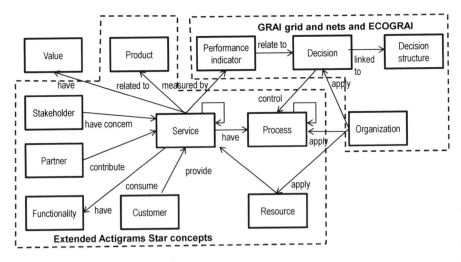

Figure 6. *Modelling languages at the BSM level*

MDSEA proposed to associate relevant modeling languages at each level in order to represent confidently the existing system and the future service product and service system. To achieve this goal, the standards for process modeling are gaining more and more importance, which gave rise to several process modeling languages and tools to enhance the representation of enterprise processes. To choose among the languages, the level of abstraction required is important.

At the BSM level, the modeling language must be simple to use, powerful and understandable by business oriented users. Moreover, this (or these) language(s) must cover process and decision with coherent models.

As indicated in figure 6, for process modeling at business level, Extended Actigrams Star (EA*) extended, from GRAI extended Actigram, that was itself derived from IDEF0, was chosen to model processes at BSM level due to its independence regarding IT consideration, its hierarchical decomposition and the fact it can model three supported resources: material, human and IT.

Moreover, GRAI Grid and nets were selected for modeling governance in a service system. GRAI Grid aims at proposing a cartography of company's decisions which controls business processes, as proposed for instance in the ISO 9000-2008 standard. The interest of GRAI Grid is to represent all decisions and their coordination, from the strategic to the operational levels. This representation is very important for business users because the results of decision making are also at the origin of performance evolution and achievement. GRAI nets allow us to detail the decision process execution, as the procedure description for the BP.

3.2. The Technology Independent Modelling level and related constructs and languages

Technology Independent Modelling (TIM) aims to represent the models at a second level of abstraction independent from the technology used to implement the system. It gives detailed specifications of the structure and functionality of the service system that do not propose technological details. More concretely, it focuses on the operation details while hiding specific details of any particular technology in order to be suitable for use with several different technologies. At TIM level, the detailed specification will be elaborated with respect to the components in the domains of IT, Organisation and Human and Physical means for a service system. So, the IT related modelling part aims at detailing the model of the enterprise application, but mainly in terms of functionalities which will be implemented and without defining which application will be chosen. The functionalities will be of course derived from the models at the BSM level. These functionalities will be classified according to their importance in order to prepare the future selection at the lower level. The functionalities can also cover the requirements in terms of interoperability with other systems implemented in one company of the ecosystem. The Physical mean part will be related to the means to add value to the product and to support the service production. At this level, the functionalities of a specific machine and the expected performances can be proposed but no name of specific machine is proposed. As for the IT part, the functionalities can be prioritized and synthetized in order to propose a questionnaire that would be sent to the various machine providers.

This is obvious that the functionalities are derived from the models, in particular the models of the physical system and business processes. The human resource part aims at defining the kinds of skills that are required according to the models. At this level, the name of a specific resource is not given but his/her place in the organization, his/her role in this organization and performance to reach must be detailed. This is obvious that this information can be derived, mainly from the decisional modelling and the business process modelling as well as from the physical models mainly for the persons directly involved in the product manufacturing and the service distribution. Moreover, this information will be sued for the recruitment or the move of specific human resource as well as for the planning of the training of existing resource.

Based on these principles, the following constructs are proposed to be represented in the models at this level:

o   Service

o   Process

o   Organisation

o   Resource

o   Organisation unit

o   Enterprise Application

o   Information

o   Human

o   Physical mean.

Based on these concepts, several modelling languages can be used to represent the virtual organization at the TIM level as indicated in figure 7 below:

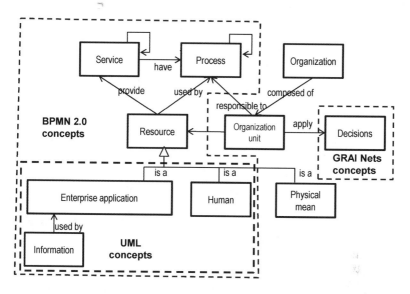

Figure 7. *Modelling languages at the TIM level*

At the TIM level, BPMN 2.0 was chosen in particular because this language offers a large set of detailed modeling construct, including IT aspects and benefits from the interoperability of many BPM IT platforms allowing the deployment and automated transformation to execution of BPMN processes. Moreover, BPMN enables also to represent human and technical resources which are required in the MDSEA principles of representation. BPMN has also the advantage to provide a meta-model developed by OMG which facilitates the implementation of the language. GRAI nets are proposed in order to detail the decision processes in coherence with the decisions identified in the GRAI Grid but with adding technical and organization information as the decision rules, the decision makers, and the decision support modules.

UML models are also proposed in order to model the enterprise applications related to information and human resources.

3.3. *The Technology Specific Modelling level and related constructs and languages*

Technology Specific Modelling (TSM) aims to combine the specification in the TIM model with details that specify how the system uses a particular type of technology (such as for example IT platform, Physical Means or Organisation with Human profile). At TSM level, modelling and specifications must provide sufficient details to allow developing or buying software/hardware components, recruiting human operators / managers or establishing internal training plans, buying and realizing machine devices, for supporting and delivering services in interaction with customers. For instance for IT component, TSM adds to the TIM, technological details and implementation constructs that are available in a specific implementation platform, including middleware, operating systems and programming languages. So, the IT related modelling part aims at detailing the model of the enterprise application, but mainly in terms of detailed functionalities which will be bought or developed in the chosen enterprise application. The functionalities will be of course derived from the functionality modelling at the TIM level. The detailed functionalities can also cover the requirements in terms of interoperability with other systems implemented in one company of the ecosystem. The Physical mean part will be related to the choice of a specific physical mean. At this level, the functionalities of a specific machine and the expected performances will be verify and tested. As for the IT part, the functionalities will be very detailed and detailed actigrams could be used. This is obvious that the functionalities are derived from the models at the TIM level. The human resource part aims at defining the specific resource which will be selected, to verify the appropriateness with his/her place in the organization, his/her role in this organization and performance to reach defined at the TIM level. This is obvious that this information can be derived, in coherence with the decisional modelling and the organization models at the TIM level

Based on the specifications given at TSM level, the next step consists in the realization and the implementation of the designed service system in terms of IT components (including coding) for automated information processing, machine/device components for material handling, and human resource and organization ensuring human related tasks/operations.

Based on these principles and the strong relationship with the TIM level, the following constructs are proposed to be represented in the models at this level:

- o   Service
- o   Process
- o   Organisation
- o   Resource
- o   Organisation unit
- o   Enterprise Application
- o   Information
- o   Human

o   Physical mean,

o   Layout

Based on these concepts, several modelling languages can be used to represent the virtual organization at the TSM level as indicated in figure 8 below:

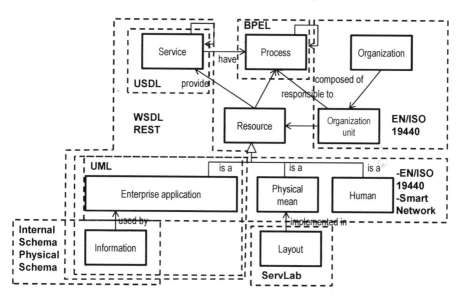

Figure 8. *Modelling languages at the TSM level*

4. Templates to describe the concepts at the BSM level

For each modeling construct defined in Figures 6 to 8, a template is also defined to describe in detail its attributes. The use of the whole or part of attributes is determined by each case and the objectives of the modeling.

The advantage of using the template is to avoid the ambiguity in the construct semantic.

The example of service construct template is given below in figure 9. The service template aims at describing service information collected from end-users. Because the service is here defined as a complementarity of the product, the concept is different than the one used in IT in the SOA approach or in the Service Oriented Modelling.

Header	
Construct label	['Service']
Identifier	[Identifier of the service instance]
Name	[name of the service instance]
Body	
Description	[Short textual description of this service instance]
Objective	[Short textual description]
Constraint	[Short textual description]
Relationships to other model elements	
PRODUCT	[Identifier/name of Product concerned by the service: described by Product template]
FUNCTIONALITY	[Identifier/name of functionality of the service: described by Functionality template]
RESOURCE	[Identifier/name of Resource providing the service: described by Resource template]
PROCESS	[Identifier/name of Process providing the service: described by Process template]
CUSTOMER	[Identifier/name of Customer consuming the service: described by Customer template]
PERFORMANCE INDICATOR	[Identifier/name of the performance of the service: described by Performance template]
VALUE	[Identifier/name of the Value of the service: detail will be described by Value template]
STAKEHOLDER	[Identifier/name of the Stakeholder: detail will be described by Stakeholder template]
PARTNER	[Identifier/name of the Partner: detail will be described by Partner template]
Other Relationships	
RELATED TO MODEL LEVEL	[Refer to BSM, TIM, TSM modeling level]: BSM
RELATED TO SLM PHASE	[Refer to service lifecycle phases]: Requirement

Figure 9. *Service template at the BSM level*

5. Conclusion

In order to face the competitiveness, companies must progressively migrate from traditional product-centric business to product-based service-oriented virtual enterprise and ecosystems. In order to do so, they must create different virtual manufacturing enterprises all along the service life cycle. To support the migration, enterprise modelling must be used to allow a progressive implementation of these VME in the frame of a common architecture as MDSE architecture proposed in this work with ensuring a continuum in the modelling, coherent from the business to the technological level and to separate the preoccupations of different actors of the system design and exploitation. The related constructs required to represent at each modelling levels are derived from the servitization and virtual organization principles. Chosen modelling languages are proposed at each modelling level as well as templates to detail each concept and avoid misunderstanding in the modelling.

Several applications are now conducted to apply the MDSEA and the related modelling languages.

The main perspectives of this work concern the transformation of languages from BSM to TIM and from TIM to TSM in order to reach the final implementation of the service system.

6. References

FP7 – FoF-ICT-2011.7.3 - Manufacturing SErvice Ecosystem Project- Annex 1 description of work – July 29th 2011

http:// www.ibm.com/ developerworks/spaces/ssme.

Jagdev, H. S.; Browne, J.: "The Extended Enterprise. A Context for Manufacturing". In: Production Planning & Control, 9 (1998) 3, S. 216-229

Lovelock, Christopher, Jochen Wirtz and Denis Lapert - Marketing des Services, Paris, France: Prentice Hall, 2004, 2nd ed., pp 619 ISBN 2-7440-7026-2

MDA - The Architecture of Choice for a Changing World [Online] // Object Management Group. - January 2008. - http://www.omg.org/mda/.

MDI: Model Driven Interoperability; Available at: http://www.modelbased.net/mdi/; Accessed on: 15th March 2010.

Thoben, K.-D., Jagdev, H., Eschenbächer, J. (2001) Extended Products: evolving traditional product concepts. In: K.-D. Thoben, F. Weber and K.S. Pawar (ed.) Proceedings of the 7th International Conference on Concurrent Enterprising: "Engineering the Knowledge Economy through Co-operation" Bremen, Germany, June 2001.

A Set of Templates for MDSEA

David Chen

IMS, University of Bordeaux
351 Cours de la libération, 33405 Talence, France
david.chen@ims-bordeaux.fr

ABSTRACT: *This paper presents a set of templates defined as part of a service modelling language for the design and implementation of service system in a Virtual Manufacturing Enterprise (VME) environment. The templates are defined under the Model Driven Service Engineering Architecture (MDSEA) at its three modelling levels: BSM (Business Service Modelling), TIM (Technology Independent Modelling) and TSM (Technology Specific Modelling). Metamodels of modelling constructs, for which the templates are defined, are presented as well. Conclusions are given at the end of the paper.*

KEYWORDS: *service modelling, enterprise modelling, model driven architecture, template*

1. Introduction

Within the frame of the European FP7 MSEE Integrated Project (Manufacturing Service Ecosystem) [5], a Model Driven Service Engineering Architecture (MDSEA) and a service Modelling Language are developed to support service system engineering in Virtual Manufacturing Enterprise (VME) environments. This paper aims at presenting a set of templates which are part of proposed service modeling language. Those templates are used to capture and structure relevant model information of a service system. The paper is organized as follow: section 2 recalls modeling language constituents as defined in EN/ISO 19440 and presents MDSEA. Section 3 gives an overview on the service modeling constructs defined at BSM level and its associated templates. Section 4 deals with service modeling constructs defined at TIM and TSM levels and their related templates. Section 5 gives the conclusions and discusses future works.

2. Basic concepts and principles

The templates presented in this paper have been defined in the service modeling language under MDSEA architecture [7].

A modeling language is defined by a set of modeling constructs. Construct(s) can be represented by: (a) graphical representation, (b) template description, and (c) text. This paper focuses on templates and other parts of the language can be found in [6]. A template contains a header part to identify a construct instance, and a body part to describe the particular instance with descriptive and relationship attributes [3]. The proposed service modeling language is consistent to enterprise modeling language constituents defined in EN/ISO 19440 standard [3].

A Model Driven Service Engineering Architecture (MDSEA) is elaborated on the basis of MDA/MDI [1],[2],[4] to allow supporting the needs of modelling the three types of service system components (IT, Human and Physical Means). This MDSEA is considered as adaptation and extension of MDA/MDI to the engineering of product related services in virtual manufacturing enterprise environment. Similar to MDA/MDI, the proposed MDSEA defines three abstraction levels [6]:

- Business System Modelling (BSM), which specifies the models, at the global level, describing the running of the enterprise or set of enterprises as well as the links between these enterprises.

- Technology Independent Modelling (TIM), which are the models at a second (lower) level of abstraction independent from the technology used to implement the system.

- Technology Specific Modelling (TSM) that combines the specification in the TIM model with details that specify how the system uses a particular type of technology (such as for example IT platform, Physical Means or Organisation with particular Human profiles).

3. Service modelling constructs and templates at BSM level

A set of service modelling constructs[1] are identified to represent service system at BSM level. Figure 1 shows those constructs and their relationships.

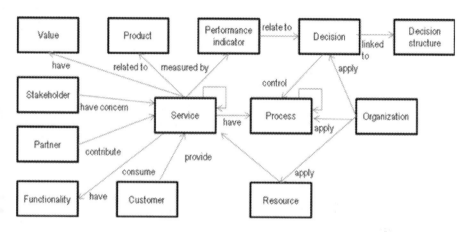

Figure 1. *Modelling constructs*
and their relationships at BSM level

Because of the page limit, only some of the templates are presented in the paper. Interested authors can read [6] for complete specification of all the templates.

Figure 2 presents Customer template. It aims at describing generic characteristics of targeted customers consuming the service. The header part gives the identity of a customer instance to describe. The body part contains a set of attributes to be specified at the BSM level of MDSEA. Additional attributes can also be added according to the needs of modeling. Customer information will be used to better define the service and the system that will provide the service.

---

1. Construct = Concept + its representation (template, graphics, text).

Header	
Construct label	["Customer"]
Identifier	[Identifier of the customer instance]
Name	[name of the customer instance]
Body	
Categories	[Worker, farmer, student,...]
Level of education	[short textual description]
Gender and age	[Short textual description]
Annual revenue range	[Short textual description]
Targeted frequency of service use	[Short textual description]
Wish and requirement	[Short textual description]
Constraint	[Short textual description]
Relation to other model elements	
SERVICE	[Identifier/name of Service concerned by the customer: described by Service template]
Other Relationships	
RELATED TO MODEL LEVEL	[Refer to BSM, TIM, TSM modelling level] : BSM
REALTED TO SLM PHASE	[Refer to service lifecycle phases] : Requirement

Figure 2. *Customer template*

Figure 3 presents process template. Process defines the sequence of execution of a set of sub-processes and activities. In a service system, various types of services are necessary such as service booking process, service delivery process, service planning service, supply service, maintenance process etc.

Header	
Construct label	[Process]
Identifier	[Identifier of the process instance]
Name	[name of the process instance]
Body	
Objective	[Short description of the process objective]
Trigger	[Condition this process instance is triggered]
Result	[Output of this process instance]
Constraint	[Constraint that may apply on this process instance]
Sub-process	[List of sub-process] [Graphical representation] Example: IDEF3 Process diagram
Relations to other model elements	
SERVICE	[Identifier/name of service concerned by the process: described by Service template]
RESOURCE	[Identifier/name of resource used by the process: described by Resource template]
Other Relationships	
RELATED TO MODEL LEVEL	[Refer to BSM, TIM, TSM modelling level] : BSM
REALTED TO SLM PHASE	[Refer to service lifecycle phases] : Requirement

Figure 3. *Process template*

NOTE: At the BSM level, process can be further detailed and modeled using some existing business-user oriented process modeling languages such as IDEF3, GRAI extended actigram, process language of ARIS and IEM, etc.

4. Service modelling constructs and templates at TIM/TSM level

The set of constructs defined at BSM level need to be mapped or feather detailed at TIM level. Figure 4 shows the set of constructs to use at TIM level. The modeling objective at TIM level focuses on detail characterization of resources needed to provide the required service.

According to ISO 19440, resources are of three types: IT related, Human related and Machine related (physical means). A service can be provided by one or any combination of these three types of resources.

The modeling constructs at TSM level are basically the same than those defined at the TSM level with complementary information for implementation and they are not presented in the paper.

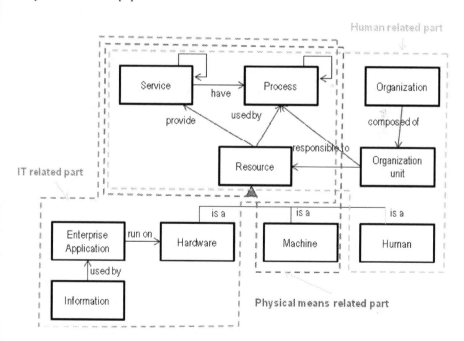

Figure 4. *Modelling constructs*
at TIM level

Figure 5 shows the Service template defined at the three levels of MDSEA. Generally speaking, information collected at BSM level mainly comes from business people, while at TIM and TSM levels, they are concerned with technical people and engineers.

Header		
Construct label		['Service']
Identifier		[Identifier of the service instance]
Name		[name of the service instance]
Body		
BSM	Domain	[Domain of the service]
	Description	[short textual description of this service instance]
	Objective	[Short textual description]
	Constraint	[Short textual description]
	Nature	['Physical' or 'Information' or 'human']
TIM	Decomposition	[List of decomposed sub-services]
	Composition	[List of services that compose this service]
	Access	[Specify how, where and when is a service made available]
	Consumption	[Specify what is expected where and when by different parties participating in service]
	Automation level	[Specify the decided automation / computerization level]
TSM	Material handling	[Implementation description on material handling aspect] Example: Material handling (for illustration only)
	Information processing	[Implementation description on automated information processing aspect]
	Human intervention	[Implementation description on human activity aspect]
	Other aspects	[Any other implantation issues]

Figure 5. *Service template*

Figure 6 presents the process template defined at TIM and TSM levels. Process modeled at BSM level will be detailed with complementary information in order to get an executable process model at TSM level for implementation.

Figure 7 presents Organisation template defined at the three modelling levels. Organisation modelling aims at specifying how responsibility and authorization are defined and implemented in a service system. At the BSM level, organisation structure is defined at high abstraction level (type, main functions and relationships). At the TIM level, more technical details on the organisation structure will be given in terms of who is responsible for what and who is authorized to do what. At TSM it is necessary to give complementary information on various implementation issues such as for example to assign responsibility to persons in the service system.

	Header	
	Construct label	[Process]
	Identifier	[Identifier of the process instance]
	Name	[name of the process instance]
	Body	
BSM	Objective	[Short description of the process objective]
	Trigger	[Condition this process instance is triggered]
	Result	[Output of this process instance]
	Constraint	[Constraint that may apply on this process instance]
	Sub-process	[List of sub-process] [Graphical representation] Example: IDEF3 Process diagram
TIM	Workflow	[Description of workflow] Example: BPMN Workflow Diagram
SIM	Execution	[Description of process execution] Example: BPEL process

Figure 6. *Process template*

	Header	
	Construct label	[Organization]
	Identifier	[Identifier of the Organization instance]
	Name	[name of the Organization instance]
	Body	
BSM	Type	[Hierarchical, networked, decentralized, centralized,...]
	Description	[Give a graphical representation of the organization structure]
TIM	Responsibility relationships	[Textual description and graphical representation] Example: Responsibility matrix
	Authorization relationships	[Textual description and graphical representation] Example: Authorization matrix (IBM)
TSM	Additional implementation descriptions	[Description on where/how the organization is to be implemented]

Figure 7. *Organisation template*

5. Conclusion and perspective

This paper presents the templates defined as part of the service modeling language under MSDEA architecture. A template allows capturing and structuring model information in a neutral format, thus facilitating transformation and interoperability. It is complementary to the graphical representations used in some existing modeling languages. Model information can be stored in template form independently of its graphical representation. A particular graphical representation can be reconstructed from template according to the need of a specific end user. Future work consists in performing some significant case studies to refine and validate the templates. Another work to be done is to define explicit links between templates at BSM level and templates at TIM and TSM levels in the case where automate transformation/mapping between those levels are required.

6. References

D. Chen, Y. Ducq, G. Doumeingts, G. Zacharewicz and T. Alix, 'A model driven approach for the modelling of services in a virtual enterprise', *Proceedings of I-ESA'12 international conference*, 2012.

EN/ISO 19440, Enterprise Integration – Constructs for Enterprise Modelling, International Standardisation Organisation, 2007.

MDA – The Architecture of Choice for a Changing World [Online] // Object Management Group – January 2008 – http://www.omg.org/mda/.

MDI: Model Driven Interoperability; Available at: http://www.modelbased.net/mdi/; Accessed on 15 March 2010.

Miller Joaquin and Mukerji Jishnu MDA Guide Version 1.0.1 [Report] – [s.l.]: OMG, 2003 – Document Number: omg/2003-06-01.

MSEE Deliverable 11.1, Service concepts, models and method: Model Driven Service Engineering, 2011.

MSEE, Manufacturing SErvice Ecosystem, Annex I - "Description of Work", project agreement n°284860, 29 April 2011.

Workshop 2

Interoperability to Support Business–IT Alignment

Report Workshop 2

Ip-Shing Fan* — Victor Taratoukhine** — Martin Matzner**

* Cranfield University
Bedford MK43 0AL, United Kingdom
1i.s.fan@cranfield.ac.uk

** ERCIS – Headquarters, Münster, Germany
Leonardo-Campus 3
48149 Münster, Germany
victor.taratoukhine@ercis.uni-muenster.de
martin.matzner@ercis.uni-muenster.de

The workshop attracted a wide ranging set of papers covering the geographical areas of German, Russia, South Africa and UK; representing developed Europe, BRIC and developing countries. The papers also have a wide range of business applications and covered aircraft maintenance, IT support incidents, printing and oil and gas. The 14 workshop participants had lively exchanges as each paper was presented and shared thoughts at the plenary. The following summarises the discussion along the key themes.

1. Future Business Scenario

Business IT alignment needs to consider developing and future business scenarios and applications. The key contexts that need to be considered are mobile platforms, cloud computing and the technology maturity and culture of developing countries. The particular challenges of developing countries where small business cannot afford on premise assets and have to lean on large corporate entities like telcos, banks to create the business eco-system infrastructure represents a business dynamics not seen in developed countries. However, this is an interesting model for creating innovative new services.

2. Interoperability challenges

The associated interoperability has to address the technical challenge of large scale and disparate infrastructure, and the business challenges of intellectual property protection and financial payment systems.

3. Business Process Modelling methods

It was agreed that there is still no universal common modelling language. Tools that are reported in the papers and in discussion included BPMN 2.0, BP Canvas, DEMO IBM Websphere Business Modeller and OctoProz.

Pen and paper, open brainstorming and mind mapping were also used as effective ways to capture process description from stakeholders. They are easy to use but suffer from difficulties to scale up to large models.

The ideal BP modelling tool should allow checks to ensure model consistency, allow re-use of model elements and support easy export to data modelling and programming tools.

The availability of BP reference models to allow compliance check would be desirable. Further work on ontology and semantic interoperability should bring domain expertise to the modelling tools.

4. Conclusion

Business model as a tool to align business operation and IT was an implicit assumption in the workshop. The discussion brought together the wide range of expertise and experience from the participants and sparked ideas for further work.

Interoperability as a Catalyst for Business Innovation

J.H.P. Eloff* — M.M. Eloff** — M.T. Dlamini* — E. Ngassam*** D. Ras*

* SAP Mobile Empowerment
Department of Computer Science, University of Pretoria
Pretoria, South Africa
jan.eloff@sap.com
moses.dlamini@sap.com
dirk.ras@sap.com

** ICC, University of South Africa, South Africa
eloffmm@unisa.ac.za

*** SAP Mobile Empowerment, Pretoria, South Africa
Faculty of ICT, Tshwane University of Technology, Pretoria, South Africa
ernest.ngassam@sap.com

ABSTRACT: *The core notion for enforcing, supporting and enabling communication and collaboration amongst stakeholders in a given business ecosystem can be regarded as Interoperability. Interoperability is not a new concept nor is there a standardised definition for the term interoperability. From a scientific and business point of view interoperability was already discussed as early as in 1990's. Developing a common understanding of interoperability is a difficult task. However, while businesses perceive interoperability as the realisation of collaborative partnerships amongst peers, a closer look at the terminology from a technological perspective may regard interoperability as an enabler of business collaboration. This paper seeks to demonstrate how interoperability can serve as a catalyst for business innovation. This is achieved by exploring its core definitions and illustrating relevance and applicability thereof through a use case that enforces value co-creation amongst business ecosystem partners (and therefore business innovation).*

KEYWORDS: *interoperability, business innovation, mobile-cloud, business services, SMMEs*

1. Introduction

Current trends in conducting business on a worldwide level are materialized through sound partnership establishment and enablement of effective and efficient communication and collaboration relationships amongst role players in the business ecosystem. Whether one looks at it from a B2B, B2C or B2B2C perspective, collaboration in businesses has become a critical business success factor. In fact, it is regarded as one of the key elements for business sustainability and growth. Therefore, there are seldom enterprises in these modern days that can claim to do business in isolation.

The core notion for enforcing, supporting and enabling communication and collaboration amongst stakeholders in a given business ecosystem can be regarded as Interoperability. In this case, attention has to be given in terms of technical interoperability and business interoperability. From a business point of view, collaboration and communication amongst business ecosystem partners following a set of standardised protocol agreements regarding business transactions can be considered as enterprise interoperability. However, from a technical perspective, interoperability may be regarded as a paradigm aimed at enforcing cooperation amongst software agents designed to support businesses' operational goals. Many reports from businesses abound on the Internet indicating that the main challenge regarding interoperability is the seamless operation and interfacing of various components sourced from different and multiple providers.

A renewed focus is necessary to investigate how to enable interoperability in today's advanced technological landscape. Therefore, this research sets itself the goal of investigating the benefits of interoperability for business innovation.

The remainder of this paper is structured as follows: In Section 2 explores the concept of interoperability further, culminating in a working definition for this research. Our working definition refers to cloud infrastructures and it also forms the implementation platform for the Business in Your Pocket (BiYP) use case discussed later on in this paper. It is for this reason that Section 3 provides a discussion from a positioning point of view with regard to interoperability and cloud infrastructures. In Section 4 we demonstrate the significant contribution of cloud computing to interoperability from a business and IT network perspective.

2. Interoperability defined

Interoperability refers to the capability of different systems to work together. Some of the initial interoperability research date back to the 1980s with work done by Lavean (1980) on interoperability in defence communications. Another area indirectly related to interoperability is Computer Supported Co-operative Work, which gained popularity during the 1990s with software programs such as Lotus Notes (Lotus Notes, 2013). Lotus Notes is a multi-user client-server cross platform application developed by IBM, creating an integrated environment for applications such as email, calendars, instant messaging and even a full office productivity suite to name but a few.

Interoperability is defined by IEEE as: "The ability of two or more systems or components to exchange information and to use the information that has been exchanged" (IEEE Standard Computer Dictionary, 1990). This definition mention two aspects namely the exchange of information and then the use of such information. Another definition states, "Being able to accomplish end-user applications using different types of computer systems, operating systems, and application software, interconnected by different types of local and wide area networks" (O'Brien *et al*, 2008) which mentions specific components.

Enterprise interoperability is defined as the ability of enterprises to interact within a collaborative process, (Mallek *et al*, 2012) or "a field of activity with the aim to improve the manner in which enterprises, by means of Information and Communications Technologies (ICT), interoperate with other enterprises, organisations, or with other business units of the same enterprise, in order to conduct their business. This enables enterprises to, for instance, build partnerships, deliver new products and services, and/or become more cost efficient" (Li *et al*, 2006).

The European Commission's definition states Interoperability as "the ability of ICT systems and of the business processes they support, to exchange data and to enable the sharing of information and knowledge" (European Interoperability Framework, 2004)

To a certain extent the above definitions are all similar and collectively contain all the elements. Therefore, the following working definition will be applicable in the cloud computing environment as discussed in this paper:

> *Interoperability is defined as the ability of two or more different entities to effectively communicate, interact within a collaborative process through the flexible exchange of data and information and through knowledge sharing, where an entity includes, but are not limited to, an organisation, a network of businesses and/or infrastructures such as cloud, enterprise, device, system, communication channel, or a software tool.*

This definition needs to address the challenges of interoperability in the cloud environment, which follows in the paper.

3. Interoperability and cloud infrastructures

Establishing an interoperable business environment taking into consideration state-of-the-art IT infrastructures, supporting today's business environments, will be incomplete without recognizing the important role that advancements in cloud computing can play. It is therefore important to consider key interoperability concerns that arise from the cloud-computing paradigm. Most of these concerns stems from two competing goals:

– Consumers of services in cloud environments want to have the flexibility and mobility to seamlessly move from one business to the other

– Providers of services, businesses who are channelling their services to consumers via clouds, increasingly want to lock consumers of services into their proprietary solutions for maximizing their revenue streams.

This section provides a review of the current research efforts aimed at finding a balance between these two competing goals and thereby promoting the interoperability feature of cloud infrastructures

According to Gartner's hype cycle curve, cloud computing has passed the peak of inflated expectations (2 – 5 years towards mainstream adoption) and is now moving beyond the hype into the trough of disillusionment (5 - 10 years toward mainstream adoption) (LeHong et al, 2012). This is the point where every firm seems to be strategically positioning themselves toward a cloud-centric approach and getting ready to reap the benefits thereof. Cloud computing is a relatively young market that is still at its infancy in terms of adoption stages and fast moving toward mainstream adoption. In support Loutas et al. (2011) asserts that cloud computing is young, chaotic and highly fragmented with just a handful of dominant providers (i.e. Amazon, Google, SalesForce, Microsoft, VMware) who are fighting to gain market dominance and promote their incompatible standards and formats.

Furthermore, to demonstrate that this market is young, there are several definitions of cloud computing that exist in literature and for a snapshot of these, the reader is directed to the work of Wyld (2009). It must be noted though that most researchers make reference to the widely used definition provided by NIST (Mell et al, 2009). However, there is still no standard definition of cloud computing. Hence, Jansen et al, (2011) argue that cloud computing means different things to different people, which somehow explain the different variants of cloud services in the market.

It is therefore no coincidence that the early adopters of this computing paradigm are faced with the problem of too many different cloud service providers offering heterogeneous services, with a variety of APIs (Application Programming

Interfaces), different implementations for similar cloud service offerings, heterogeneous data formats etc. For example, different providers offer different hypervisors, such as Amazon's EC2, Microsoft's Hyper-V, VMware's ESX and ESXi, Citrix's XenServer etc. Each of these uses heterogeneous formats of virtual machines.

Due to the heterogeneity problem, users are faced with many uneven and inconsistent cloud systems. Therefore, users or cloud-based applications of such systems are forced to interact with them using different APIs. Each time a user thinks about moving their data to the cloud, they are required to first find out if the intended cloud provider will have the necessary APIs for them to connect their on-premise applications to be able to process the cloud hosted data. This has also led to the proliferation of cloud APIs (Lawton, 2009; Parameswaran *et al*, 2009).

The heterogeneity problem is stifling the growth and adoption of cloud computing (Parameswaran *et al*, 2009). This has exacerbated the problem of vendor lock-ins, which stifles mobility and makes it hard for users to migrate their data or applications from one cloud platform to the next. This also inhibits users from leveraging on other cloud services provided by other vendors. Hyek *et al*. (2011) argues that the biggest issue is related to how clients' on-premise infrastructure, applications and data interact with cloud based systems resources. As an example, consider a client's database that has been migrated to the cloud, which might still require interaction with on-premise systems. The other issue stated in Hyek *et al*. (2011) stems from orchestration of resources from multiple providers to be able to provide coordinated services that scale with the demands of the clients.

Hence, there is a big gap between cloud clients and providers and also between the various cloud providers themselves that has made clients' data and applications to remain in pockets of fragmented cloud silos. This has created a surging need for research efforts that would help breakdown the cloud silos and closes this gap to provide seamless interoperability among and between cloud providers and their clients. Loutas *et al*. (2011) argues that interoperability can help overcome the heterogeneity challenge in order to unlock greater innovation on the cloud, level the field of play and create a healthy competitive cloud environment that result in the creation of Intra- and Inter-cloud the cloud of clouds (which they refer to as the interconnected cooperating and collaborating clouds). Similar to how the Internet was formed, this would potentially lead to the establishment of an open cloud vision.

Hence, several researchers (Gasser *et al*[1], 2012; Gasser, *et al*[2], 2012; Petcu, 2011; Schubert *et al*, 2012; Claybrook, 2011; Hyek *et al*, 2011; Parameswaran *et al*, 2009) are beginning to seriously consider the overlooked issue of interoperability in the cloud. They rank this issue on a high priority amongst other key challenges (such as security, privacy, multi-jurisdiction, multi-tenancy etc.) inhibiting a widespread adoption of cloud services and argue that it must be afforded the necessary attention that it deserves.

In response, several standards and industry consortia are working toward developing specifications and best practices that would enable interoperability on the cloud in all dimensions (Lawton, 2009). These include the Cloud Computing Interoperability Forum (CCIF); Distributed Management Task Force (DMTF); Open Virtualization Format (OVF); Open Cloud Manifesto (OCM); Open Cloud Consortium (OCC); Global Inter-Cloud Technology Forum (GICTF); Open Cloud Computing Interface (OCCI); Open Cloud Interoperability Framework (OCIF); Object Management Group (OMG); Cloud Computing Working Group (CCWG); Intel's Open Data Center Alliance (ODCA) etc. For more information the reader is directed to the work of Loutas *et al.* (2011).

Furthermore, the European Commission under the banner of Future Internet Assembly has funded a number of research projects aimed at unpacking and addressing the issue of cloud interoperability. These include the Standards and Interoperability for e-Infrastructure Implementation Initiative (SIENA); Cloud4SOA; mOSAIC Contrail; SAIL; IoT-A; REMICS.

What have we learned? Considering all the above aspects depicting the interplay between interoperability and cloud computing the conclusion easily can be that it lacks structure-enabling enterprises to implement an interoperable networked-business environment. Should the focus be on end-to-end integration on the protocol level or should it be on interoperable services? Hence, this research proposes a generic architecture that enterprises can use not only to improve their understanding of the matter but also to develop their own roadmap for implementing interoperability. This generic architecture for interoperability is presented in the figure below.

The generic architecture presented above clearly shows that the heterogeneity of cloud services makes new the research efforts into cloud interoperability timely and relevant. As reflected in the discussions above, the research efforts directed to the interoperability of cloud services are slowly picking up and we are expecting more outputs in the near future. However, all such efforts are being hampered by the fact that again there are just too many fragmented efforts aiming to solve this problem. Therefore, as introduced, this generic architecture is an attempt to consolidate matters. In the next section a use case is presented that demonstrates the contribution that cloud computing can potentially make to new interoperable business models.

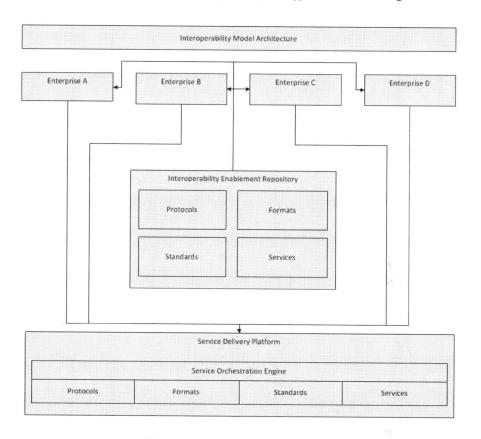

Figure 1. *Interoperability Architecture*

4. Business in Your Pocket (BiYP) – a use case for Interoperability

Business in Your Pocket (BiYP) is the result of an extensive innovation project undertaken by SAP Research in South Africa (Ngassam *et al*, 2013). The vision of the project was to enable very small enterprises (VSEs) to run their business better, thereby participating collaboratively in the formation and contribution into a large business network comprised not only of their peer VSEs, but also of large/small/medium enterprises as well as individual end-users with interest in the business network.

From a business point of view, the enablement of a business network through BiYP provides an opportunity for ecosystem partners to achieve their business objectives through collaboration (and therefore interoperability) with other partners. The enforcement and realisation of the foregoing business objective on the technical level is through the development of applications that support such collaboration. To this end, Service Oriented Architecture (SOA) and Service Oriented Computing (SOC), that represent the technical paradigm for Software as a Service (SaaS), formed the key foundation toward the realization of BiYP.

The collaborative processes created in the BiYP container are based on real-world requirements from businesses operating in the Emerging Economies. With regard to BiYP, interoperability is mainly defined by means of the needs of consumers interacting with multiple businesses in a mobile–cloud infrastructure. The remainder of the BiYP use case discussion is structured as follows:

4.1 Interoperability in today's world cannot be achieved in the absence of a well-grounded understanding of SOA, therefore we highlight a few important SOA principles that contributed to the realization of BiYP

4.2 Internationally recognized industry standards are fundamental in creating an interoperable networked-business environment.

4.3 Services are the building blocks for implementing collaborative processes. We briefly discuss the way BiYP approached the structuring of services.

4.4 Advances in cloud architectures underpin a successful interoperable environment. The 4-tier cloud architecture employed for the implementation of BiYP is discussed.

4.1. *BiYP - Service Oriented Architecture*

The proposed solution relied on SOA and Service Engineering concepts in order to develop appropriate services for supporting the collaborative vision for the formation of a business network. The intention was to leverage SOA characteristics with cloud computing, thereby offering SaaS and cost effective mobile applications to VSEs and ecosystem partners. The BiYP container is similar to that of a customizable on-line application distribution system, commonly referred to as an app-store. However, BiYP requires that the services that form the backbone of application generation are loosely coupled and interoperable. The underlying principle of BiYP was based on state-of-the-art advancements made in SOA and SOC (Erl, 2005).

SOA refers to an architecture where the applications are defined as independent services with well-defined interfaces (Ngassam *et al*, 2013). These services are consumed by end-users not knowing about the complxities of computing resources. Interoperability of services in a SOA is implemented through standards such as Quality of Service (QOS) and trust (Erl, 2005; Studer *et al*, 2007) (Ngassam *et al*, 2013).

SOA can be both an architecture and a programming model (Ngassam *et al*, 2013). Interoperability and loose coupling being one of the most fundamental characteristics of SOA and SOC, the design of a SaaS such as for BiYP required a paradigm shift from a development perspective. As such, after gathering requirements, developers had to enforce the notion of first paying attention to developing basic building block (referred to as atomic services) that can be utilized in the formation of the intended app either through service composition (in order to produce more complex services) or by aggregation (through composition) of identified atomic services to make up the app.

Therefore, according to (Ngassam *et al*, 2013) the software to be built is composed out of an aggregated set of atomic web-services that are grouped into clusters in order to achieve each aspect of the intended business goal of the planned application. As an architecture, SOA facilitates interoperability on the systems level (refer to our working definition in an earlier part of this paper), the design of software systems that provide services to other applications through published and discoverable interfaces, and where the services can be invoked over a network (Ngassam *et al*, 2013).

BiYP aligns with the following, amongst others, SOA characteristics (Erl, 2005) with the aim in creating an interoperable business environment:

– As stated in (Ngassam *et al*, 2013) services are loosely coupled; this helps to minimize dependencies between services and enhance reusability within the BiYP container. This facilitates customization of end-user's requirements (Ngassam *et al*, 2013) and it becomes the main catalyst for designing and implementing the concept of a collaborative process being one of the main components of interoperability, as reflected in our working definition for interoperability

– Each service is exposed to other services through its interface. Well defined interfaces contribute to data and information exchange which is a critical success factor for creating an interoperable environment.

– Services can be atomic or complex in which case they are composed out of many services. With regard to interoperability implemented by means of a cloud infrastructure this is of primary importance that there is a logic decomposition of re-usable services on the services tier of the cloud architecture.

– Contractual: adhere to standards. Knowledge sharing which is one of the most important benefits to be derived from an interoperable environment can only be achieved across multiple businesses platforms by means of industry standards.

– Autonomous: control the business logic they encapsulate, this is an important property for the collaborative process feature of interoperability.

– Abstract: hide the business logic from the service consumers, again contributing to the seamlessly provisioning of collaborative processes.

4.2. *BiYP - Standards*

Furthermore, and in order to comply with our working definition of interoperability, the services in BiYP are described, in a standardized way, by syntactic and semantic representations (Ngassam *et al*, 2013). For syntactic descriptions XML is used, with specific reference to WADL (Hadly, 2009) for REST Services. For semantic descriptions WSMOLite (OWL, n.d; Roman *et al*, 2005) is used. BiYP service representations are published in ebXML.

The intention again is to enforce the notion of reusability of loosely coupled and autonomous services that make up each atomic service developed in BiYP. Following this approach it becomes incrementally less complex to come up with a domain ontology of core concepts of BiYP. Our primary focus was to develop a SaaS in the domain of the retail sector, providing apps such as Shop (regarded as a lean procurement app), Payment, lean CRM and the like. The initial domain ontology would therefore focuses on the definition of concepts pertaining to the specific domain of retail. After completing this aspect of SaaS, we intend to evolve BiYP into other business domains such as service, manufacturing, construction, etc. by just reusing atomic services already defined in the core and extending the domain ontology by incorporating other specialized services identified in the new domain to be incorporated.

This clearly demonstrates the enforcement of the notion of standardization in our development paradigm, although this is done on an incremental fashion in order to avoid dealing with highly complex ontological domain definitions.

An illustration to the development approach is that in the service sector, a VSE that requires the Payment app would be able to do so without loss of generality, in the sense the developers will only reuse the payment functionality already implemented during our initial iteration. During the implementation of services required for the service sector, only specialized services at complex level are implemented such as scheduling, job card, etc. A similar approach is used for the integration of another sector in the overall BiYP solution.

Based on the foregoing, the paradigm used in developing BiYP is expandable and may not necessarily be coined to a given operational industry where VSEs and ecosystem partners operate. Instead, the solution is customizable during the on-boarding process of ecosystem partners and would ensure the enforcement of the formation of a large business network that enables non intra-sector collaboration but also cross-sector collaboration. The foregoing represents in our view a true reflection of Enterprise Interoperability (and therefore Business Innovation).

4.3. *BiYP - Services*

BiYP would consist of "a range of autonomous web services exposed in the service registry that can be invoked by other services to fulfil the business needs of VSE consumers. The BiYP container will expose a range of services to the consumers for customization as explored in subsequent sections. BiYP thus requires a flexible approach for the conceptualization of the underlying domain ontology for facilitating the syntactic and semantic interaction amongst services" (Ngassam *et al*, 2013) (Studer *et al*, 2007)

The materialisation of BiYP as a collaborative process environment is achieved by a well-structured domain ontology differentiating between core and context. Core is shared by all business domains accommodated in the BiYP interoperable container whilst context caters for specific business sectors e.g. retail and construction.

In terms of deployment, the most effective way is a cloud implementation, through the use of Platform-as-a-Service (PaaS). A PaaS offers the opportunity to develop and deploy interoperable applications in the cloud without scalability concerns. PaaS such as cloud foundry, cloud fusion, SAP Netweaver cloud and the like can be employed for this purpose.

"In general, BiYP can be regarded as a container of apps grouped together and supported by a range of loosely coupled services. These are implemented based on the end-users requirements, captured in the form of scenarios. The grouping of apps depends on user's needs and is restricted to the required dependencies established amongst supporting services that constitutes an app" (Ngassam *et al*, 2013).

4.4. *BiYP – Cloud Architecture*

BiYP services model is depicted in the next figure (Ngassam *et al*, 2013).

The Presentation Layer: This is the mobile front end.

The Application Layer: The application layer is the app store.

The Service Layer: Services that ought to be compounded to make up an app.

The 3rd Party Layer: This layer is the extension of the API services.

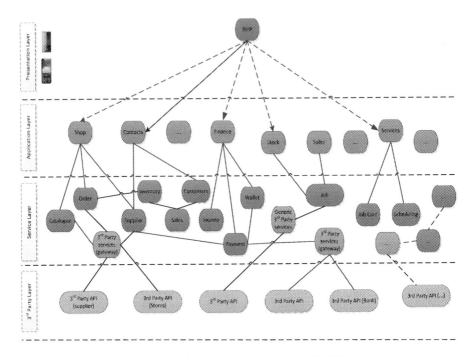

Figure 2. *4-Tier cloud architecture of BiYP*

5. Conclusion

It is shown in this paper that interoperability can contribute to business innovation. An important contribution is the generic architecture for interoperability reflecting the underlying building blocks such as interoperability enablement repositories and service delivery platforms. The BiYP use case clearly indicates that interoperability should not only be addressed on the technical integration level but also on the interoperable business level. Furthermore BiYP provides an opportunity to business participation as ecosystem partners to achieve their business objective through collaboration (and therefore interoperability) with other partners. It is therefore concluded that businesses should drive a new wave of innovation by focusing on new business models harnessing the benefits of interoperability in the cloud.

6. Acknowledgements

The support of SAP Research Pretoria towards this research is hereby acknowledged. Opinions expressed and conclusions arrived at are those of the authors and not necessarily to be attributed to the companies mentioned in this acknowledgement.

7. References

Claybrook B., "Cloud interoperability: Problems and best practices", 2011, available at: http://www.computerworld.com/s/article/9217158/Cloud_interoperability_Problems_and _best_practices?taxonomyId=158&pageNumber=1, accessed: 11 March 2012.

Erl, T. *Service-Oriented Architecture: Concepts, Technology, and Design. Upper Saddle River*, NJ, USA: Prentice Hall PTR, 2005.

European Commission, European Interoperability Framework for Pan-European eGovernment Services, IDABC Program, European Commission, 2004 Available at: http://ec.europa.eu/idabc/servlets/Docd552.pdf?id=19529.)

Gasser U., Palfrey J., Becker M., "Mapping Cloud Interoperability in the Global Economy: The Theory and Observations from Practice", The Berkman Center for Internet & Society, Harvard University, Research Publication No.:2012-19, December 2012.

Gasser U., Palfrey J., Interop: *The Promise and Perils of Highly Interconnected Systems*, Basic Books-A member of the Perseus Books Group, New York, 2012.

Hadley M., "Web Application Description Language (WADL)," Sun Microsystems Inc., 2009.

Hyek P., Munakata Y., Norris R., Tsang J., Flynn C., Price K., Steger J., "Cloud computing issues and impacts", Ernst & Young, Global Technology Industry Discussion Series, 2011.

IEEE (Institute of Electrical and Electronics Engineers): Standard Computer Dictionary- A Compilation of IEEE Standard Computer Glossaries. 1990

Jansen W., Grance T., "Guidelines on Security and Privacy in Public Cloud Computing: Draft Special Publication 800-144" National Institute of Standards and Technology, U.S. Department of Commerce, Computer Security Division, Information Technology laboratory, USA, 2011.

Lavean, Gilbert E., "Interoperability in Defense Communications", IEEE Transactions on Communications, 28(9) 1445 – 1455. 1980

Lawton G., "Addressing the challenge of cloud computing interoperability", 2009, available at: http://www.computer.org/portal/web/computingnow/archive/news031, accessed: 12 March 2013.

LeHong H., Fenn J., "Hype Cycle for Emerging Technologies, 2012", Gartner, Report No. G002339317, Stamfordvol, 31 July 2012.

Li MS, Cabral R, Doumeingts G, Popplewell K., "Enterprise interoperability research roadmap- an Enterprise Interoperability community document". Work coordinated by the Enterprise Interoperability Cluster of the Information Society and Media Directorate-General, European Commission." Published by European Commission. 2006

Lotus Notes, Available online at Lotus Notes http://www-142.ibm.com/software/ products/us/en/ibmnotes, last accessed on 13 March 2013

Loutas N., Kamateri E., Zotou M., Zeginis D., Tarabanis K., Bocconi S., Mogulkoc E., Polydoras P., Strube P., "Requirements Analysis Report", Seventh Framework programme of the European Community, Cloud4SoA Project, Contract No.:257953, available at: http://www.cloud4soa.eu/sites/default/files/Cloud4SOA%20D1.1%20Requi rements%20Analysis.pdf, accessed 12 March 2013.

Mallek S., Daclin N., Chapurlat V., 'The application of interoperability requirement specification and verification to collaborative processes in industry", *Computers in Industry* 63 (2012) 643–658). 2012

Mell P., Grance T., "The NIST Definition of Cloud Computing" The NIST, 2009.

Ngassam E., Eloff J.H.P., Kok D., Venter E., Slavova M., Przewloka M., "Business in Your Pocket - BiYP: Empowering Very Small Enterprises in South Africa", submitted to *Journal of Electronic Commerce in Organizations*, March 2013

O'Brien J., Marakas G., *Introduction to Information Systems*, McGraw-Hill/Irwin; 14th Edition. 2008

OWL Services Coalition, "OWL-S: Semantic Markup for Web Services."

Parameswaran A.V., Chaddhi A., "Cloud Interoperability and Standardization", SETLabs Briefings, Vol.7, No.7, pp.:19 -26, 2009.

Petcu D., "Portability and Interoperability between Cloud: Challenges and Case Study", Springer-Verlag Heidelberg, *LNCS* 6994, pp.:62 – 74, 2011

Roman D., Keller U., Lausen H., de Bruijn J., Lara R., Stollberg M., Polleres A., Feier C., Bussler C., and Fensel D., "Web service modeling ontology," *Applied Ontology*, vol. 1, no. 1, pp.:77–106, 2005.

Schubert L., Jeffery K., "Advances in Clouds: Research in Future Cloud Computing", European Union, Expert Group Report, Public version 1.0, 2012

Studer R., Grimm S., Abecker A., *Semantic Web Services: Concepts, Technologies, and Applications*. Springer, 2007.

Wyld D.C., "Moving to the Cloud: An Introduction to Cloud Computing in Government", E-Governemt Series, IBM Center for the Business Government, IBM7, available at: http://inls525fall2011.web.unc.edu/files/2011/09/DavidWyld.pdf, accessed: 12 march 2013.

Process-Oriented Business Modeling – An Application in the Printing Industry

A. Malsbender* — K. Ortbach* — R. Plattfaut* — M. Voigt* — B. Niehaves**

* European Research Center for Information Systems
University of Muenster
Leonardo-Campus 3
48149 Muenster, Germany
{andrea.malsbender\kevin.ortbach\ralf.plattfaut\matthias.voigt}@ercis.uni-muenster.de

** Hertie School of Governance
Friedrichstraße 180
10117 Berlin, Germany
niehaves@hertie-school.org

ABSTRACT: *Business modeling frameworks are important means for developing new business ideas. Resulting business models can assist in decision making on whether to implement an innovation. We argue that business modeling frameworks have to be process-oriented. Process-orientation in business modeling has two major advantages: Different stakeholders' perspectives may be integrated and business model information may easily be reused in the later innovation process. In this article we introduce the process-oriented business model framework Octoproz and its application in an innovation workshop in a real life scenario of a printing industry case company. Our qualitative results suggest that Octoproz assists business modelers in detailing and structuring business ideas in a meaningful and comprehensive way. However, we identified a pain point in financial calculations in process-oriented business modeling. Our framework requires improvement to provide for guidance in the calculation process. Moreover, we found that Octoproz is limited in its applicability for purely digital business models. We finally indicate directions for future research.*

KEYWORDS: *business modeling, process-orientation, business process management, case study*

1. Introduction

Business models, understood as conceptual models representing business ideas, are important for both changing existing businesses and creating new ones. As markets change, organizations have to adapt the way they create value. This adaptation has to be supported by suitable methods and technology in order to improve decision making. Business models are an important tool for business innovation. Information used in the business model should incorporate the perspectives of different stakeholders or departments, that is, IT, organization, HR, finance, or marketing. Moreover, the information should be reused in the later stages of a business innovation process. Both aspects call for a process perspective in business models.

In this article, we report on the merits and drawbacks of a process-oriented business modeling framework (Octoproz) for creating business models. We briefly present the framework and discuss its application in a real life case in the printing industry. On the basis of three existing business ideas, our case organization applied Octoproz to create process-oriented business models, and on that basis, decided which idea to implement in the organization. We strive to answer the following research question: In how far is a process-oriented business modeling framework valuable for an organization when selecting the best of several business innovation ideas? Results suggest that Octoproz is valuable for our case organization because it helps to include different stakeholders and supports information reuse in later innovation stages. In addition, top management of the organization argued that the framework was useful for structuring and comparing ideas and that it helped to take a well-argued decision.

In the next section we will introduce related work on business modeling and briefly present Octoproz. Then, we present the case setting and the methodology. This position paper ends with a presentation and discussion of the results.

2. Business Modeling and Process Orientation

2.1. *Business Modeling*

Business modeling is an approach for developing and structuring new business ideas (Magretta 2002). While the term business model and the associated process of business modeling is widely known, definitions vary significantly (Al-Debei and Avison 2010). Two major conceptualizations of the term can be identified: On the one hand, the term is referred to as "a loose conception of how a company does business and generates value" (Porter, 2001). In this understanding, it is used to describe the way a company is doing its business (Galper 2001; Gebauer and

Ginsburg 2003). On the other hand, authors have stressed the modeling aspect in their definition of business models (e.g., Osterwalder 2004). Here, business models are understood as a conceptual tool that expresses the business logic of a firm (Osterwalder, Pigneur, and Tucci 2005). Gordijn et al. (2000) refer to it as a conceptual model that shows how a network of actors creates, exchanges and consumes objects of value by performing value adding activities. Thus, not the key objectives of the company are at the core of the definition but instead the graphical representation that describes and structures them. We follow this second definition.

2.2. *Process-Oriented Business Modeling*

While there has been a discourse about the term itself, there have also been discussions about the distinction from business process modeling (Al-Debei & Avison, 2010). It is argued that business models "are centered around the notion of value, while in process modeling concepts focus on how a process should be carried out" (Gordijn et al., 2000). However, there is evidence that this theoretical boundary cannot hold up in practice. While many of the existing business model frameworks do not focus on the value creation process, they integrate some process-related aspects. For instance, Osterwalder and Pigneur (2010) introduce the concept of key activities, Johnson (2010) has key processes as one element in his model, and Bouwman et al. (2008) allow for detailed description of activities by means of a 'walk-through'. Going further, the e³-value approach (Gordijn and Akkermans 2001) allows a mapping of values to business process models, while the UML based approach of Eriksson & Penker (2000) even considers processes as the core of the modeling convention and assigns resources or goals to the different process steps. However, within the latter approach, models become complex rather quickly and are difficult to use in managerial environments. Including process-related aspects in business models or even structuring the business model along the process of value creation has a variety of benefits. Firstly, detailed concepts of a business model usually require the modeling of key processes in a later development step. Thus, taking a process-oriented perspective in business modeling may increase reusability. Secondly, process thinking is a great device for structuring the development process itself and may lead to more accurate models. These potential benefits led to the development of the process-oriented business modeling framework Octorpoz.

2.3. *The Process-Oriented Business Modeling Framework Octoproz*

The framework Octoproz consists of four components (see Figure 1): In the process component, consumer activities, business activities, and channels, which facilitate the interaction between them, are captured. Channels may refer to technical communication (e.g., Telephone, E-Mail) or personal communication. The process should be modeled in a straight forward manner, reducing the service process to the most fundamental activities. In the value proposition component, both customer values (Timmers, 1998) and business values (Betz, 2002) are defined separately and are related to process activities and channels. In the resource component, both internal and external resources are defined for all process activities and channels. Internal resources are those owned by the business while external resources are goods and services provided by external partners. In the financial component, all costs and revenues of one single (average) service delivery (i.e. one service run) are modeled. The goal of the component is to provide for basic but consistent information on the expected overall profit or loss of the new service. Costs are defined for each of the defined resources. Revenues relate to the process activities which deliver value to the customer. Business functions that are independent of a single service delivery, but, nevertheless, are indispensable for performing the process, can be added to the process component as central functions. These functions represent support processes (Harmon, 2007) such as IT services and HR. They are also related to specific resources (central resources), which cause costs and revenues occurring on a fixed basis (fixed costs & revenues). For visualization, related tuples of activities, values, resources, costs, and revenues are positioned in one row of the framework.

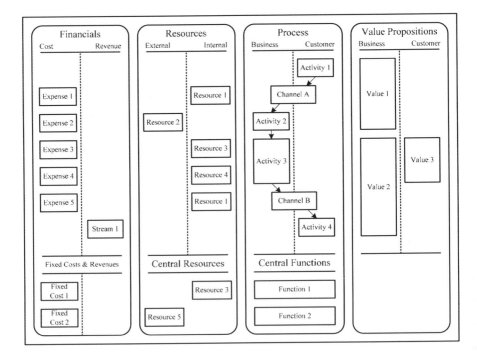

Figure 1. *The Octoproz Framework*

In the next section, we introduce our research methodology for the evaluation of the Octoproz framework.

3. Methodology

We applied and evaluated our process-oriented business modeling framework in an innovation workshop of a medium-sized company in the printing industry. The company offers printing solutions on the B2B market, including fast and high quality prints of hard- and soft-cover books, flyers, and posters. The innovation workshop is held on an annual basis, with the goal to discuss and decide on future product portfolio strategies. The workshop had nine participants from different organizational departments, including IT, accounting, production, sales, and management. We were asked to facilitate and moderate the workshop with a specific task: the company had three innovation ideas which were still on a low level of detail. The goal of the workshop was to decide on which innovation to implement in order to grow in the B2B market.

The nine participants were split in three cross-functional teams. Each team had to model exactly one innovation idea. The task was to interpret the innovation ideas as new services. Each idea was described from two perspectives: The innovation idea had to be specified from a B2B perspective, and from a B2C perspective, thus considering not only the direct customer of the printing company, but also the customer who finally makes use of the printing service.

The workshop was conducted as follows: First, we held a presentation of 30 minutes, introducing the Octoproz business modeling framework. Then, we split up the participants into groups which then individually developed different business models on brown paper for approximately 90 minutes. The groups were moderated by our research team, taking the role of method experts. They provided guidance in the application of our framework while the discussion of the innovations was left to the groups. After developing the business models, we asked all participants for feedback on the framework for about 10 minutes including a little survey. After the workshop, our research team discussed the observations of the group sessions, which revealed strengths and weaknesses of our approach.

4. Case Study at a Printing Company – Results and Discussion

The application of our process-oriented business modeling framework led to well-structured and mainly comparable business models. Based on roughly sketched ideas, the participants were able to generate comprehensive models in the allocated time. The first group developed two business models: The first one demonstrates the setup process of the new service, describing what needs to be adapted or changed in the organization to make the delivery of the service possible. The other one presents the run process focusing on the service delivery process itself. The second group was able to address the business idea in depth, including a whole business casing scenario. The third group focused on the presentation of the whole service process and utilization of the resources needed to realize the business idea.

Overall, the conducted case study at the printing industry led to the manifestation of prior theoretical assumptions and serves as evaluation of the developed process-oriented business modeling framework Octoproz. From the workshop groups' point of view, each business model development process provided by Octoproz was experienced as a *"good structure to review [business] ideas and make them comparable."* The group process was supported as the structured modeling procedure obtained by the framework led to an efficient and productive teamwork.

From the individual participants point of view, the framework served as a good basis for the generation of a decision supporting business model. One participant stated within the evaluation process that the *"structure [of the framework] is really helpful, method really expedient."* Beyond, he remarked that an *"assessment of sales potential as well as risk assessments are missing"* within the framework. Another participant stated that *"the structure is really good. Management of time is crucial."* As he also recognized that *"a well done preparation of the executing organization is needed – market analysis, targeted customer".* This is recognized by the moderators as one possible explanation for the fact that the preparation of the business models was partly beset with a time bottleneck. Although a creative process step was conducted prior to the case study, a comprehensive market analysis was missing. Nevertheless, seven of nine participants felt almost completely or completely supported by Octoproz during the development of business ideas (Likert-Scale-5 Point: Result 4 and 5 of 5 points). This is confirmed in the overall rating of Octoproz with high satisfaction values.

From the method experts and moderators point of view, the modeling process was experienced to be efficient. Participants were able to focus on relevant information needed for the generation of the business model. Crucial process steps could be identified during the modeling process, raising awareness for bottlenecks of resources and risk circumstances. However, some drawbacks of Octoproz have been identified. First, it was commentated by one of the method experts that the manual financial perspective does not fulfill the requirements of a decision supporting financial calculation. Furthermore, as the business idea was focused on a business to business model, the mapping of common process steps like the design of cooperation agreements was identified as difficult to model for the participants. Finally, Octoproz proved to be of limited applicability for purely digital business models, since process activities in online processes hardly imply resource consumptions. In other words, Octoproz is specifically applicable for business models that involve 'offline' activities and resources, such as delivery services and means for transportation. Summarizing, the presented process-oriented business modeling framework Octoproz has a high benefit for practice as business ideas can be structured in a meaningful and comprehensive way. Furthermore, different scenarios can be applied and both setup models (setup process) and process delivery models (run process) can be visualized. Within the presented case study, the resulting decision of our case organization was to implement none of the developed business models. Instead, they rather opted for an alternative business strategy. We conclude that the process-oriented framework is detailed enough to take decisions on profitability and feasibility of a business idea.

Nevertheless, the case study uncovered some limitations which need to be addressed by further research. First, the framework does not provide a specification for the level of detail of the service process. In our case study, this led to complications in the comparability of the three business models that had been developed. Second, the financial perspective needs further improvements, as it is the main perspective for deciding upon implementation or rejection of a business idea. Third, Octoproz is specifically applicable for business models that involve 'offline' activities and resources. Finally, as the framework was filled out manually, the missing assistance for business casing becomes obvious. It was noted, that a tool would need to include business casing functionalities in order to fill out this gap of missing guidance. This needs to be addressed by future work as the whole framework can be implemented in a tool supporting each step in detail.

5. Acknowledgements

This research was funded by the German Federal Ministry of Education and Research (research project KollaPro, promotional reference 01FL10004).

6. References

Al-Debei, M. M., & Avison, D. (2010). Developing a unified framework of the business model concept. *European Journal of Information Systems*, *19*(3), 359–376.

Betz, F. (2002). Strategic business models. *Engineering Management Journal*, *14*(1), 21–27.

Bouwman, H., Faber, E., Haaker, T., Kijl, B., & de Reuver, M. (2008). Conceptualizing the STOF Model. In H. Bowman, H. de Vos, & T. Haaker (Eds.), *Mobile Service Innovation and Business Models* (pp. 31–70). Berlin, Heidelberg: Springer.

Eriksson, H., & Penker, M. (2000). *Business modeling with UML: Business Patterns at Work*. John Wiley & Sons.

Galper, J. (2001). Three Business Models for the Stock Exchange Industry. *Journal of Investing, 10*(1), 70–78.

Gebauer, J., & Ginsburg, M. (2003). The US wine industry and the internet: an analysis of success factors for online business models. *Electronic Markets, 13*(1).

Gordijn, J., & Akkermans, H. (2001). Designing and Evaluating E-Business Models. *IEEE Intelligent Systems,* (August), 11–17.

Gordijn, J., Akkermans, H., & Vliet, H. V. (2000). Business Modeling is not Process Modeling. *Proceedings of the Workshops on Conceptual Modeling Approaches for E-Business and The World Wide Web and Conceptual Modeling* (pp. 40–51). London, UK: Springer.

Harmon, P. (2007). *Business Process Change* (2nd ed.). Burlington, MA, USA: Morgan Kaufmann.

Hedman, J., & Kalling, T. (2003). The business model concept: theoretical underpinnings and empirical illustrations. *European Journal of Information Systems, 12*(1), 49–59.

Johnson, M. W. (2010). *Seizing the White Space - Business Model Innovation for Transformative Growth and Renewal.* Cambridge, MA: Harvard Business Press.

Magretta, J. (2002). Why Business Models Matter. *Harvard Business Review, 80*(5), 86–92.

McGrath, R. G., & MacMillan, I. (2000). *The entrepreneurial mindset: Strategies for continuously creating opportunity in an age of uncertainty.* Cambridge, MA: Harvard Business School Press.

Osterwalder, A. (2004). The Business Model Ontology - A Proposition in a Design Science Approach. Business. Universite de Lausanne.

Osterwalder, A., & Pigneur, Y. (2010). *Business Model Generation.* New Jersey: John Wiley & Sons.

Osterwalder, A., Pigneur, Y., & Tucci, C. L. (2005). Clarifying business models: Origins, present, and future of the concept. *Communications of the AIS, 16*(1), 1–25.

Porter, M. E. (2001). Strategy and the Internet. *Harvard business review, 79*(3), 62–78, 164.

Timmers, P. (1998). Business Models for Electronic Markets. *Electronic Markets, 8*(2), 3–8.

A Comparative Study of Modelling Methodologies Using a Concept of Process Consistency

E. Babkin — E. Potapova — Y. Zelenova

B. Pechorskaya 25/12 Str., N. Novogorod, 603155, Russia
National Research University Higher School of Economics
eababkin@hse.ru

ABSTRACT: *In our research we are interested in a comparative study of application modelling methodologies for analyzing non trivial and hard-to-reach properties of the business processes. Our attention was attracted to such a non trivial property as the consistency of business processes. Poor consistency of business processes can affect company profits and lead to the loss of regular customers and reputation in the market.. Checking this property of the business process helps to reveal hidden bugs in the process model, but requires considerable labor costs and analytics. In our research we compared two approaches to verifying consistency of business processes. The first approach is based on generating object life cycles for each object type used in the process and supported by such special tool as an extension for IBM WebSphere Business Modeler. Another one is a proposition to use DEMO methodology for verifying consistency. The results of the research show that DEMO methodology significantly reduces labor costs and improves quality of analysis.*

KEYWORDS: *modelling methodology business process, consistency, object life cycle*

1. Introduction

In modern practice of business analysts and IT-architects a plethora of modelling languages and methodologies is available to define various elements of business models, enterprise structure and IT-landscape. Existing modelling approaches offer different foundational concepts and represent variations in the abstraction levels. However most of enterprise modelling approaches intensively such a notion as business process.

Among different modelling methodologies there is a moderate agreement with the regard to the scope and semantics of the notion of business processes. A business process is an activity or set of activities that will accomplish a specific organizational goal. A successfully operating business process should have a number of properties. Some of these properties can be easily achieved, but some properties are very difficult to verify.

In our research we are interested in a comparative study of application modelling methodologies for analyzing non trivial and hard-to-reach properties of the business processes. Undoubtedly different modelling methodologies should be able to grasp the same key properties of business processes. Of cause differences in expressiveness and the abstraction level of each modelling methodology introduce differences in the modelling and analysis results. We may compare the level of efforts and quality of the results obtained during application of different modelling methodologies for analysis of the business processes' properties. The outcomes of such comparative analysis help to objectively measure quality and appropriateness of the modelling methodology for particular tasks.

Our attention was attracted to such a non trivial property as the consistency of business processes. The problem of consistency has already been extensively studied (Ryndina *et al*, 2007a) (Pijpers *et al*, 2008) (Engels *et al*, 2001) (Ryndina *et al*, 2007b), (Wang *et al*, 2008). This property plays an important role for alignment of business strategy and operational activities because inconsistencies can lead to many problems: increasing costs, unsatisfied customers or compliance violations. Therefore, most companies tend to make their business processes consistent. It should be pointed out that the concept of consistency is not inherent in the business process. We cannot just look at a business process and explicitly say whether it is consistent or not. The concept of the consistent business process arises by comparing the considered business process with some reference model. "Best practice" business processes can be considered as a reference consistent model. In this article in the capacity of reference model we used ITIL business processes (The Open Guide, 2012).

In this paper we present the first results of the comparative study in which two different modelling methodologies are applied for consistency analysis. The same set of the 'best practice' and real business processes are analyzed by (1) the methodology of IBM WebSphere Business Modeler and (2) a highly abstract DEMO methodology based on the principles of Enterprise Ontology (Dietz, 2006). We are aiming to know how much an abstraction level of modelling technique may influence efficiency of business process analysis.

The results are presented as follows. In Section 2, we introduce the consistency analysis method based on using object life cycle (Laengle *et al*, 2007). In Section 3 and 4 we describe a proposed solution that analyzes business processes using DEMO models. Analyzing the business process for consistency, we propose to abstract from its datalogical and infological details and focus on its ontological essence, which is crucial for business. Then, we compare results of analysis based on two different approaches. Finally, we discuss the results of research and make a conclusion in Section 5.

2. Measuring Process Consistency Using Object Life Cycles

Business process models represent business process in terms of tasks that need to be performed to achieve a certain business goal. Business process models show the flow of business objects in a process. In such works as (Ryndina *et al*, 2007) and (Tabares *et al*, 2009) consistency is considered in terms of object life cycle which shows complete behavior of business objects and represent how business objects go through different states during their existence. In this case, consistency is considered as the ideal life cycle, which is logical, compatible and complete.

Accordingly, the business process is consistent if it provides transformability of objects within a process from one state to another, and also provides the opportunity for business objects to pass all their stages in accordance with their initial ideal life cycle. The method which was suggested consists of four principal steps. An overview of a proposed solution is shown in Figure 1.

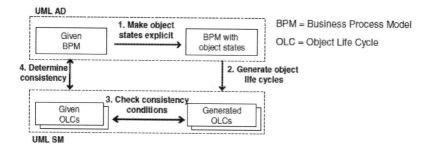

Figure 1. *Solution Overview*

In Step 1 an analyst should make the overlap between a business process model and object life cycle. It is necessary to add object state information to the business model. Next in Step 2, there is a generating a life cycle for each object type used in the model. Then (Step 3) we can determine the consistency between the generated life cycle and the given ones (the ideal life cycle). The result of the previous stage allows us determining the consistency between the business process model and the given life cycles (Step 4).

In (Ryndina *et al*, 2007b) K. Ryndina, J. M. Küster and H. Gall propose two consistency notions for the business model and the object life cycle: life cycle compliance and coverage. Life cycle compliance means that the business process initiates only those state transitions for objects that are defined in the given life cycle. It allows objects of the given type to traverse only a part of their given life cycle in the process. Authors define a state correspondence between two states in different object life cycles if the states are equal (i.e. have the same name), if they are both initial states or they are both final states. A transition correspondence is defined between two transitions if there are state correspondences between their sources states and between their target states.

On the other hand, coverage means that objects traverse the entire given life cycle in the process, but additional transitions not defined in the given life cycle may also be incurred in the process. Every transition in the generated object life cycle should have a transition correspondence to some transition in the ideal life cycle. Furthermore, business objects must be created and reach their final states within the process boundaries. Depending on the circumstances, one or both of the mentioned consistency notions should be met.

It is necessary to point out that two states in the different object life cycles should have the same name otherwise it will be marked as a fact of inconsistency even if these object states are correct logically. In the result of analysis our prototype displays so-called inconsistencies view with a list of detected inconsistencies. There are two categories of inconsistency: non-conformance and non-coverage. A non-conformance inconsistency indicates that some manipulation of the business item does not conform to the given object life cycle. A non-coverage inconsistency is detected when some parts of the given object life cycle are not covered by the process model.

Using the results of analysis the analyst should decide how to change the business process to resolve a particular inconsistency, but at the same time he or she also needs to ensure that these changes do not introduce new inconsistencies as a side-effect. The approach of establishing consistency of business process based on using object life cycle is a quite effective method. Supporting technique for the generating of object life cycles from process models enables consistency checking and considerably simplifies the work of analyst. In addition the consistency has two notions: life cycle compliance and coverage which enable to explore the quality of a process.

In (Ryndina *et al*, 2008) a prototype was suggested as an extension to the IBM WebSphere Business Modeler that allows to capture object states in business process models, generate life cycles from process models and check the consistency conditions. Object Life Cycle Explorer is a set of plug-ins for WebSphere Business Modeler, a tool that natively supports modelling of business processes, business objects, resources, etc. WebSphere Business Modeler additionally allows to define a set of possible states for a business item and associate states with object flows in a process model. The results of modelling and analysis using notation of IBM WebSpehre Business Modeler became first part of our comparative study. The modelling methodology of IBM Business Modeler represents a traditional type of business process modelling which may be set in correspondence with such methods as BPMN, UML.

In the current study we follow the principles of the business object life cycle, and also analyze a number of different business processes of incident management in terms of the life cycle. The generated object life cycle for the business object "ticket" is shown in Figure 2. As was mentioned earlier, ITIL business models play the role of the reference model. The object life cycle for the business process of incident management designed according to ITIL requirements is shown in Figure 3.

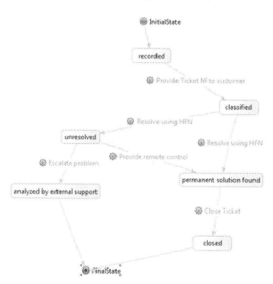

Figure 2. *Generated object life cycle for business object "ticket"*

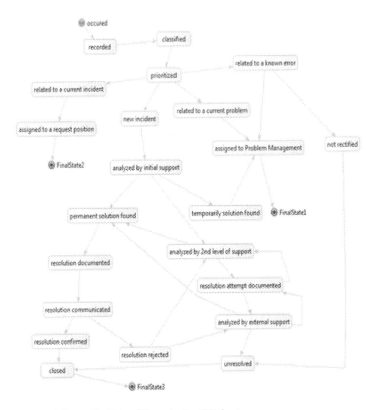

Figure 3. *Object life cycle for ITIL business process*

3. DEMO Methodology as an Alternative Mean for Analysis of Process Consistency

DEMO (Design & Engineering Methodology for Organizations) is a methodology for the design, engineering, and implementation of organizations and networks of organizations. The entering into and complying with commitments is the operational principle for each organization. These commitments are established in the communication between social individuals, i.e. human beings (Dietz, 2006).

In DEMO the basic pattern of a business transaction is composed of the following three phases. An actagenic phase during which a client requests a fact from the supplier agent. The action execution which will generate the required fact. A facagenic phase, which leads the client to accept the results reported.

Basic transactions can be composed to account for complex transactions. The DEMO methodology gives the analyst an understanding of the business processes of the organization, as well as the agents involved. The analysis of models built on the methodology of DEMO allows the company to obtain detailed understanding of the processes of governance and cooperation and serves as a basis for business reengineering and information infrastructure development, consistent with the business requirements.

As was mentioned earlier the concept of "consistency" is not inherent in the business process, it occurs only in comparison with a reference model. The approach based on DEMO methodology uses the same principle. There is a business process that should be verified, and there is the ideal business process. DEMO models are built for both processes and analyst can detect inconsistency in the analyzed business process comparing both models.

In this approach, consistency is considered in terms of DEMO models, which show only the ontological essence of the process. In this case, consistency is regarded as an ideal DEMO model where all transactions are logical, compatible and complete. Accordingly, the business process is consistent, if it contains all transactions that are in the reference DEMO model and if the execution of the transaction is in the same order. There are two types of inconsistency: excess transactions and links between objects and the lack of transactions and links that exist in the reference DEMO model.

DEMO models are very compact and take no more than a sheet of paper. Analyst does not need any special tools, in some cases a pen and paper is enough.

In the majority of cases visual comparison is enough to detect inconsistency in a business process. The reason of it is the fact that DEMO models operate with less amount of data eliminating infological and datalogical process information which often overload models.

Each DEMO model has practical importance and useful for the analysis of the whole organization. The analyst can build all five DEMO models for each business process, but the study found out that the process model, the action model and the state model do not bring appreciable benefits during the analysis of consistency. Therefore we analyzed business processes using only the interaction model and the interstriction model, such approach significantly saves the time of analysis.

Under this approach, the first step of the analysis of consistency is constructing the interaction model and the interstriction model to the referent business process and the analyzed business process correspondingly. Then the analyst should compare these models and draw some conclusions.

The interaction model (IAM) is the most compact ontological model. It shows area of responsibility of actors and the transactions that are important in terms of business operation. Also the analyst should make a transaction result table which represents transaction and the result of this transaction. Consider the process that has been examined earlier. The transaction result table (TRT) and actor transaction diagram are shown below.

transaction type	result type
T01 Incident gathering	R01 Incident has been gathered
T02 Remote resolving	R02 Remote resolving has been done
T03 On-site resolving	R03 On-site resolving has been done
T04 Ticket closing	R04 Ticket has been closed

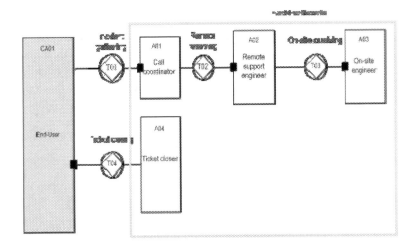

Figure 4. *The TRT and the Actor transaction diagram of the analyzed business process*

Then the analyst should make a transaction result table and the actor transaction diagram of the corresponding business process from ITIL.

transaction type	result type
T01 Incident recording	R01 Incident has been recorded
T02 Incident classification	R02 Incident has been classified
T03 Incident matching	R03 Incident has been matched
T04 Incident investigating	R04 Incident has been investigated
T05 Investigation escalating	R05 Investigation has been escalated
T06 Incident closing	R06 Incident has been closed

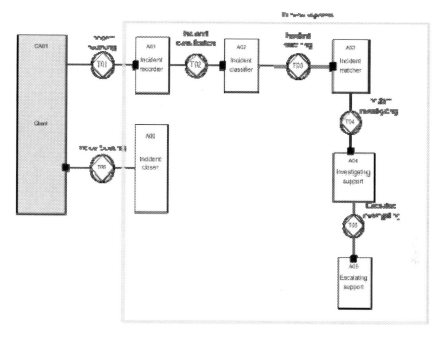

Figure 5. *The TRT and the Actor transaction diagram of the referent ITIL business process*

The comparison of two models shows that the analyzed business process is inconsistent, it has not some transactions described in the reference model and it has some superfluous transactions.

The interstriction model (ISM) besides benefits of the IAM contains information links between actor roles and the external banks to which the enterprise needs to have access. The bank contents table (BCT) and organization construction diagram of analyzed business process are shown below.

object class, fact type, or result type	P-bank
INCIDENT	CPB11
Incident has been gathered	PB01
Remote resolving has been done	PB02
On-site resolving has been done	PB03
Incident has been closed	PB04
Incident type	CPB12
CUSTOMER	CPB13
customer information	CPB13

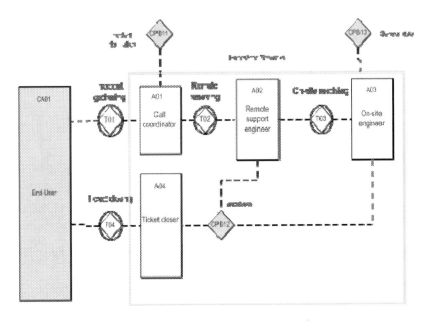

Figure 6. *The BCT and the Organization construction diagram*
of the analyzed business process

The bank contents table (BCT) and organization construction diagram of the business process from ITIL are shown on figure 7.

object class, fact type, or result type	P-bank
INCIDENT	CPB11
Incident has been recorded	PB01
Incident has been classified	PB02
Incident has been matched	PB03
Incident has been investigated	PB04
Investigation has been escalated	PB05
Incident has been closed	PB06
Incident type	CPB12
Error type	CPB12
Problem type	CPB12
CLIENT	CPB13
type_of_client	CPB13

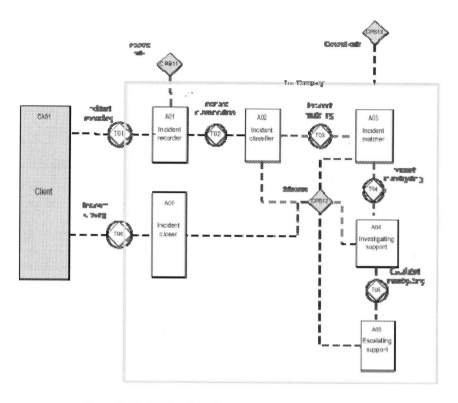

Figure 7. *The BCT and the Organization construction diagram
of the referent ITIL business process*

The comparison of the models shows which links between actors and banks are redundant or are not available. As the result the analyst can make a conclusion about consistency of analyzed business process referring to the reference DEMO models.

4. Comparative study of two approaches to the consistency analysis

As a result of the research strengths and weaknesses of two methods were identified. Also we obtained empirical factual data of labor costs and estimated the complexity of the analysis. There are some advantages of the approach based on the properties of the object life cycle.

First, intuitive understanding of the modeled business processes and object life cycles. The business process model, representing a sequence of related activities and logical transitions are closer to understanding and interpreting. New methodologies that require deep understanding of the essence of the method are often rejected because of their complexity and incomprehensibility. Second, a prototype as an extension to the WebSphere Business Modeler provides quality support for the analyst and excludes much of routine work.

The approach has some disadvantages. First, this is dependence on software support. If the analyst has not WebSphere Business Modeler it will be impossible to use Object Life Cycle Explorer for analysis. Without this tool every step of methodology contains a lot of routine work and takes too much time.

Second, the analyst should operate with a large number of occupational data, be able to use and understand the professional vocabulary which is inherent in a particular business process.

Third, the methodology and software required similar terminology in generated life cycle and life cycle of the reference model, otherwise the analysis of consistency is impossible. Therefore, it is often required to modify the original terminology of business process.

Fourth, detailed modeling of business processes overloads the diagram of excess information and dramatically complicates the analysis (by several times). Generated life cycles are quite cluttered because of including stages and transitions that do not play any key role in the analysis of consistency.

The approach based on DEMO methodology has considerable benefits in comparison with the previously described one. First, DEMO methodology does not require software support for modeling and diagrams easily fit on a sheet of A3 format paper. Second, the diagrams are easy for visual comparison due to its compactness and using only the desired data. Third, diagrams contain only transactions of ontological level that focus on decision-making or creating a new product. Infological and datalogical data do not overload such diagrams, it greatly facilitates and speeds up the analysis. Fourth, DEMO methodology does not require one-to-one correspondence between two business processes. It facilitates the construction of models and saving important data.

As for disadvantages, it is necessity to examine the theory of DEMO methodology and notation conventions, which are necessary to construct models.

The diagram below presents the results of several experiments where we measured efforts (in terms of labor costs) needed for practical work following each of the two presented approaches.

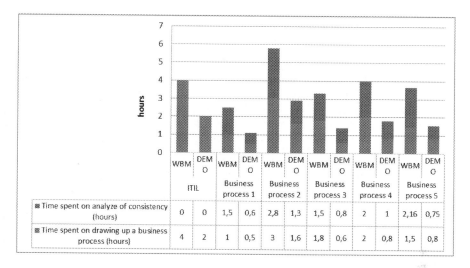

Figure 8. *Trade-offs and labor costs*

The approach based on DEMO methodology is more effective then method based on constructing object life cycles and allows to quickly and accurately analyze business processes of consistency without using special software. The usage of DEMO methodology reduces labor costs approximately by two times, even including the time needed for construction of the business process and analysis of consistency.

5. Conclusion

Consistency of the business process needs to be analyzed in order to avoid various problems. In this paper we compared two different methods of analyzing consistency of business processes: the approach based on using object life cycles and the approach based on applying DEMO methodology. Each method has its strengths and weaknesses.

DEMO methodology allows looking to the problem of inconsistent business processes from the ontological point of view. The results of research show that DEMO methodology significantly reduces labor costs and improves quality of analysis. However, for more comprehensive comparison the business-related metrics should be taken into account during evaluation of the results of consistency analysis. Such metrics measure real business impact of processes modification determined by detected process inconsistencies. Following that direction we are going to continue our research.

6. References

Dietz J. L. G. *Enterprise Ontology: Theory and Methodology*, Springer, 2006.

Engels G., Küster J.M., Groenewegen L., Heckel R., A Methodology for Specifying and Analyzing Consistency of Object-Oriented Behavioral Models, Proceedings of the 8th European software engineering conference held jointly with 9th ACM SIGSOFT international symposium on Foundations of software engineering, Vienna, Austria, 2001, p. 186–195.

Laengle, S., Seguel H., Theoretical and Practical Consistency in Business Process Optimization, Sigifredo Laengle home site / Facultad de Economía y Negocios, Universidad de Chile, Santiago, Chile, 2007.

Open Guide, The, http://www.itlibrary.org/index.php?page=Incident_Management, page accessed – December 2012.

Pijpers V., Gordijn J., Consistency Checking Between Value Models and Process Models: A Best-of-Breed Approach, Proceedings of the Third International Workshop on Business. – IT Alignment and Interoperability (BUSITAL'08) held in conjunction with CAiSE'08 Conference, 2008, p. 58-72.

Ryndina K., Küster J.M., Gall H., *Consistency of Business Process Models for Object Life Cycle Compliance*, Lecture Notes in Computer Science / Business Process Management. – Springer-Verlag Berlin Heidelberg, 2007.

Ryndina K., Küster, J.M., Mono A., Object Life Cycle Explorer for WebSphere Business Modeler, IBM Zurich Research Laboratory, 2008.

Ryndina, K., Küster J.M., *Improving Inconsistency Resolution with Side-Effect Evaluation and Costs*, MoDELS, LNCS 4735, Springer, 2007, p. 136–150.

Tabares M. S., Arango F. Achieving Consistency and Completeness of Business Process Models throughout the Lifecycle, Proceedings of Memorias de la XII Conferencia Iberoamericana de Software Engineering (CIbSE 2009), Medellín, Colombia, 2009, p. 145-150.

Wang E.T.G., Shih S.-P., Jiang J.J., G. Klein G. The consistency among facilitating factors and ERP implementation success: A holistic view of fit, The Journal of Systems and Software, no. 81, 2008, p. 1609–1621.

Maintenance Support throughout the Life-Cycle of High Value Manufacturing Products. Interoperability Issues

Alena Fedotova* — Victor Taratoukhine** — Yury Kupriyanov***

* The Bauman Moscow State Technical University, Department of computer automation and European Research Centre in Information Systems (ERCIS) Lab Russia at Higher School of Economics
afedotova@acm.org

** University of Muenster, European Research Centre for Information Systems (ERCIS) HQ and ERCIS Lab Moscow at Higher School of Economics
victor.taratoukhine@ercis.uni-muenster.de

*** European Research Centre in Information Systems (ERCIS) Lab Russia at Higher School of Economics National Research University Higher School of Economics, Faculty of Business-Informatics
yukupriyanov@hse.ru

ABSTRACT: *This paper reviews existing methods and techniques addressing the problem of maintenance support throughout the life cycle for high value manufacturing products. As part of this doctorate research the analysis of current Enterprise Asset Management systems (EAM) systems is conducted, including gap analysis and to-be model for future complex product life-cycle management. In order to contribute towards a more comprehensive solution, an advanced approach (algorithm) of periodic maintenance is presented. Doctorate candidates believe that this approach will reduce the cost of maintenance of high value manufacturing products. The algorithm based on constraint programming methods is briefly presented and the future research directions are discussed.*

KEYWORDS: *EAM systems, SAP, long-life equipment, maintenance, cost engineering, methods of constraints satisfaction problems*

1. Introduction

At the present time modern development of high value manufacturing products includes whole set of information technologies, which should works efficiently and support all stages of product lifecycle, providing IT landscape from product idea and marketing till further utilization.

In Figure 1 you can see a simplified structure of information technologies, which can be used during development on all stages of product lifecycle. Thus, problem of IT systems interoperability is very important for supporting of high value manufacturing products lifecycle.

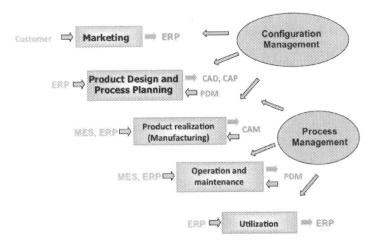

Figure 1. *IT landscape in Product Lifecycle Management*

New approaches to organization of information systems to supporting of equipment and Enterprise Asset Management (EAM systems) are considered in this paper.

The increasing requirements for products quality and fluctuations in customer demand, as well as dynamic competitors impose significant requirements on the ability of manufacturers to provide customers with products in the required quantity, quality and for competitive price [1, 2]. Also, the cost and environmental impact of keeping long-life equipment and capital systems operating efficiently will have a key role [3], especially in high – value products such as aerospace industry, automotive, and other industries. The high value products and infrastructure are typically technology intensive, expensive and reliability critical requiring engineering services, such as maintenance support throughout the life cycle [4].

High value manufacturers are looking for additional cost savings through performance-based service contracts and by taking responsibilities for their product performance through-life. The ability of owners and service providers to deploy best-in-class maintenance capability will be increasingly critical to meeting shareholder and public demands in tomorrow's world [5]. This requires a new and integrated focus on research in maintenance within the high value manufacturing companies and their supply chains.

This means higher reliability technological capacities of the company and their continued willingness to work at the peak of its features. Thus considerably increases the efficiency of the importance of processes of maintenance and repair of equipment (maintenance), and with them the whole set of processes for asset management companies. The most significant results to improve the efficiency of processes in the region can be achieved by providing integration platform to bring together ERP data and Enterprise Asset Management (EAM systems), based on current industry information platform [6].

In recent years, the importance and relevance of the problems of construction of system configurations for multicomponent systems has increased dramatically in many application areas: unit planning, resource allocation system, logistics system. Case studies EAM systems in the world testifies to their extremely high returns of investments. According number of studies the vast majority of the projects paid off in less than a year or two. Model is a reduction of 20% or more of the cost of maintenance, which is achieved by [7]:

- increase the availability, reliability and efficiency of plant and equipment / machinery (increase in production of 0.5% -1%);

- improving the accuracy of planning maintenance of equipment (planned repairs share in the total number of repairs increased from 30% to 80%);

- reducing the inefficiencies of human resources and materials and equipment (down the costs by 2% -5%);

- to improve transparency and fairness including the cost of work on the management and maintenance of fixed assets;

- increasing the validity of estimates of the cost of planned management and maintenance of fixed assets;

- the construction of a single (correct and consistent) directory nomenclature capital assets.

Currently on the market there are over 400 suppliers EAM systems, most of which focused on the development of systems solutions for narrow local problems.

The leading and presented in most regions are products of companies are IBM, IFS, Infor, Mincom, Oracle and SAP. The strengths of these systems are:

- the integration with ERP-systems from different vendors;

- most support systems functioning on a variety of platforms;

- support for extensive functionality;

- high scalability;

- the company's presence in all global markets.

Specific analysis of EAM systems was conducted for SAP AG solutions. For instance, the SAP Enterprise Asset Management (SAP EAM) solution helps organizations efficiently and sustainably manage the whole lifecycle of physical assets by means of interoperability IT systems. Tools for managing production equipment, roads, machinery, vehicles, facilities, and power grids help reduce operating costs, minimize risk, and manage capital expenditures more effectively. Powerful reporting functionality and analytics improve asset usage and performance. Core Business Processes interoperability supported by SAP EAM: Planning, Building, and Commissioning; Asset Visibility and Performance; Asset Operations and Maintenance; Operational Risk Management; Real Estate Lifecycle Management [8].

Despite that most of popular EAM systems can be considered as industry standards (in variety of the sectors of the economy), as part of the analysis we defined some of the key challenges:

- the high cost of implementation;

- limited investment in vendor development of innovative technologies;

- the low prevalence of specialists and consultants to implement;

- the product is not available in many areas;

- the lack of support for integration with other vendors' products;

- support the operation only on the platform and limited use of advanced mathematical methods for periodic and non-periodic;

- preventive maintenance.

Future literature review, industry interviews and case studies defined that it is a significant gap between current practice, integrated in EAM systems and new approaches for maintenance of high value manufacturing products.

The competitiveness of the aircraft is influenced by a number of factors, including the operating system maintenance and repair of equipment.

Maintenance and repair of equipment is an operation or a complex of operations intended to keep an item in the proper condition when used for intended purpose, on standby, for storage and transportation [9]. British Standard Glossary of terms (3811:1993) defined maintenance as the combination of all technical and administrative actions, including supervision actions, intended to retain an item in, or restore it to, a state in which it can perform a required function [10]. European Federation of National Maintenance Societies may be defined maintenance, repair, and operations as, "all actions, which have the objective of retaining or restoring an item in or to a state in which it can perform its required function. The actions include the combination of all technical and corresponding administrative, managerial, and supervision actions."

The increasing requirements for products quality and fluctuations in customer demand, as well as dynamic competitors impose significant requirements on the ability of manufacturers to provide customers with products in the required quantity, quality and for competitive price. From a purely industrial point of view, this means higher reliability of a company's technological capacities and their constant availability at the peak of their features. Thus the importance of maintenance effectiveness considerably increases, as well as the whole set of a company's asset management processes.

Generally speaking, there are three types of maintenance in use:

- Preventive maintenance, where equipment is maintained before break down occurs. This type of maintenance has many different variations and is subject of various researches to determine best and most efficient way to maintain equipment. Recent studies have shown that Preventive maintenance is effective in preventing age related failures of the equipment. For random failure patterns which amount to 80% of the failure patterns, condition monitoring proves to be effective. It can be divided into two subgroups: Scheduled maintenance (planned maintenance) and Condition-based maintenance. The effectiveness of the aircraft maintenance are determined mainly by scheduled maintenance.

- Corrective maintenance, where equipment is maintained after break down. This maintenance is often most expensive because worn equipment can damage other parts and cause multiple damage.

- Reliability centred maintenance often known as RCM, is a process to ensure that assets continue to do what their users require in their present operating context.

One of the most advanced concept is the concept of Integrated Vehicle Health Management (IVHM). IVHM is seen as a potential solution for many maintenance-related problems. The concept of IVHM was first created by NASA and looks at complete health management solution and addresses infrastructure assets as well as moving vehicles. An IVHM System is made up of different building blocks such as sensors, fault diagnosis and prognosis systems and communication links. It needs to have a rigorous business case representing the diverse stakeholder requirements [11]. Despite the fact our research focus on improving the traditional approach - Scheduled maintenance.

The main parameters that characterize the perfection of the maintenance system are the scope and frequency of maintenance work, which have a direct impact on operating costs and the intensity of the aircraft operation. It is obvious that the smaller the amount of work and the greater the frequency of their performance, the lower the operating costs and the stronger the aircraft operation. The share of the maintenance cost can vary from 10 to 50 percents of total operating costs [12]. The aircraft design features, the technical operation methods, regulatory and procedural requirements, the quality of work, operating parameters, environmental conditions and other factors influence on the scope and frequency of maintenance.

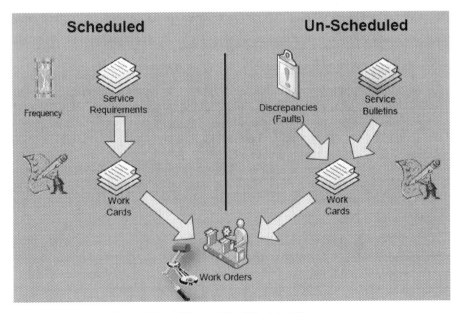

Figure 2. *Scheduled and Un-Scheduled Maintenance.*
(c) Siemens AG, PLM Software Group

The scope and frequency of work are determined by the maintenance program. It should be noted that the requirements for the content of the maintenance program in Russia differ from those operating abroad. In the Russian Federation the maintenance program is a developer's document, common to the aircraft type, whereas the maintenance program abroad is a document developed by the operator for each individual aircraft taking into account the conditions and parameters of its operation and maintenance system adopted by the operator based on the minimum maintenance requirements specified in the process of type certification.

The objectives of an efficient airline maintenance program are:

- To ensure realization of the inherent safety and reliability levels of the equipment.

- To restore safety and reliability to their inherent levels when deterioration has occurred.

- To obtain the information necessary for design improvement of those items whose inherent reliability proves inadequate.

- To accomplish these goals at a minimum total cost, including maintenance costs and the costs of resulting failures.

These objectives recognize that maintenance programs as such cannot correct deficiencies in the inherent safety and reliability levels of the equipment. The maintenance program can only prevent deterioration of such inherent levels. If the inherent levels are found to be unsatisfactory, design modification is necessary to obtain improvement [13].

In the general statement in the presence of all the necessary initial information quantitative confirmation of maintenance program effectiveness is to provide a set of probabilistic aircraft safety performance, while minimizing maintenance cost (e.g., maintenance cost per flying hour). In this approach, the main difficulty is the quantitative confirmation of compliance with the aircraft requirements, which requires an adequate mathematical model allowing us to assess the impact of maintenance on the aircraft safety and effectiveness.

Real alternative to the quantitative approach is the rational combination of quality engineering analysis of the choice of technical operation methods and the aircraft maintenance with a quantitative optimization of maintenance frequency on based on the mathematical model scheduled maintenance influence on the on-board systems reliability and safety. This allows us to analyse the impact of possible system failures and their components on the aircraft flight safety, regularity and efficiency [14].

2. Main goal

Based on this analysis, the main goal of this research was defined as: *to create a method and algorithm for improving of scheduling of periodic maintenance actions* (*works*) as universal service procedures. This will greatly simplify the support of the whole system, expand the area of its use, and hopefully will reduce the maintenance cost of complex products.

3. Problem solution

Based on industry case studies and number of practical research conducted with number of the aerospace companies we defined an advanced approach for improving the regular maintenance of complex, high value manufacturing products, described generally in number of stages:

- The functional decomposition of the work into a hierarchy of components and the composition of the work scope (servicing/repair work domain ontology) [15].

- Description of regularities determining the inclusion of this work in the periodic maintenance as constraints.

- Starting a mechanism to monitor the resulting complex maintenance work based on constraint satisfaction programming (CSP) [16]:

> *First stage*: satisfaction of the constraints that are associated with the known parameters of the components. Method NC-1 [17, 18].

> *Second stage*: the pairwise comparison of directory components, which is aimed at removing the components not compatible with each other. Method of pre-screening Forward Checking [19, 20].

> *Third stage*: the calculation and verification of compliance with the requirements of the design parameters. Backtracking method [21].

To - be model for future complex product life-cycle management and full mathematical description of the approach will be presented in extended version of the paper.

4. Conclusion and future work

In this research the analysis of current Enterprise Asset management (EAM) systems was conducted. The key challenges and opportunities were defined. Advanced approach (algorithm) for periodic maintenance were shortly described. The algorithm is based on constraint programming methods. The next step will be a creation of practical case studies for specific industry (aerospace industry) which will liable us to evaluate the effectiveness of the proposed framework. Also, cost reduction analysis [5] will be conducted to evaluate economic effectiveness of the proposed method. Finally, integration of the proposed solution to current ERP/EAM systems as joint co-innovation program between Bauman Moscow State University/ERCIS Lab Moscow and SAP will be considered.

5. References

1. Chapman, S. N.: *The Fundamentals of Production Planning and Control*. Pearson Prentice Hall, 2006.

2. Scheer, A.-W.: *Computer Integrated Manufacturing: Towards the factory of the future*, 3rd ed. Berlin u.a., 1994.

3. Becker, J.; Taratoukhine, V.; Vilkov, L.; Rieke, T.: Process Driven Value Assessment of ERP Solutions: An Overview on the Extended SAP Methodology. In: Proceedings of the 2nd International Conference on Information Management and Business (IMB2006). Sydney, Australia, 2006. S. 225-235.

4. Becker, J.; Vilkov, L.; Taratoukhine, V.; Kugeler, M.; Rosemann, *M. Process management,* Moscow, Russia.Eksmo. 2007.

5. Taratoukhine V, Roy R., Mishra K., Souchouorkov R., Knowledge in the Commercial and Engineering Activities within Cost Estimating. 9th ISPE International Conference on Concurrent Engineering: Research and Applications, Netherlands: A.A. Balkema Publisher, 2002.

6. Scheer, A.-W.: *Business Process Engineering - Reference Models for Industrial Enterprises*. 2nd ed. Berlin u.a., 1994.

7. Kupriyanov, Y.V.: Research note. EAM-systems: Tasks, functionality, providers. –OXS, Moscow, 2007

8. SAP Enterprise Asset Management Maximize Return on Assets, Manage Risks, and Improve Equipment Effectiveness: http://www.sap.com/community/ebook/2012_05 _EAM_Max/en/index.html#/page/1.

9. GOST 18322-78. System maintenance and repair of equipment. Terms and definitions. 1978.

10. British Standard Glossary of terms (3811:1993).

11. Ip-Shing Fan, Ian Jennions. Asset Health Management System Design. Conference Proceedings. 17th International Conference on Concurrent Enterprising. (ICE 2011), Germany.

12. Airline Maintenance Program Development Seminar, Fleet Maintenance Seminars, Boeing, Seattle, Washington, USA. 2008.

13. ATA MSG-3. Revision 2007.1. Operator/Manufacturer Scheduled Maintenance Development. ATA. - 2007.

14. Guidelines "Guidelines for the analysis of logistic support aircraft production," Research Center of CALS-technologies, "Applied Logistics" 2010. M.: - 204p.

15. Ovsyannikov M., Bukhanov S. Configuration management with using the method constraint programming. *News of higher educational institutions. Mechanical Engineering. № 14,* 2012 pp. 70-75.

16. Rossi F., van Beek P., Walsh T. (eds.) *Handbook Of Constraint Programming.* Elsevier, 2006. 978 p.

17. Benhamou F., Older W. Applying Interval Arithmetic to Real, Integer and Boolean Constraints. Journal of Logic Programming 32 1997, pp.1-24.

18. Cleary. J. Logical Arithmetic. Future Comput. Syst. 2 (2) 1987, pp. 125–149.

19. Gent Ian, Artificial Intelligence: Constraint Programming [Electronic resource] / Gent Ian.- Access mode: http://www.dcs.st-and.ac.uk/ipg/AI/.

20. Bartak R. On-line guide to Constraint Programming [Electronic resource] / Bartak R.- Access mode: http://ktilinux.ms.mff.cuni.cz/~bartak/constraints/.

21. Dechter R., Frost D. Backjump-based backtracking for constraint satisfaction problems. Artificial Intelligence, 136(2): pp. 147–188, 2002.

Using Enterprise Architecture to Align Business Intelligence Initiatives

Ip-Shing Fan* — Sara Warner**

Cranfield University
Cranfield, Bedford, MK43 0AL
United Kingdom
* i.s.fan@cranfield.ac.uk
** sara.warner@sky.com

ABSTRACT: Between 70% to 80% of corporate Business Intelligence projects fail. There is evidence that the maturity of Enterprise Architecture within an organisation can improve the success of information technology. This paper groups the non-technical issues of Business Intelligence initiatives into four classifications: strategic alignment, change management at a strategic level, change management at a tactical level and process engineering. The list of non-technical issues demonstrates that the success of Business Intelligence in an organisation is not limited to the success of the technology, but involves a paradigm shift in the information culture of the organisation. Recommendations are made to mitigate risks in Business Intelligence initiatives by implementing a mature Enterprise Architecture.

KEYWORDS: business intelligence, enterprise architecture, strategic alignment, change management, information culture

1. Introduction

In 2005, Gartner (Hostmann et al.) published a paper detailing seven 'Fatal Flaws' in Business Intelligence implementations. They are still using that same list of 'Fatal Flaws' today except now there are nine flaws (Hostmann et al., 2008). The issues detailed in this Gartner paper are predominantly people and processes, not technical. They cover areas such as organisational culture, managing expectations, change management, process engineering and strategic alignment. Within the 2005 report, Gartner states that understanding these flaws will not ensure success so it appears necessary to find a method that will improve the likelihood of success. Enterprise Architecture professes to connect the Business, Applications, Data and Technology (The Open Group, 2009) and to provide a solid foundation for change.

The purpose of this paper is to establish if Enterprise Architecture has the potential to overcome the recurring non-technical issues within Business Intelligence Implementations. The paper first examines current literature in Enterprise Architecture and Business Intelligence. The recurring non-technical problems in Business Intelligence implementations are analysed and similarities are identified to group and classify these issues. Using these classifications, the paper then considers how the principles and practices of mature Enterprise Architecture could improve the likelihood of success in Business Intelligence initiatives.

2. Enterprise Architecture

The purpose of Enterprise Architecture is to integrate and optimise business processes to ensure that the business can respond to change (Open Group, 2009). The principle of Enterprise Architecture is to ensure that the core functions of the business are stable and reliable and enable efficiencies that will not limit the business, but provide a basis for flexibility and agility in the business. The starting point on the timeline for Enterprise Architecture is commonly recognised as John Zachman's publication (1987) of "A Framework for Information Systems Architecture". As the use of computers in business became a necessity through the 1990's, there were many technical publications (Ryan and Santucci, 1993; Spewak, 1993; Cottey and Chang, 1996; Zachman, 1997) that began to include the terms Enterprise Architecture or Information Architecture; they mainly described the concepts from a technical point of view. Frameworks and methodologies began to be developed such as the Zachman Framework, Federal Enterprise Architecture, Gartner (formerly the Meta Framework) and The Open Group Architecture Framework (TOGAF) (Sessions, 2007a).

In the last five years, more has been published on Enterprise Architecture as a separate entity to the IT function of a business. One of these is the book "Enterprise

Architecture as Strategy" (Ross et al., 2006) which is specifically aimed at 'all executives', not just senior IT managers. Roger Sessions (2008) discusses the principles of simplifying the 'complex enterprises' as a best practice for Enterprise Architecture. While many of the definitions of Enterprise Architecture suggest that Enterprise Architecture involves documenting every system, structure and process, he recommends that the focus should be on areas that add business value.

The necessity to implement new systems, processes and technology without hampering the daily running of the business is a constant challenge for businesses. Ross et al. (2006) recommends that companies move through their stages of Enterprise Architecture maturity by building a "foundation for execution". The four stages are:

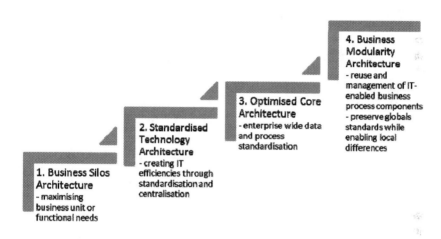

Figure 1. *Four stages of Enterprise Architecture maturity
(adapted from Ross et al., 2006)*

3. Business Intelligence

The use of the term "Business Intelligence" became significant in the early 1990's and was often used to describe the applications that delivered the reporting and analysis of the data within a data warehouse. Business Intelligence applications now include reporting, analysis, dashboard, scorecards, and data mining tools. The Data Warehouse Lifecycle Toolkit (Kimball et al., 2008) explains the relationship between data warehousing and business intelligence. It also explains that the use of each of these terms remains fluid within the industry but that the key is that "the data warehouse is the foundation for business intelligence". Parr Rud (2009) says that Business Intelligence is "a term that encompasses all the capabilities required to turn data into intelligence". Sabherwal and Becerra-Fernandez (2011) define Business

Intelligence as "providing decision makers with valuable information and knowledge by leveraging a variety of sources of data as well as structured and unstructured information". Gartner (2011) defines Business Intelligence as "an umbrella term that spans the people, processes and applications/tools to organize information, enable access to it and analyse it to improve decisions and manage performance."

The recent consensus is that Business Intelligence is more than a technology or an application. The one aspect that few definitions seem to capture is that Business Intelligence is the enterprise wide organisation and presentation of business information designed to support the business in delivering the business strategy. Without that essential link to delivering the business strategy, Business Intelligence initiatives may provide capabilities for understanding data and information but at the same time fail to deliver any business value (Williams and Williams, 2007).

3.1. *Measuring Business Intelligence Success*

One of the main issues with Business Intelligence initiatives has always been defining or measuring success, in particular, predicting or proving return on investment (ROI). Williams and Williams (2007) describe adding business value as being about improving management or operational processes in order to increase revenues, decrease costs or both. The benefit of Business Intelligence is not measured in terms of the information provided but in terms of the impact that information has in changing business strategies and processes.

Yeoh and Koronios (2010) define success using five measures: three infrastructure measures of system quality, information quality and system use, together with two process measures of budget and time schedule.

As Williams and Williams (2007) discuss, the challenge comes in isolating the value of Business Intelligence from the value of the strategies. The very nature of Business Intelligence being enterprise wide means that the impact of Business Intelligence cannot be isolated to one process or one strategy.

3.2. *Business Intelligence Success Factors*

The most comprehensive research found that explores critical success factors in Business Intelligence implementation is Yeoh and Koronios (2010). They use a two-stage methodology using the Delphi method to determine the critical success factors and five case studies to test the relationship between these success factors and the success of the Business Intelligence implementation. They found that the one overriding factor for success is having a business-oriented approach.

Seah et al. (2010) reported a case study on the role of indigenous leadership in implementing a business intelligence system. Kašćelan (2011) discusses the outcomes of a single case study and concludes that the relationship between the business and the development team and the cross skilling of this team were key to the project success. Also mentioned are the need to change the approach to information and the re-engineering of business processes. Over time and with growing complexity in the information systems, businesses have abdicated responsibility for not just the information technology (Ross and Weill, 2011) but for the information content, expecting the IT function to produce what they needed to run the business in the form of reports. Expensive Business Intelligence projects were failing to deliver so the business bought more expensive tools, hired and fired IT personnel from consultants to directors (Feld and Stoddard, 2011) and still the projects were failing.

Davenport (1999) discusses three issues with information management:

- "Information evolves in many directions, taking on multiple meanings."

- "People don't share information easily."

- "Changing an IT system won't change a company's information culture."

Each of these emphasises points to information management is a human centred initiative, and should not be ignored. Gartner published a report in 2005 (Hostmann et al.) that outlined seven 'Fatal Flaws' which has since been updated to nine flaws (Hostmann et al., 2008). These flaws are in the most part all about people and processes and echo the same sentiments that Davenport discussed in 1999. Williams and Williams (2007) look at Business Intelligence readiness factors and describe the aspects that need to be in place within the business to provide a foundation for creating business value from Business Intelligence. They list fifteen mistakes of which only three are technical. Gartner (Hostmann et al., 2005; Hostmann et al., 2008) and Williams and Williams (2007) publish the real issues summarised from their experience working with businesses, where Yeoh and Koronios (2010) determined their critical success factors using a panel of experts and a handful of case studies. Warner(2012) organised these issues and success factors together with notes from Seah et al. (2010) and Kašćelan (2011) relating to success criteria.

4. Non-Technical Issues and Success Factors Classification

Analysis of the non-technical issues groups them into four classifications: strategic alignment, strategy level change management, tactical level change management, and process engineering

4.1. *Strategic Alignment*

Strategic alignment is often mentioned as a requirement for success in Business Intelligence. Williams and Williams (2007) list four main points: Understand strategic drivers and goals; determine the business questions that Business Intelligence needs to answer to achieve these goals; identify tools, methods and frameworks to inform decisions and measure performance; and deliver the information required to take actions to support the goals. Strategic alignment ensures the design of the reporting supports business decision making.

4.2. *Change Management*

The Change Management issues often relate to the change in culture that is required to realise the business value of the Business Intelligence initiative.

Business Intelligence is a culture of defined reporting based on business strategy and using the results of that reporting to redefine future strategy. This change in the level of involvement required by the business is something many organisations struggle to achieve. It changes the balance of power in relation to the control and ownership of data and information. The main issue is the change in the information culture. As such, change management become fundamental to the success of any Business Intelligence initiative. This change in information culture needs to be led by the business executive and not IT (Ross and Weill, 2011) therefore change management is required at a strategic level. The tactical level is to effect the changes. The strategic changes need to be supported, and if necessary, enforced, so change management is also critical at a tactical level. If the information culture within the business is to change then the new culture needs to be supported and incentivised and the bad practices need to be exposed and disincentivised (Davenport, 1999). Davenport (1999) states that "Changing the company's information culture is the best way to implement IT, but it's also the hardest to carry out".

Organisational change is easier if there is both certainty and agreement about not only where the organisation is currently but about where the organisation needs to be (Eaton, 2010). Using an Enterprise Architecture such as TOGAF 9 (The Open Group, 2009) can provide the necessary roadmap to define the 'as-is' and future states and enable the planning for how to achieve the future state. The documents created within the framework can aid communication by providing a common language across functional groups. In this way a mature Enterprise Architecture provides a foundation for change and can support the communication and process changes required as part of the changes.

4.3. *Process Engineering*

One area which is often overlooked in this context is process. If the aim is to change the information culture then what is actually changing is the way in which people interact with systems and each other with respect to information. In simple terms, the processes need to change. Process engineering enables the capture of the 'as-is' state for processes. This in turn enables the future state to be mapped out and the route from 'as-is' to future to be planned and managed. Williams and Williams (2007) are supportive of the case for business process engineering as a complement to strategic alignment and an enabler of change management. They refer to the degree of process engineering as the difference between good practice and best practices and therefore a key factor in the success of a Business Intelligence initiative capturing business value. If Enterprise Architecture documents the 'as-is' status for the whole enterprise it will include the processes, therefore enabling the process engineering.

5. How Enterprise Architecture Can Improve Business Intelligence Initiatives

Enterprise Architecture contributes by ensuring that the technology infrastructure is able to support the operating model of the organisation. Ross et al. (2006) talks of digitising the core. Where the core of the business is both digitised and standardised, this provides a foundation for Business Intelligence in both the technology and more importantly by enabling the technology and data to be aligned to the business strategy. Enterprise Architecture ensures that in addition to better understanding of business processes there is enterprise ownership of these processes. By standardising technology, as in stage 2 of the maturity model (Ross et al., 2006), the business has already gone through the complex process of defining common language and definitions for processes and information, delivering strategic alignment and negating the majority of the strategic alignment issues. The change that the business will have undertaken in order to achieve Enterprise Architecture maturity will also provide a foundation for the delivery of change management at both a strategic and tactical level as required by the Business Intelligence lifecycle. If the business is thinking as an enterprise, rather than as separate business silos then the implementation of enterprise wide Business Intelligence will be easier to market to the business as a whole in order to obtain organisational support. While there will still be challenges to be faced in changing business processes, Enterprise Architecture can support and drive the automation of core processes, freeing people from the more tedious tasks, and increase business satisfaction. Business Intelligence contributes to that automation in addition to benefiting from it. It is clear that by achieving a good or mature Enterprise Architecture some of the obstacles to Business Intelligence are reduced or removed. There is also some overlap, as Enterprise Architecture and Business Intelligence share some common challenges, such as the need for change management.

6. Business Intelligence Initiatives Risk Check

Within each class, the issues and success factors have been reformulated into a list of sample questions.

Classification of Issues and Success Criteria	Sample Questions
Strategic Alignment	Is Business Intelligence seen as part of the core function of the business (not a one off IT project)? Is there a committed Business Intelligence sponsor from the business? Is there a Business Intelligence strategy? Is the Business Intelligence Strategy aligned to the business strategy? Is there a business analyst defining the business information requirements that form the Business Intelligence strategy? Are the metrics to be developed aligned to the business strategies?
Change Management - Strategic	Is there data quality management? Is there Business Intelligence governance? Is the Business Intelligence vision / strategy well communicated through the whole organisation? Is the organisation incentivised to support the Business Intelligence strategy? Is there a plan to encourage / enforce a change in information culture? Are there sufficient resources (funding, people, skills, systems)?
Change Management - Tactical	Is Business Intelligence development part of a continuous improvement cycle? Is the plan to encourage / enforce a change in information culture being implemented / championed? Do the users have the appropriate skills and support? Are data quality improvements being implemented?
Process Engineering	Is there a process for Business Intelligence development which is business driven? Is data quality management built into day to day processes? Are end users accountable for data quality? Are the day to day business processes using the Business Intelligence reporting? Are end users held accountable on a day to day basis using the Business Intelligence reporting?

These questions are structured so that a negative response would suggest a significant risk to a Business Intelligence initiative.

7. Conclusion

The Business Intelligence issue classes form a framework for risk analysis that the Business Intelligence initiative would need to mitigate before beginning. This is a realistic short-term solution but in the longer term the organisation would need a strategy that would prevent such a long list of risks in order to ensure a more certain outcome from Business Intelligence initiative and to provide a more stable foundation.

One method for providing a business environment, which would enable the implementation of an enterprise wide Business Intelligence initiative, would be a mature Enterprise Architecture. It is clear that there are parallels and overlaps between Enterprise Architecture and Business Intelligence that suggests that they are interdependent.

8. References

Cottey, P. T. and Chang, R. A. (1996), "Plan your enterprise architecture", *InformationWeek*, , no. 585, pp. 75.

Davenport, T. H. (1999), "Saving IT's Soul: Human-Centered Information Management", in *Harvard business review on the business value of IT*, Harvard Business School Press, Boston, MA.

Eaton, M. (2010), "Achieving successful organisational change ", *Training Journal*, , pp. 38.

Feld, C. S. and Stoddard, D. B. (2011), "Getting IT Right", in Harvard Business Review (ed.) *Harvard Business Review on Aligning Technology with Strategy* Harvard Business School Publishing Corporation, Boston, MA, pp. 25.

Gartner Inc (2011), *IT Glossary: Business Intelligence*, available at: http://www.gartner.com/technology/it-glossary/business-intelligence.jsp (accessed 09/03).

Hostmann, B., Buytendijk, F. and Friedman, T. (2005), *Avoid the 'Fatal Flaws' of Business Intelligence and Corporate Performance Management* G00129090, Gartner Inc.

Hostmann, B., Buytendijk, F. and Friedman, T. (2008), *Gartner Reveals Nine Fatal Flaws in Business Intelligence Implementations*, available at: http://www.gartner.com/it/page.jsp?id=774912 (accessed 08/12).

Kašćelan, L. (2011), "Advantages and Limitations in Implementation of Business Intelligence System in Montenegro: Case Study Telenor Montenegro", *Economic Review: Journal of Economics & Business / Ekonomska Revija: Casopis za Ekonomiju i Biznis*, vol. 9, no. 2, pp. 19-30.

Kimball, R., Ross, M., Thornthwaite, W., Mundy, J. and Becker, B. (2008), *The data warehouse lifecycle toolkit* 2nd ed, Wiley, Indianapolis.

Parr Rud, O. (2009), *Business Intelligence Success Factors:Tools for Aligning Your Business in the Global Economy*, John Wiley & Sons, Inc, Hoboken, New Jersey.

Ross, J. W. and Weill, P. (2011), "Six IT Decisions your IT People Shouldn't Make ", in Harvard Business Review (ed.) *Harvard Business Review on Aligning Technology with Strategy* Harvard Business School Publishing Corporation, Boston, MA, pp. 1.

Ross, J. W., Robertson, D. C. and Weill, P. (2006), *Enterprise architecture as strategy: creating a foundation for business execution*, Harvard Business School Press, Boston.

Ryan, H. and Santucci, J. (1993), "Building an enterprise information architecture", *InfoWorld*, vol. 15, no. 12, pp. 57.

Sabherwal, R. and Becerra-Fernandez, I. (2011), *Business intelligence: practices, technologies, and management* Wiley; John Wiley distributor, Hoboken, N.J.; Chichester.

Seah, M., Hsieh, M. H. and Weng, P. D. (2010), "A case analysis of Savecom: The role of indigenous leadership in implementing a business intelligence system", *International Journal of Information Management*, vol. 30, no. 4, pp. 368-373.

Sessions, R. (2007a), A Comparison of the Top Four Enterprise-Architecture Methodologies, available at: http://msdn.microsoft.com/en-us/library/bb466232.aspx (accessed 05/31).

Sessions, R. (2007b), Enterprise Architecture - A 20 Year Retrospective: Exclusive Interview with John Zachman, available at: http://www.objectwatch.com/whitepapers/ IASANewsletterApril2007.pdf (accessed 05/31).

Sessions, R. (2008), *Simple Architectures for Complex Enterprises* Microsoft Press, Washington.

Spewak, S. H. (1993), *Enterprise architecture planning : developing a blueprint for data, applications and technology*, QED Publishing Group.

The Open Group (2009), *TOGAF Version 9* Van Haren Publishing, Zaltbommel, Netherlands.

Warner, S. (2012) Enterprise Architecture: the Next Step for Business Intelligence, MSc thesis, Cranfield University.

Williams, S. and Williams, N. (2007), *The Profit Impact of Business Intelligence*, Morgan Kaufmann Publishers, San Francisco.

Yeoh, W. and Koronios, A. (2010), "Critical Success Factors for Business Intelligence Systems", *Journal of Computer Information Systems*, vol. 50, no. 3, pp. 23-32.

Zachman, J. A. (1987), "A Framework for Information Systems Architecture", *IBM Systems Journal*, vol. 26, no. 3, pp. 276.

Zachman, J. A. (1997), *Enterprise Architecture: The Issue of the Century*, available at: http://www.aeablogs.org/eakd/files/EA_The_Issue_of_the_Century.pdf (accessed 09/03).

Towards Enterprise Architecture Using Solution Architecture Models

Vadim Agievich* — **Rinat Gimranov**** — **Victor Taratoukhine*****
Jörg Becker***

* Higher School of Economy, National Research University
ul.Myasnitskaya, 20
101000 Moscow, Russia
Agievich_VA@Surgutneftegas.ru

** Surgutneftegas, OJSC,
ul.Grigoriya Kukuevitskogo, 1, bld.1
628415 Surgut, Russia
Gimranov_RD@mail.ru

*** ERCIS – Headquarters, Münster, Germany
Leonardo-Campus 3
48149 Münster, Germany
victor.taratoukhine@ercis.uni-muenster.de

ABSTRACT: *This position paper is focused on an issue of development of a baseline Enterprise Architecture for a large company. The paper outlines a new method of baseline Enterprise Architecture modelling using Solution Architecture models.*

KEYWORDS: *enterprise architecture, solution architecture, large company*

1. Introduction

The Enterprise Architecture (EA) discipline, although more than 15 years old is still uncertain in its application in real world enterprises. There are many EA frameworks, methods and tools but the EA practice still has areas that are not as formalized as practitioners would expect. At the moment a number of different Enterprise Architecture frameworks and tools exist but challenges still remain both from framework and organizational perspectives as H.Shah and M.Kourdi describe in [Shah 2007]. One of the challenges of EA development for large companies is organizing baseline EA development.

Enterprise Architecture is often referred as a blueprint for how an organization achieves the current and future business objectives using IT. It examines the key business, information, application, and technology strategies and their impact on business functions. It provides the framework for planning and implementing a rich, standards-based, digital information infrastructure with well-integrated services and activities [Dahalin et al., 2010]. It's a strategic information asset base, which defines the mission, the information necessary to perform the mission, the technology, and the transformational processes for implementing new technologies in response to the changing mission needs [Schekkerman 2009]. Solution Architecture (SA) discipline is closely related to EA but is typically used in a different context. Moreover, they are often seen as different disciplines and different practices. As M.Ricca related in [Ricca 2011], of the two, EA is sometimes regarded as the rich and decadent relative while SA is the honest, reliable, and hard-working one. Enterprise Architecture is a bird's-eye view of the business and it's IT. It is like city plan. Solution Architecture in this respect is like a building plan of the city. It reflects some parts of IT and their connections to the business. Thus they describe the same things but from different prospective and in different granularity. These considerations (along with some other arguments shown below) let authors to make a conclusion that a baseline Enterprise Architecture (in its' IT part) can be built automatically from Solution Architecture models data within an integrated modelling tool.

2. Enterprise Architecture Models

There is no common way of Enterprise Architecture modelling. The models are described by corresponding Enterprise Architecture frameworks. Enterprise Architecture frameworks define the scope of the Enterprise Architecture and decompose various elements of the architecture onto structured levels and elements [Shah et al., 2007]. These elements and their relations are described in a metamodel that is the core of most Enterprise Architecture frameworks. According to [The Open Group 2011] a metamodel is a model that describes how and with what the architecture will be described in a structured way.

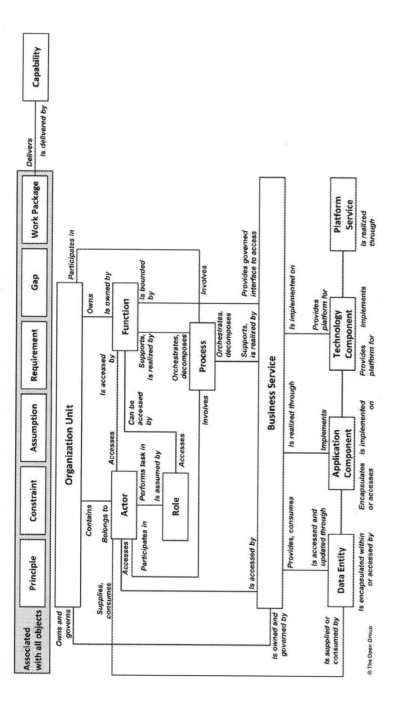

Figure 1. *TOGAF core metamodel*

Models in an EA repository are organized in a way that provides a complete set of objects and relationships between them according to the metamodel definition. Fig. 1 presents the metamodel of The Open Group Architecture Framework (TOGAF) that is one of the most well-known and highly-adopted EA frameworks.

3. Connecting Solution Architecture with Enterprise Architecture

According to [The Open Group 2011] Solution Architecture is a description of a discrete and focused business operation or activity and how IS/IT supports that operation. A Solution Architecture typically applies to a single project or project release, assisting in the translation of requirements into a solution vision, high-level business and/or IT system specifications, and a portfolio of implementation tasks.

In order to use Solution Architecture models data for Enterprise Architecture models the models should be compatible and consistent. Therefore the compatibility and consistency should be provided in granularity, language and model components.

According to the standard ISO/IEC 15288 "Systems and software engineering – System life cycle processes" [ISO 2002] architectural design processes include logical architecture (or high-level) design and physical architecture design. Also the standard indicates types of models that solution architects may use for logical design phase.

The models of Solution Architecture that are created on the phase of high-level design are close to Enterprise Architecture development in the sense of granularity. Thus these models may be used then in Enterprise Architecture modelling.

Requirements for Solution Architecture descriptions are specified in ISO/IEC/IEEE 42010: Architecture descriptions are used by the parties that create, utilize and manage modern systems to improve communication and co-operation; enabling them to work in an integrated, coherent fashion. Architecture frameworks and architecture description languages are created as assets that codify the conventions and common practices of architecting and the description of architectures within different communities and domains of application [ISO 2011].

4. Solution Architecture Modelling

M. Lankhorst in the paper notes that enterprise modeling should focus on bringing together already existing techniques and integrating these at the appropriate level of abstraction [Lankhorst et al., 2004].

In order to stay compatible with EA models SA models may and should be based on the same architecture framework. There are several methods and languages of modelling for Solution Architectures and System Architectures that support creating models compatible with some Enterprise Architecture frameworks ([Frankel et al., 2003], [OSI 2008], [OSI 2011], [The Open Group 2012]).

After the authors' study of such languages they came to a conclusion that the most suitable language for the purpose described above is Archimate [The Open Group 2012]. It is supported by The Open Group and is able to serve as a modeling language for of the most common EA frameworks used in large companies – TOGAF [The Open Group 2011].

In order to provide necessary data compatibility SA and EA modelers should use the same vocabulary of objects (object catalogs). It is possible only within a special integrated modelling tool.

An EA framework used in a company may contain some elements that are out of the scope of Solution Architecture descriptions, e.g. enterprise drivers and goals, non-automated functions (see fig.1). That is why Enterprise Architecture may be built from Solution Architectures only in IT part and should be complemented with business models in order to be complete. Hence if we have business models in the repository and make SA and EA models using a unified toolset based on unified building blocks (object catalogs) we may present a baseline EA as a projection of initial Business Architecture and all Solution Architectures of the company (see Fig.2).

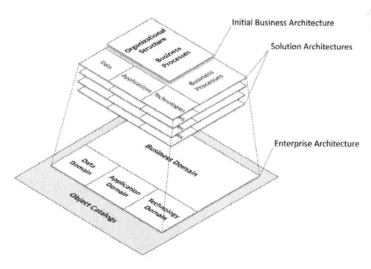

Figure 2. *Enterprise Architecture as a projection of Solution Architectures*

5. Conclusion

The authors stated the theses that an Enterprise Architecture may be created using Solution Architecture models despite the differences between the two disciplines. Also the method of developing EA using Solution Architectures was shortly outlined.

6. References

Becker, J., Kugeler, M., Rosemann, M.: *Process Management: A Guide for the Design of Business Processes*, Springer, 2003.

Dahalin, Z.M., Razak, R.A., Ibrahim, H, Yusop N.I., Kasiran, M.K.: An Enterprise Architecture Methodology for Business-IT Alignment - Adopter and Developer Perspectives. CIBIMA 2010, Article ID 222028, 2010.

Frankel D., Harmon P., Mukerji J., Odell J., Owen M., Rivitt P., Rosen M., Soley R.M: The Zachman Framework and the OMG's Model Driven Architecture. Business Process Trends. 2003. №9.

ISO/IEC 15288:2002 Systems and software engineering – System life cycle processes, 2002.

ISO/IEC/IEEE 42010:2011 Systems and software engineering – Architecture description, 2011.

Lankhorst, M.M.: Enterprise architecture modeling - the issue of integration, *Advanced Engineering Informatics* 18, 205–216, 2004.

Office of System Integration (OSI): OSI Solution Architecture Framework. http://www.bestpractices.osi.ca.gov/sysacq/documents/OSISolutionArchitectureFramewo rk.pdf, 2008.

Office of System Integration (OSI): Solution Architecture Framework Toolkit. http://www.bestpractices.osi.ca.gov/sysacq/documents/solution_architecture_framework_ toolkit.pdf, 2011.

Open Group, The, TOGAF 9.1, http://pubs.opengroup.org/architecture/togaf9-doc/arch/, Published 2011.

Open Group, The: ArchiMate 2.0 Specification http://pubs.opengroup.org/architecture /archimate2-doc/, 2012.

Ricca, M.: Bridging the Gap Between Enterprise Architecture and Solution Architecture for Maximum Benefit, http://www.oracle.com/technetwork/articles/entarch/ricca-bridging-ea- sa-457138.html, Published September 2011.

Schekkerman, J.: *How to Manage the Enterprise Architecture Practice*. Trafford Publishing, 2009.

Shah H., Kourdi M.: Enterprise Architecture Frameworks, IEEE IT Professional, Vol 9, No 5, 2007.

Shah, H., Kourdi, M.: Frameworks for Enterprise Architecture, IT Pro September - October 2007.

Workshop 3

Standardisation for Interoperability in the Service-Oriented Enterprise

Report Workshop 3

Martin Zelm* — David Chen**

* INTEROP-VLab, Belgium
martin.zelm@t-online.de

** IMS, Bordeaux University
351 Cours de la libération, 33405 Talence, France
david.chen@ims-bordeaux.fr

The objective of this workshop at the IWEI 2013 has been to disseminate/diffuse standardisation activities of the European project MSEE (Manufacturing Services Ecosystem) and to increase awareness of standards development with focus on the service oriented enterprise. New research topics in the frame of Ecosystems have been presented, discussed and some proposed for standardization, namely service modeling languages, service life cycle management and a reference ontology for manufacturing as well as tools for Negotiating Interoperability Solutions. The first paper titled "Standardisation in Manufacturing Service Engineering" presented by Martin Zelm (Interop-VLab; Belgium) reported on a survey in the FP7 project MSEE to establish the level of understanding and experience with standards, for instance 93 % of the responses say that standards are important. The areas of required future service standards have been identified as Service Modelling Languages, Service Lifecycle and EI Framework. An early involvement in the standardisation process is explored, since the normal standardisation process usually starts after completion of a development project and due to lack of funding is not any more supported by the developers. The discussion went about how to best start this process. For example in the OMG, a "Request for project" (RFP) can be produced early in a project and takes about one year to agree.

The second paper titled "An approach to standardise service lifecycle management" prepared by Mike Freitag et al (IAO Fraunhofer Institute, Germany) discussed an approach to standardize Service Lifecycle Management in order to support manufacturing companies to develop their services on a systematic way. A framework and the phases of Life Cycle Management are proposed, applicable to the next steps in the servitization process as well as the challenges to be considered when it comes to the conditions for service innovations. These concepts have some commonality with the ISO/STEP standards for the product life cycle. As brought up in the discussion the requirements of the Service provider versus that of Service user needs to be considered and balanced.

The third paper titled "Open business model and service innovation with VDML and ServiceML". presented by Arne Berre (SINTEF, Norway) addressed a platform developed in the FP7 NEFFICS project on Open Business Model , Process and Service innovation for networked enterprises. The platform is based on a business model framework with six views, where each view is supported by a corresponding diagram view from the Value Delivery Modeling Language (VDML). The AT-ONE method provides an insight into service innovation and is developed for end users and consultancies for further development of corresponding executable models and simulation models. All specifications up to the latest version VDML 2012 are public available. The final version is planned for Sept 2013.

The fourth paper titled "Service Modelling Languages and potential for a new standard" presented by David Chen (University of Bordeaux, France) discussed the added value for end user of modelling languages is that he knows how to build a system, but not in a systematic way. Further, it is not easy to re-engineer an existing system, The proposed modelling approach makes this easier. Early proposals for a specification can be made. Further, there are similarities between the SML approach and the VDML approach, as an excellent opportunity to bring the work into OMG along with the VDML work. First action will be a mapping exercise, which needs resource and active participation.

The fifth paper titled "Reference ontologies for manufacturing" presented by Robert Young, (Loughborough University, UK) discussed ideas towards the development of a reference ontology for manufacturing which could provide a basis for the validation of the interoperability compliance either between systems or between standards. The methodology of service templates presented shows some similarity with that used for the SML in the fourth paper. The question how to insure interoperability between reference ontologies for ontologies and between the modelling languages needed to build them i.e. OWL, CL etc needs further work. Finally, Carlos Coutinho, (Universidade Nova de Lisboa, Portugal) presented in a paper titled "Standardisation tools for Negotiating Interoperability Solutions" an effort to develop a standardized Sustained Interoperability Framework based on agents and rules to achieve solid and stable integration of solutions in the manufacturing supply chain, using existing standards, via the deployment of a strong and formal negotiation mechanism. Further, a prototype based on the Java Development Framework (JADE) is proposed to prove that the interoperability between two or more systems is more controllable and stable with the above negotiation method. In the discussion, the question came up which SDOs can be involved in this negotiation technique and who may be interested in the early work.

Standardisation in Manufacturing Service Engineering

Martin Zelm — Guy Doumeingts

c/o INTEROP VLab, Belgium
martin.zelm@t-online.de
guy.doumeingts@interop-vlab.eu

ABSTRACT: *Product related service is a key element of any service-oriented manufacturing system. The paper presents methods to capture standardization knowledge in the European Integrated Project Manufacturing SErvice Engineering (MSEE), with the goal to initiate development of standards in the domain of manufacturing engineering services.*

For this purpose, a project internal survey has been performed to identify areas of potential standardization that can lead to future standards. With the survey, a coordinated follow-up within the project and subsequent external promotion are foreseen. An early involvement in the standardisation process is explored, since the normal standardisation process usually starts after completion of a development project and due to lack of funding is not any more supported by the developers.

KEYWORDS: *manufacturing service engineering, standardisation process, enterprise modelling*

1. Introduction

In the past, manufacturing industry has considered the physical product as their main deliverable to the customer. Today manufacturing at large is undergoing a change from the production of physical goods to a service oriented portfolio. With changing market requirements, it has become necessary to offer to the customer services linked to the product called "Extended Product" (Thoben et al. 2001). Such services include for example warranty support, repairs, updates or maintenance services. The FP7 Integrated Project MSEE (Manufacturing Service Ecosystem)1 aims to create new Industrial Models for the Virtual Factory. The vision of MSEE is characterised by new management methodologies in the business infrastructure of the Future Internet that will enable self-organization in distributed ecosystem. The components of such ecosystem are merged dynamically and delivered as services, along the global value chain.

Standardisation - the creation and use of standards - is an important means to stabilize enterprise activities and insure interoperation between enterprises. Standards should complement the development of technical specifications beginning during the research activities in order to ease the implementation of new products and services. But standardisation is built on voluntary collaboration among industry, academia, consumers, public authorities and other interested stakeholders and is very often handicapped by budget constraints of the academic developers. A specific issue of interaction between research and standardisation in the ICT domain has been elaborated in the COPRAS2 study namely, how can research results contribute to standardisation and how can the research results benefit from standards. The COPRAS Guidelines provide three recommendations:

- standardisation is one opportunity for ICT research projects to disseminate their results

- standardisation efforts (identify work items and planning involvement) should be started at the beginning of an ICT project

- direct involvement of the project partners in standardization bodies is highly recommended.

We employ these recommendations as an orientation in the MSEE project work.

2. State of the Art in Service Engineering

Since several years, SDOs (Standards Development Organizations) as ISO, IEC, and industry consortia like W3C, OMG and OASIS that have been active to standardize different aspects of services as for example service functionalities,

---

1 MSEE www.msee-ip.eu/
2 COoperation Platform for Research And Standards (COPRAS), http://www.w3.org/2004/copras/

service behaviour or quality of services. Complementary to the work of SDOs, initiatives from academia have concentrated on developing ontologies and formal languages for specifying services. The initiatives below are relevant for standardization of services in the domains of MSEE.

Service Oriented Architecture (SOA) is a concept existing since long time and comprises a set of principles and methodologies for designing and developing software in the form of interoperable services. These services are well-defined business functionalities that are built as software components. A number of standards is already available many more are in development mainly in the Object Management Group (OMG).

Digital Business Ecosystem (DBE) is a distributed open socio-technical system with properties of self-organisation, inspired from the knowledge of natural ecosystems. From a practical viewpoint, *DBE* 3 is a free, open source and distributed software platform. The platform is based on Internet technologies and is designed to enable SMEs to create, integrate and provide services - both in real world business and in software-.

Service Science Management and Engineering (SSME) has been proposed by IBM as an emerging discipline of integrated research in the fields of measuring, representing and cataloguing services and skills to be applied in service workforce management and in effective computer supported service automation. From life cycle perspective, MSEE 4envisages an Integrated Service Lifecycle Management reference model, which could become a standard by itself.

Similar standards on *Product Lifecycle Management (PLM)* exist as for instance ISO 10303 'Automation systems and integration - Product data representation and exchange' a standard, which was further adapted into the open standard STEP (STandard for Exchange of Product data model) and implemented with various sector oriented Application Protocols (AP) via the industry consortia PDES, Inc and ProSTEP.

User Specifications of Enterprise Business Services: Standards for the service economy have been elaborated with the Fraunhofer IAO Institute and the German Institute for Standardization DIN5 (Deutsches Institut für Normung e.V.). The standards have been published as Publicly Available Specifications (PAS, 2008-2011). Examples of manufacturing oriented services are for instance PAS 1018: 'Essential structure for the description of services in the procurement stage' or PAS

---

3 http://www.digital-ecosystem.org/
4 http://www.MSEE-ip.eu, Description of Work, WP2
5 http://www.DIN.de

1019: 'Structured model and criteria for the selection and evaluation of capital services'

Two major research initiatives addressing the Future Internet should be mentioned: The *FI-WARE*6 project is introducing an innovative infrastructure for cost-effective creation and delivery of services The *IERC* European Research Cluster on the Internet of Things is bringing together EU-funded projects with the aim of defining a common vision and the IoT technology.

3. MSEE approach to standardisation

MSEE is aiming to achieve early awareness of potential service standards in the context of the research work. A particular workpackage has been setup under the title 'Access and contribution to standards' with the following goals:

1. to motivate and support MSEE researcher in the process of transforming project results into new standards. Information about MSEE standardisation results will be actively disseminated inside and outside of the MSEE project.

2. to develop relations with SDOs and Industry consortia active in standardisation, in order to understand better new ways to develop standards.

3. to promote the transfer of MSEE research results into standardisation by helping to identify potential subjects capable to create specific standards in the relevant project domains of SME networks. This requires for the workpackage partners both, an early involvement in the project life cycle and a clear understanding of the standardisation process.

Work has started with a MSEE related survey to elaborate a common level of knowledge about the state of the art and requirements for standardisation work among the project partners.

4. The standardisation survey

The goal of the survey was to understand the level of knowledge about standards and the involvement of the MSEE partners in standardisation. The survey was performed as an online questionnaire with seven questions to be answered by 18 project partners. The survey shows that 93% of the answers state a need for standardisation in the project. More detailed results say that the recommended area should be in enterprise services e.g. primarily in service languages and ontologies.

---

6 http://www.fi-ware.eu

However only 50% of the partners have already been involved in standardisation work of SDOs, which indicates that education is necessary to increase the level of involvement in standardisation. The survey results are presented in Table 1. Some remarks identify domains where standards are needed.

Question	Number of answers, Results Yes/No	Remarks
1. ID of answering person?	18 answers received	N/A
2. Have you been involved in the development of standards?	18/18 answers received 9 Yes, (50%), 9 No	N/A
3. If yes, in which domains? (e.g.: Enterprise Services, Enterprise Interoperability, Internet Technologies)	12/18 answers received 6 Yes (50%) 6 No	2 Enterprise Services, 2 Enterprise Interoperability 2 Internet Technologies
4. Have you been in contact with Standards Development Organisations (CEN, National organisations, OMG...)?	12/18 answers received 6 Yes (50%) 6 No	
5. In your opinion, do you see needs for standardisation within the MSEE project?	15/18 answers received 14 Yes (93%) 1 No	
6. If yes, in which domain(s) do you think that MSEE can propose new standards?	Enterprise Interoperability Framework 7 Service modelling and LC 12 Infrastructure Structural Services 2	Other areas proposed: XML, QML, USDL, Languages for Services / for Systems, Methods for SSME, Maturity Models
7. If yes, what SDO do you recommend?	CEN 9 National 1	Other proposed: OG, OASIS, W3C, ISO TC 184, CEN CWA

Table 1. *Answers and results per question*

Additional comments have been received from the project partners within the survey. They are shown in Table 2 as examples.

Question	Comments
1. ID of answering person?	N/A
2. Have you been involved in the development of standards?	N/A
3. If yes, in which domains? (e.g.: Enterprise Services, Enterprise Interoperability, Internet Technologies)	- Internet technologies cad/cam lectra & gerber technology for cutter interoperability eBIZ textile: http://ebiz-tcf.eu/ - Product/service lifecycle management - Business Modelling and Integration - Semantic Web Services, Semantic WEB - Enterprise Interoperability, Enterprise Modelling - UBL2.0 SBS in 2007
4. Have you been in contact with Standards Development Organisations (CEN, National organisations, OMG...)?	- CEN for clothing sizing charts - Yes. I am Planning and Policy Committee member in ISO TC184/SC4, and active as project leader developing standards in this committee. I am also the head of the Portuguese Delegation - Yes, I have been working in cooperation with BSI, as far as translation and review of standards are concerned
5. In your opinion, do you see needs for standardisation within the MSEE project?	N/A
6. If yes, in which domain(s) do you think that MSEE can propose new standards?	- It would be useful to interface with the ongoing standardization that we are carrying out on product-service lifecycle management, called QLM, within the OpenGroup - User oriented Service modelling for Service Life Cycle Manufacturing - Propose Languages for modelling services and service system
7. If yes, what SDO do you recommend?	- USDL standardization efforts seem to move towards the Linked Open Data approach. Creation of an "USDL Manufacturing Profile" could be an appropriate way to position MSEE requirements in the area of service description as a de-facto standard. - ISO. As an experience from the past, which resulted in 29 ISO standards, I would recommend to create a CEN Workshop, and then develop CEN Workshop Agreements (CWAs) to be submitted immediately after to ISO for international standardisation

Table 2. *Comments per question*

Overall, the survey indicates that standardisation activities are ongoing or can be proposed. Priorities for new work items will be analysed with the partners. Three areas for potential standards development have been identified from the survey results: Enterprise Interoperability/Enterprise Modelling for an extension of CEN/ISO 11543 to address Maturity Models in Manufacturing Service Ecosystems ; Service modelling languages including USDL (Universal Service Description Language) and Service Life Cycle Management; Semantic WEB Services for the manufacturing domain. Proposals for standardisation are mainly expected from the MSEE Sub Projects SP1 involved in Service Modeling for Service Lifecycle Management and from SP2 working on Reference Frameworks for Service based Ecosystems. Standardisation groups to take up MSEE requirements could be for instance CEN TC 310 'Advanced Automation Technologies and their Applications' or ISO 10303 'STEP Data Modelling and Access' or Linked Open Data or the Open Group.

5. Conclusion and Further Work

Besides a brief introduction to manufacturing service engineering and the MSEE project, the results of a standardisation survey conducted in the project have been reported. From the survey results, opportunities for three domains of potential standards development have been identified, namely Enterprise Frameworks/ Enterprise Modelling, Service modelling / Service Lifecycle Management and Semantic WEB Services for manufacturing.

Further work will concentrate on setting priorities for new work items and on support of new or increased participation in SDOs, with the goal to develop reference specifications and finally international standards. For this effort owners of the standardisation process must be identified. They have to define with an expert group the work item, to find the acceptance in the voting and to manage the development/

In parallel the new standardisation knowledge will be promoted via workshops and scientific conferences as part of the dissemination plan of the project.

The paper is mainly based on work performed in the project MSEE - Manufacturing SErvice Ecosystem. MSEE is an Integrated Project funded by the European Commission within the ICT Work Programme under the European Community's 7th Framework Programme (FoF-ICT-2011.7.3).

6. References

European Commission, "Modernising ICT Standardisation in the EU – The Way Forward", COM 324, 2009

Framework for Enterprise Interoperability, CEN/ISO 11354 , (2010)   ISO TC 184/ SC5, http://www.iso.org

King, J., Lyytinen, K. (Eds), " Standards making: A critical research frontier for information systems",. *MSI Quarterly Special Issue*, 2003

Open systems application integration framework, ISO 15745 (2003), ISO/TC184/SC5, http://www.iso.org

Product Life Cycle Management - the QLM Working Group (2012) of the OpenGroup, available from https://collaboration.opengroup.org/qlm

Service-oriented Architecture Standards, SOA Work Group (2012), The Open Group, available from http://www.opengroup.org/standards/soa

Unified Service Description Language (USDL), W3C USDL Incubator Group, (2011), available from http://www.w3.org/2005/Incubator/usdl/

Web Ontology Language (OWL). World Wide Web Consortium, available from http://www.w3.org//2004/OWL

7. Appendix: Standards Development Organisations

CEN	Comité Européen de Normalisation
CENELEC	European Committee for Electrotechnical Standardisation
ETSI	European Telecommunication Standards Institute
IEC	International Electrotechnical Commission
IEEE	Institute of Electrical and Electronics Engineers
IERC	European Research Cluster on the Internet of Things
ISO	International Organisation for Standardisation
NIST	National Institute of Standards and Technology
OASIS	Organization for the Advancement of Structured Information Standards
OMG	Object Management Group
UN/CEFACT	United Nations Centre for Trade Facilitation and Electronic Business
W3C	World Wide Web Consortium

Service Modelling Language and Potentials for a New Standard

David Chen

IMS, University of Bordeaux
351 Cours de la libération, 33405 Talence, France
david.chen@ims-bordeaux.fr

ABSTRACT: This paper presents a service modelling language for the design and implementation of service system in a Virtual Manufacturing Enterprise (VME) environment. The proposed approach is developed under the frame of an ongoing FP7 European Integrated Project MSEE. A Model Driven Service Engineering Architecture (MDSEA) adapted from MDA/MDI acts as a framework for the proposed service modelling language. The paper focuses on the modelling language defined at BSM (Business Service Model) level which is presented in detail. Conclusions are given in the end of the paper.

KEYWORDS: servitization, service modelling, enterprise modelling, model driven architecture

1. Introduction

This paper presents the result of a research work performed in the frame of the European FP7 MSEE Integrated Project (Manufacturing SErvice Ecosystem) [5]. Particularly, the goal of this work is to develop a service (system) modelling language to support service system engineering in Virtual Manufacturing Enterprise (VME) environments. The proposed service modeling language makes uses of existing relevant enterprise modeling techniques as a basis with necessary adaptations and extensions. Service is usually seen as interactions between customers and service provider. The service system is an integrated set of interacting components providing particular services. The language aims at modeling both service and service system.

The paper is structured as follows: section 2 presents modeling language principle based on the EN/ISO 19440 standard. Section 3 gives an overview of the proposed MDSEA architecture considered as a framework to develop the language. In section 4 the service modeling language will be presented in detail focusing on the Business Service Modelling (BSM) level. Section 5 discusses some standardization potentials of the proposed language. Section 6 concludes the paper.

2. Modelling Principle

An enterprise modeling language is defined by a set of modeling concepts/ constructs with identified interrelationships between the constructs.

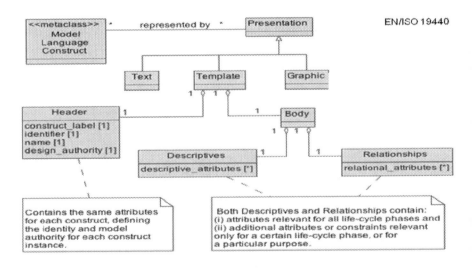

Figure 1. *Modelling language constituents [3]*

Construct(s) can be represented by: (a) graphical representation, (b) template description, and (c) text. A template will contain a header part to identify a construct instance, and a body part to describe the particular instance with descriptive and relationship attributes [3]. The proposed service modeling language is consistent to enterprise modeling language constituents defined in EN/ISO 19440 standard [3] as shown Figure 1.

3. Model Driven Service Engineering Architecture

A Model Driven Service Engineering Architecture (MDSEA) is elaborated on the basis of MDA/MDI [1],[2] to allow supporting the needs of modelling the three types of service system components (IT, Human and Physical Means). This MDSEA can be considered as adaptation and extension of MDA/MDI to the engineering of product related services in virtual manufacturing enterprise environment. The adapted MDSEA is shown figure 2 [6].

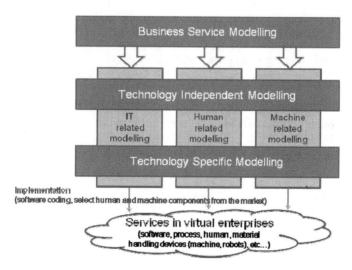

Figure 2. *MDSEA architecture*

Similar to MDA/MDI, the proposed MDSEA defines three abstraction levels [6]:

- Business System Modelling (BSM), which specifies the models, at the global level, describing the running of the enterprise or set of enterprises as well as the links between these enterprises. The models at the BSM level must be independent of the future technologies that will be used for the various resources. In this sense, it's useful, not only as an aid to understand a problem, but also that it plays an important role in bridging the gap between domain experts and the development experts that will build the service system (adapted [4]).

- Technology Independent Modelling (TIM), which are the models at a second (lower) level of abstraction independent from the technology used to implement the system. It gives detailed specifications of the structure and functionality of the service system that do not propose technological details. At TIM level, the detailed specification will be elaborated with respect to the components in the domains of IT, Organisation and Human and Physical means for a service system.

- Technology Specific Modelling (TSM) that combines the specification in the TIM model with details that specify how the system uses a particular type of technology (such as for example IT platform, Physical Means or Organisation with particular Human profiles). At TSM level, modelling and specifications must provide sufficient details to allow developing or buying software/hardware components, recruiting human operators / managers or establishing internal training plans, buying and realizing machine devices, for supporting and delivering services in interaction with customers.

4. Service Modelling Language Defined at BSM level

Based on existing relevant enterprise modeling techniques and service modeling and engineering concepts, a set of service modelling constructs[1] are identified to represent service system at BSM level. Figure 3 shows those constructs and defines the relationships between the constructs. Each construct can be further described by a template, a graphical representation and a text to explain some specific concerns and detail.

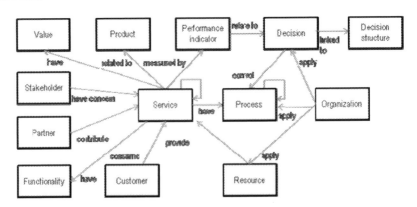

Figure 3. *Modelling constructs and relationships at BSM level*

---

1 Construct = Concept + its representation (template, graphics, text)

In a servitization process carried out by a manufacturing enterprise towards a VME, considered *Service* is related to a *Product*. To develop such a service, various *Stakeholders* (providers, intermediary, engineers, etc.) may express their specific concerns. *Partners* are integrated stakeholder of the virtual enterprise providing particular services to the overall undertaking. Service is used / consumed by *Customers*. Service provides *Functionality* (*functions*) which are utilities to fulfill customer's needs. Service has therefore *Value*(s). Service provided can be evaluated by a set of *Performance Indicators* which are related to a set of *Decisions* which control the service system, i.e. to a set of objectives, and decision variables. Decisions are related in a *Decision Structure* where consistence / coherence must be analyzed. To provide service to customer, *Process*(es) is/are in general needed to be defined and followed at run time. Generally speaking, a service system is constituted by any combination of the three types of resource (IT, Human, Physical means) which will be specified at TIM level. Finally, to ensure a good functioning of a service system, *Organization* structure (hierarchical, decentralized, ...) will be defined. Details in terms of responsibility and authorization (who is responsible for what and who is authorized to operate on what resource, process and decision-making) will be defined as well at TIM and TSM levels. Indeed, for instance, at the BSM level, the decisions are listed but not the related decision makers are linked to decision support systems. Similarly, the types of resources doing the activities are listed but not the precise name or location of those resources.

It is to note that for each modelling construct defined in the language shown in figure 3, a template is also provided to allow a detailed description of its attributes. Figure 4 shows an example of the 'Service' template to further describe the 'service' construct. The template identifies the name of the service 'Electric car battery maintenance', the service content description (clearing, repairing,...), the objective and constraints as well as the nature of the service. Additional attributes for specific cases can also be added to the template if necessary.

Header		Example
Construct label	['Service']	Serive
Identifier	[Identifier of the service instance]	S001
Name	[name of the service instance]	Electric car battery maintenance
Design authority*	[<identifier> / <name> of the person/organisation with authority to design/maintain this particular instance]	
Body		
DOMAIN	[Domain of the service]	Maintenance (after sale)
DESCRIPTION	[short textual description of the functionality / utility]	This service is to cleaning, recharging, repairing (replacing parts) of electric car battery
OBJECTIVE	[Short textual description]	keep battery function at its 90% capacity during 3 months after a maintenance
CONSTRAINT	[Short textual description]	Need 24 hours delay to deliver service, must booking the service from Web
NATURE	['Physical' or 'Information' or 'human']	Human and physical
CLASSIFICATION	[Refer to Product Service System (PSS) classification]	Additional Service

Figure 4. *Template for 'Service' modelling construct*

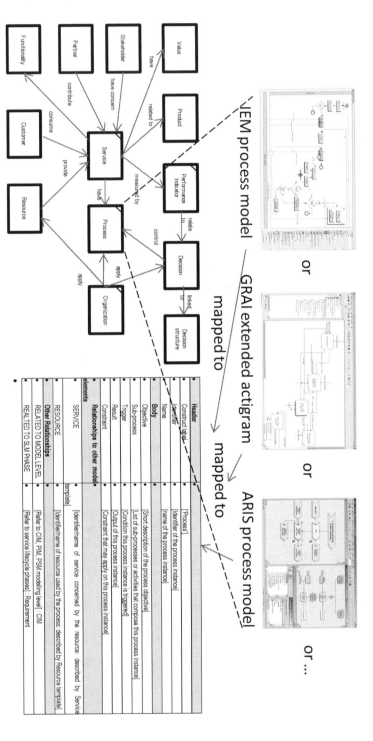

Figure 5. *Use of template - example of 'Process' modelling construct*

The proposed service modeling language supports, through the use of templates, the integration of existing modeling techniques. Model information captured and collected using a particular language/tool can be mapped to templates which are neutral. Figure 5 illustrates the use of the process template to map the modeling elements used by various process modeling language/tools. For example the process template should contain all those attributes used by main existing process modeling languages (such as IDEF3, BPMN, GRAI extended actigram, MoGo process tool, ISO 19440 process modeling construct, etc) so that only a subset of those template attributes are used when a particular existing process modeling language is used. Another purpose of template is to support model transformation between various different modeling languages and tools. Model information can be stored in template form independently of its graphical representation. A particular graphical representation can be reconstructed from template according to the need of a specific end user. To support the use of existing enterprise modeling techniques, mapping is done to define the link between proposed modeling constructs and existing languages. Generally speaking a modelling language/ tool can support one or several constructs, for examples: GRAI grid and nets supported by GRAI methodology and GraiTools allows the modelling of decisions and decision-making structure; Actigram can be used to model functions and functionality, etc. Figure 6 shows a tentative mapping of main known existing enterprise modelling languages to the BSM service modelling constructs [7].

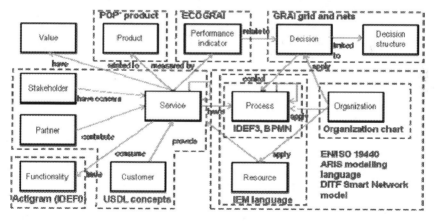

Figure 6. *Mapping existing languages to BSM service modelling constructs*

The Business Service Model (templates and graphical representations) will then be transformed to Technology Independent Model (TIM) for detail design and Technology Specific Model (TSM) for additional supplementary specifications needed to develop and implement the designed service system (see detail in [6]).

5. Potentials for Standardisation

There is no language international standard for the modelling of service system. Most of existing enterprise languages can be reused to model part of a service system. But concepts of those modelling techniques need to be integrated and mapped one to another in order to cover the whole modelling requirements for service system engineering. The standardization activities might aim to: 1) adopt MDSEA as a standard service modelling architecture under which modelling language can be developed; 2) develop metamodel of service modelling constructs at the three modelling levels under MDSEA; 3) map service modelling constructs to existing relevant enterprise modelling techniques. The relevant standardization working groups which could under take this task could be those in charged with enterprise modelling standardisation (CEN TC310/WG1 and ISO TC184 SC5/WG1).

6. Conclusion and Perspective

It has been considered that no single existing language can represent all of the various aspects that need to be described in modelling service and associated service system in a VME environment. The service modelling language presented in the paper has defined a set of constructs which are inspired from existing enterprise modelling languages. Adopting a Model Driven Approach (MDSEA) allows model transformations and reengineering based on models. The proposed service modelling language (constructs and templates) can be considered as a basis for future possible standardisation.

7. References

[1] MDA - The Architecture of Choice for a Changing World [Online] // Object Management Group. - January 2008. - http://www.omg.org/mda/.

[2] MDI: Model Driven Interoperability; Available at: http://www.modelbased.net/mdi/; Accessed on: 15th March 2010.

[3] EN/ISO 19440, Enterprise Integration – Constructs for Enterprise Modelling, International Standardisation Organisation, 2007.

[4] Miller Joaquin and Mukerji Jishnu MDA Guide Version 1.0.1 [Report]. - [s.l.]: OMG, 2003. - Document Number: omg/2003-06-01.

[5] MSEE, Manufacturing SErvice Ecosystem, Annex I - "Description of Work", project agreement n°284860, April 29th 2011.

[6] MSEE Deliverable 11.1, Service concepts, models and method: Model Driven Service Engineering, 2011.

[7] D. Chen, Y. Ducq, G. Doumeingts, G. Zacharewicz and T. Alix, A model driven approach for the modelling of services in a virtual enterprise, Proceedings of I-ESA'12 international conference, 2012.

An Approach to Standardise a Service Life Cycle Management

Mike Freitag* — **David Kremer*** — **Manuel Hirsch**** — **Martin Zelm*****

* Fraunhofer IAO
Nobelstr.12
70569 Stuttgart, Germany
Mike.Freitag@iao.fraunhofer.de
David.Kremer@iao.fraunhofer.de

** Centre for Management Research, DITF Denkendorf
Koerschtalstr. 26
73770 Denkendorf
Manuel.Hirsch@DITF-MR-Denkendorf.de

*** Martin Zelm
c/o INTEROP-VLab, Belgium
*Hempenkamp 26, 22359 Hamburg, Germany
martin.zelm@t-online.de

ABSTRACT: *Servitization is a grand challenge for all manufacturing companies to extend their business. This paper presents an approach to standardize Service Lifecycle Management in order to support manufacturing companies to develop their services in a systematic way. Companies might benefit from this approach, as it indicates how relevant characteristics have to evolve in order to take the next steps in the servitization process and what challenges have to be considered when it comes to the conditions for service innovations. However, the result of this paper still remains an approach that needs to be validated in industrial practice.*

KEYWORDS: *service innovation, life cycle, manufacturing ecosystem, service science, service management, service engineering, servitization*

1. Introduction

Servitization for manufacturing companies becomes more important in order to find new business and industrial models to meet users' expectations and customers' requirements (Freitag *et al.* 2007, Spath *et al.* 2010, Spath *et al.* 2011).

Traditional product-centric sectors, with the aim to put customers and users at the centre of their business models, are therefore evolving into service centric sectors and are embracing and adopting deep transformation processes in order to meet the new challenges: this evolutionary process is often referred to as the servitization process for non-tertiary sectors (Spath *et al.* 2010). However, the servitization process is not just a change in the business model: it involves all the aspects of the enterprise, which therefore needs methodological and technical support concerning an integrated development and management of service offerings (Freitag *et al.* 2011, Spath *et al.* 2011).

The objective of this paper is to present a general approach for manufacturing companies that want to take the chance of servitization by making use of a business ecosystem. The focus is more on an easy to use approach than a finalized methodology.

The paper is structured in two following main chapters:

- An approach to standardise a Service Lifecycle Management

- Categories to standardise a Service Lifecycle Management.

2. An Approach to Standardize a Service Life Cycle Management

The *Service Lifecycle Management* framework consists of the three axes "Phases of Service Life Cycle Management", "Role Model for Service Life Cycle Management" and "Methods and Tools for Service Life Cycle Management", with a special focus on an ontology for Service Life Cycle Management.

2.1. *Phases of a Service Life Cycle Management*

Figure 1 below gives an overview of the detailed architecture of the Service Lifecycle Management Framework. The three main phases of Service Lifecycle Management "service ideation", "service engineering" and "service operations management" consist of various components.

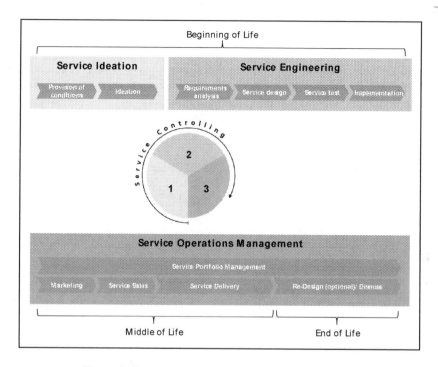

Figure 1. *Framework of a Service Life Cycle Management*

Service Ideation

Service ideation is an early phase of the SLM framework and does not have an explicit beginning, thus it is quite delimitable. Service ideation should always and continuously take place in companies, which want to focus on service business.

Service ideation is rather a state of mind closely linked to perception than a typical SLM phase, such as for example service engineering. In the open-mindedness of the ideation phase companies need to aspirate various influences coming from the surroundings of the enterprise that may have effect on their service business or at least should be respected within it.

These *idea providing* influences may be changing customer needs, new emerging technologies, transformations of the company environment, and other causes or drivers of change. For service ideation they serve as triggers or stimuli.

When a collection of service ideas is handed over to the first phase of service engineering, "idea management", it comes to a structured collection and subsequent evaluation of the service ideas provided by the phase of *service ideation*.

Service Engineering

The service engineering process of Fraunhofer IAO is a *waterfall model* for the development of new services. It first was introduced at the end of the 1990s and then was detailed and modified in the subsequent years, for example by Meiren and Barth (2002). In order to avoid some overlappings the phase "Service Engineering" consists here of four phases: Requirements analysis, Service design, service test and service implementation.

The *requirements analysis* as the first process phase marks the start of the actual development project. Here, the internal and external requirements with respect to the new service to be developed have to be considered.

The second phase of the service development process is called *service design*. The main goal of this phase is to define and describe the new service in detail.

In the third phase the service should be *tested* by customers or by using a simulation tool or at least by a checklist.

The *implementation* of the service also includes the operative realization of the previously elaborated marketing concept. Furthermore, the involved employees need to be trained as planned, necessary but up to now missing resources have to be procured.

Service Operations Management

The primary activities "Service sales & marketing" lead to the acquisition of customers respectively service projects. After the acquisitions phase the service needs to be delivered to the customers. This happens within "service delivery".

The support activities for Service Operations Management have been changed in comparison to the support activities of Porter's value chain. With respect to the architecture of the framework and its stage-gate-character, there remain two significant support activities, "service portfolio management" and "service operations controlling".

2.2. Role Models for the Service Lifecycle Management Phases

In organizations, the breakdown of work between employees or organizational units among one another is often defined by means of roles. Roles bundle one or more tasks and can be assigned to one or more employees or organizational units. For example, in the role model illustrated in figure 2, the owner of the role "Service Manager" is responsible for a set of tasks: He has to evaluate proposed service ideas on a strategic level, to come to a decision quickly, to allocate resources for the service development project, and to control if the decision is executed effectively. The role of the Service Manager can be assigned to a single person as well as to an organizational unit like a committee, an expert team, a board of directors, or others.

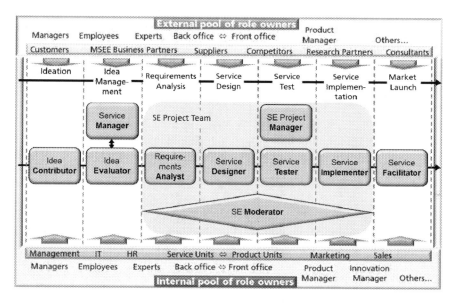

Figure 2. *Role Model for the "Service Ideation" and "Service Engineering" Phase of Service Lifecycle Management Framework*

Consistent with the "Service Ideation" and "Service Engineering" phase of the Service Lifecycle Management Framework, figure 2 depicts an array of roles, which can be assigned either to an internal pool of potential role owners (examples for possible functions and positions at the bottom of the figure) or to an external pool (indicated at the top of the figure). For a specific company, role assignment as well as task definition for roles should match the company's parameters of processes, organizational structure, and competences of employees or organizational units, respectively.

The first role *Idea Contributor* relates to "Feeding in new ideas for services to the company". This relates to the transfer into the company of new service concepts that occur in the environment of the company. Prerequisites here are access to relevant sources of information and knowledge owners, the ability to make a preliminary assessment of technological and market opportunities and knowledge of the relevant in-house contact. The Idea Contributor role throws up parallels to the concept of the boundary spanner (Tushman, 1977). Boundary spanners bridge organizational interfaces and are responsible for interactions and the exchange of information across corporate boundaries. The prerequisite is access both to external networks from which the information can be obtained and access to the company's internal networks, which receive information.

The second role is called *Idea Evaluator*. Information about new service concepts received from the Idea Contributor requires preliminary assessment and selection before it is forwarded to the relevant decision-makers so that an assessment can be made as to whether a further study of the new service opportunities is likely to be successful. This also includes delegating the check as well as working out new service concepts and approving the relevant resources. The Idea Evaluator role corresponds to the function of the "gatekeepers", which – according to Reid and de Brentani (2004) – is the central contact for new technology (here: service) concepts and forms the interface between the boundary spanner and the decision-makers in the company.

The *Service Manager* role includes the decision about the elaboration, trialling and implementation of the new service concept and the corresponding approval of resources. The fourth role called *Requirements Analyst* accounts for the production of feasibility and cost efficiency analyses as well as the acquisition of knowledge on preconditions required for successful service rollout.

The *Service Designer* role is responsible for the actual development of the new service concepts, using Service Engineering Methodologies to provide a systematic and sustainable service design. As *Service Tester*, the relevant role bearer conducts one or more market tests to evaluate the acceptance of customers regarding the new service concept. This can be done by means of a presentation, process simulation, pilot study, or others.

The *Service Engineering Moderator* is a cross-divisional role. The relevant role bearer integrates the specific (sometimes even contrary) perspectives and target systems of the participating operative units, business functions, and other important stakeholders. This role accounts for moderation of both the content dimension, so that arguments can be exchanged and integrated efficiently, as well the relationship dimension, clearing misunderstandings and conflicts of opinion, and maintaining good relations between the internal stakeholders.

The *Service Implementer* role finally accounts for the market rollout of the new service, after it has been tested and optimized by the Service Tester role. As successful service development projects in a dynamic context require active management, the role of the *Service Engineering Project Manager* establishes a constant flow of information, feedback loops, decisions, and tactic priorization. Bearers of this role also are responsible for keeping in contact with internal and external customers, like the Service Manager (internal) or the business customers (external).

The *Service Facilitator* prepares the market launch of the new service. As an intermediary between the company and its customers, he manages to convey the benefit of the new service to the customers. Subtasks here are actively understanding of the tangible and intangible assets of the new service on the one hand, and conveying the benefits to the customers on the other hand.

A role model for the "Service Operations Management" phase of the Service Lifecycle Management Framework is depicted in figure 3. The model allows for the spectrum of tasks in each phase to be assigned to one or more individuals or groups of process participants.

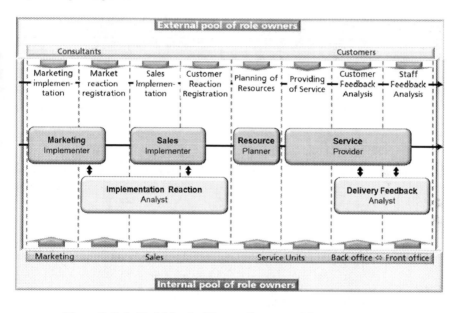

Figure 3. *Role Model for the "Service Operations Management" Phase of Service Lifecycle Management Framework*

Reflecting the Service Operations Management phases, the roles bundle the following tasks:

- Marketing Implementer: Based on the Market Launch-activities from the preceding role "Service Facilitator", here marketing activities for the new service or solution are initialized.

- Sales Implementer: Preparation and conduction of sales activities with respect to the new service/solution.

- Implementation Reaction Analyst: For both marketing and sales activities, feedback of the market (e.g., responses to advertising, development of sales performance figures) is collected, aggregated, and evaluated.

- Resource Planner: For successful service provision, the required resources (e.g., capacity, budget, infrastructure) have to be planned proactively.

- Service Provider: Service/solution provision is established and integrated in the day-to-day business of the company.

- Delivery Feedback Analyst: Corresponding to the marketing and sales phases, feedback from both external and internal stakeholders is collected and evaluated.

Compared to the role model of the Service Engineering module, the assignment of role owners to the roles depicted here is more specific: as marketing, sales, and service provision are the genuine tasks of the correspondent company departments, the pool of potential role owners should be transparent, although responsibilities for the new services or solutions have to be appropriately assigned to the role owners. Moreover, marketing and sales activities may to some extent be delegated to external consultants or external marketing/sales provider, and customers may play a substantial role in the analysis and feedback activities as well.

Depending on the company's specific design of working tasks, work processes, and organizational structure, role concepts should be tailor-made solutions to be suitable to day-to-day business requirements. Moreover, the successful implementation of role models often requires a change of behavioral patterns, fields of responsibility, and cultural aspects. The underlying change process should be actively managed and monitored.

2.3. *Formal Semantics in Service Life Cycle Management*

Formal semantics – namely ontologies – are considered to be key drivers for standardization, as ontological elements can be used to capture, structure, and further elaborate explicit as well as implicit knowledge within a certain domain. Essential ontological elements are concepts (universals), attributes as well as relations between concepts, and instances (particulars) of these concepts. Ontologies in standardization help to determinate uncertainties, handle exceptions, and reducing misinterpretation. In addition, rigid semantics of ontologies allow for automatic reasoning e. g. in order to interpret incomplete knowledge bases.

Current research argues for using ontologies in SLM in order to bridge and align (product-) service ideation, engineering, and operation (Hirsch, 2012). This is why ontologies are applied in the following to adequately support and standardize knowledge intensive tasks in Service Life Cycle Management. In this context, ontologies are used to capture formalized factual as well as rule-based knowledge about e. g. (product-) services, relevant stakeholders, and collaborative value creation activities all along the service life cycle. As a result, ontologies in SLM facilitate servitization as well as service innovation from service development to service execution (Lau *et al.*, 2013).

The following excerpt of an SLM Ontology derives from a middle-out ontology engineering approach that combines existing top-level ontologies with newly developed domain ontologies from the field of services in (manufacturing) industries. Top-level ontologies that were considered are – among others – the Process Specification Language (PSL) published in ISO 18629 (Grüninger and Menzel, 2003) and the Collaborative Innovation Ontology (CIO) on innovation-related expert knowledge (Hirsch, 2012). Domain specific semantics on product-services as well as their in-/tangible components are derived form – among others – Nance1 , PTO2, or IMKS3 as well as reference modeling frameworks like EcoGRAI (Chen *et al.*, 1997). Special focus has been put on ontological features to handle access rights and IPR levels on enterprise internal, community and future internet/market level.

The current version of the SLM Ontology comprises concepts, relations, and rules to describe dependencies between knowledge workers (*actors*), innovation-related tasks (*activities*), and (product-) services as well as their in-/tangible components (assets). To capture the maturity level and status of (product-) services in SLM, status (*abstracts*) are associated with all elements of the ontology. The SLM Ontology is compliant with other works on semantic models for service management but extends state-of-the-art compendiums with innovative findings in context of collaborative knowledge work within Manufacturing Service Ecosystems. Key Concepts of the SLM Ontology are as follows (concepts and sub-concepts are depicted in isA-relations):

- Abstract
    o   Access Rights on enterprise internal level, community/Ecosystem level, and future internet/market level
    o   Status of e.g. a Servitization Process
    o   Maturity of e. g. a (Product-)Service

---

1 http://ec.europa.eu/competition/mergers/cases/index/nace_all.html
2 http://www.productontology.org/
3 http://www.lboro.ac.uk/departments/mm/research/product-realisation/imks/Results/IMKS

- Actor
  - o Customer relations as well as
  - o Stakeholders like e. g. Service Providers
- Activity
  - o Servitization Process, incl. sub-processes
  - o Service Ideation, Engineering, and Operation
- Asset
  - o Methods for Servitization
  - o Tools for Servitization
  - o (Product-) Services as well as their
    - ▪ Intangible and
    - ▪ Tangible components

The concepts listed above will be extended towards a holistic ontological framework in the near future. The resulting ontology will be implemented as semantic reasoning tool in order to support servitization initiatives by means of a knowledge-driven SLM repository. The final SLM Ontology will furthermore cover a dedicated rule-set that captures expert knowledge on how to be successful in servitization and service innovation

3. Candidates to Standardize a Service Life Cycle Management

Standardisation means the creation and implementation of standards, a process built on voluntary cooperation among industry, academia, consumers, public authorities and other interested stakeholders. Standards complement the development of technical specifications and ease the implementation of innovative products and services.

In the context of research, standardisation supports the dissemination of research results and widens the potential of exploitation. Standardisation provides access to a large pool of external expertise. Developing new standards can help to build a competitive advantage of industrial users in the application of research results

Current research, as elaborated in Section2 of this paper, suggests to use ontologies in Service Lifecycle Management (SLM) in order to bridge and align (product-) service ideation, engineering, and operation This is why ontologies are applied in order to adequately support and standardize knowledge intensive tasks in Service Life Cycle Management. Two candidates for New Work Items are proposed:

1. A standard for Categories of Service Life Cycle Management (SLM) following the proposed SLM Framework .The benefit for the practitioner is that

Service oriented enterprises could seamless collaborate by using similar interoperating service concepts.

2. Standardisation of knowledge intensive tasks in Service Life Cycle Management Formal semantics are considered key drivers for standardization, as ontological elements can be used to capture, structure, and further elaborate knowledge within a given domain. The resulting ontologies can support, bridge and align (product) service ideation, engineering, and operation.

Work to standardise Product Lifecycle Management has been done in ISO for instance in the ISO/STEP standards for the exchange of product model data during the product lifecycle.

4. Summary

The Service Life Cycle Management framework being introduced consists of the three phases "service ideation", "service engineering" and "service operations management". Each of the three phases were described and the roles in charge of fulfilling tasks in the context of service business were presented. Based on this the standardisation approach outlined in this paper takes on ideas from formal semantics in order to capture, structure, and communicate knowledge about actors, activities, and assets within the domain of Service Life Cycle Management. The concepts will be extended towards a holistic ontological framework that can easily be applied in companies in order to handle service innovation in a systematic way.

5. Acknowledgements

The paper is mainly based on the initial work performed in the project MSEE - Manufacturing SErvice Ecosystem. MSEE is an Integrated Project funded by the European Commission within the ICT Work Programme under the European Community's 7th Framework Programme (FoF-ICT-2011.7.3).

6. References

Chen, D.; Vallespir, B.; Doumeingts, G., GRAI integrated methodology and its mapping onto generic enterprise reference architecture and methodology, In: *Computers in industry*. 33 (2), pp. 387–394, 1997.

Freitag, M., Ganz, W., *"InnoScore® service. Evaluating innovation for product-related services"*, Service Research & Innovation Institute (Hrsg): Annual SRII global conference

(SRII), 2011. March 29, 2011 - April 2, 2011, San Jose, California, USA; proceedings, IEEE, Piscataway, NJ, 214–221.

Freitag, M., Husen, C., Müller, R., *Entwicklung und Management internationaler Dienstleistungen. Studie zum Dienstleistungsexport deutscher Unternehmen*, Stuttgart, Fraunhofer IRB Verlag, 2007.

Grüninger, M.; Menzel, Christopher The process specification language (PSL) theory and applications, In: *AI Mag.* 24 (3), pp. 63–74, 2003.

Hirsch, M., *Smart Services for Knowledge Integration - Ontologiebasierte Dienste zur Unterstützung der kollaborativen Wissensarbeit in Innovationsnetzwerken*, Düsseldorf: VDI-Verlag (Fortschritt-Berichte VDI).

Lau, A., Hirsch, M., Matheis, H., From Collaborative Development to Manufacturing in Production Networks: The SmartNets Approach, In: *Robust Manufacturing Control*. Springer pp. 287–299, 2013.

Meiren, T., Barth, T., *Service Engineering in Unternehmen umsetzen. Leitfaden für die Entwicklung von Dienstleistungen*, Stuttgart, Fraunhofer IRB Verlag, 2002.

Spath, D., Fähnrich, K.-P., Freitag, M., Meyer, K., *Service Engineering internationaler Dienstleistungen*, Stuttgart, Fraunhofer Verlag, 2010.

Spath, D., Ganz, W., Taking the Pulse of Economic Development. Service Trends, München, Hanser, 2011.

Open Business Model, Process and Service Innovation with VDML and ServiceML

Arne J. Berre* — Henk de Man** — Yannick Lew*
Brian Elvesæter* — Bjørn Morten Ursin-Holm***

* SINTEF, P. O. Box 124 Blindern, N-0314 Oslo, Norway
arne.j.berre@sintef.no
yannick@ifi.uio.no
brian.elvesater@sintef.no

** Cordys, P. O. Box 118, 3880 AC Putten, The Netherlands
hdman@cordys.com

*** Induct Software AS, Rosenkrantzgate 4, NO-0159 OSLO, Norway
bmuh@inductsoftware.com

ABSTRACT: *This paper presents the NEFFICS platform which provides a foundation for cloud-based open business model innovation, process innovation and service innovation for networked enterprises. Business model innovation is supported with a basis in a business model framework with six views, where each view is supported by a corresponding diagram view from the Value Delivery Modeling Language (VDML). Process innovation is supported by VDML activity diagrams with options for mappings to Business Process Model and Notation (BPMN) and Case Management Model and Notation (CMMN). Service innovation is supported by the Service Modelling Language (ServiceML) which shares the core collaboration models of VDML for role modelling and value networks.*

KEYWORDS: *open innovation, business model innovation, process innovation, service innovation, VDML, SoaML, ServiceML, AT-ONE*

1. Introduction

This paper presents a platform for community support for open business model innovation including support for process and service innovation. This is provided through the NEFFICS platform which combines an open innovation social media platform with a business modelling and operations platform. Together this provides a foundation for cloud-based open business model innovation, process innovation and service innovation for networked enterprises. Business model innovation is supported with a basis in a business model framework with six views, where each view is supported by a corresponding diagram view from the Value Delivery Modeling Language (VDML) [OMG 2012b]. VDML has now been proposed for further standardisation within the Object Management Group (OMG). Process innovation is supported by VDML activity diagrams with options for mappings to Business Process Model and Notation (BPMN) [OMG 2011] and Case Management Model and Notation (CMMN) [OMG 2013]. Service innovation is supported by the Service Modelling Language (ServiceML) which shares the core collaboration models of VDML for role modelling and value networks. ServiceML extends the Service oriented architecture Modeling Language (SoaML) [OMG 2012a] for business architectures, i.e. Business-SoaML as described in [Chang 2012], and combines this with the five views of the AT-ONE method [Clatworthy 2008] to support service innovation. A further relationship of these languages in the context of an Enterprise Architecture framework can be found in [Berre 2012, Berre 2013b]. The remainder of this paper is structured as follows: In Section 2 we provide a description of the functionality offered by the NEFFICS platform. Section 3 introduces VDML and describes the business model innovation framework. Section 4 describes process innovation with VDML. Section 5 introduces ServiceML and describes the service innovation support. Finally, Section 6 concludes this paper and outlines further work.

2. The NEFFICS (Innovation, Modelling and Execution) Platform

This section provides a description of the functionality, i.e. services and tools, offered by the NEFFICS platform and its methodologies and frameworks. The NEFFICS platform, as shown in Figure 1, is grouped into five main areas:

- The Innovation Community provides the services for idea, challenge and innovation management with possible links to analysis models.

- The Business analysis modelling provides the collaborative cloud based, VDML implementation that enables model based Enterprise design and transformation, over and above the model driven platform that enables application development.

- The Business automation modelling provides support for models that can be automated and directly supported through business operations runtime.

- The Business operations runtime provides services for execution of models, management of work to be performed as part of model execution, and monitoring of model execution and business data generated as a result of model execution, all in a distributed service-oriented architecture context.

- The Internet of Services and Things area includes third party services that provide access to underlying services for collaboration, interoperability, sensor and RFID information. Services of enterprise applications, available on premise of use case partners, can be positioned in this area as well.

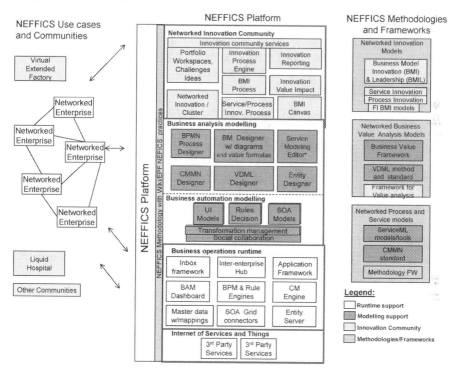

Figure 1. *The NEFFICS platform*

The NEFFICS platform provides tools and services that build upon the baseline functionality for innovation community and business operations extended with support for the NEFFICS Methodologies and Frameworks:

- The Networked Innovation Models define frameworks for different innovation types, starting from business model innovation and further supporting service, process and product innovation.

- The Networked Business Value Analysis Models define frameworks and methods for business value analysis, including the VDML specification.

- The Networked Process and Service Models define frameworks and methods for process and service modelling, supporting process and service innovation. It also includes the CMMN specification.

Accompanying the NEFFICS platform we have the public NEFFICS Methodology Wiki (neffics.modelbased.net) which provides descriptive guidelines in the form of practices for how to apply and adopt the models, methodologies and tools provided by the NEFFICS platform and frameworks.

Business Model Innovation is the core innovation activity of the business. It could be said to encompass the other innovation types such as Process and Service Innovation. One can address innovation from many perspectives and define types for it, but in the context of NEFFICS we have chosen to expand upon three particular innovation types.

- *Business Model Innovation* could be seen as the root innovation type, where all changes to a business could be seen as a new business model, or improvements to existing ones. Innovating the business model is related to changing one or more of the blocks of the business model. The NEFFICS platform enables you to innovate, implement and execute the services in the same environment, drawing upon resources from your enterprise network.

- *Process Innovation* is about innovating a process itself. In NEFFICS this type of innovation plays a very important role because the NEFFICS Business Operations Platform (BOP) is often used to facilitate live business processes and cases that support the actual business activities. Having them under the same roof as the innovation process are precursors for an efficient innovation lifecycle.

- *Service Innovation* is about establishing new or improving existing services. This is particularly relevant in the context of NEFFICS because the platform is enabling services that span the boundaries of the enterprises. The NEFFICS platform offers tools that help you approach service innovation from the users' point of view. This is complementary to the abovementioned process innovation perspective.

2.1. *Networked Innovation Community*

The innovation community provides a social media based community for the suggestion and management of ideas and challenges in a community. The innovation community was built with open innovation in mind and supports various aspects of opening up the innovation practice to be more receptive for input from other stakeholders such as customers and partners. The transition towards a more open innovation practice could manifest in many ways, such as including selected partners of customers in the front-end or back-end of your innovation practice. It could also be the place where one enable new business opportunities through sharing and opening up business models so that others can compete for a place in the value network, or extend it to change any of the components of a business model. The core objective of the innovation community is to increase innovation capacity by bridging the many users that have an innovation challenge with the users that have possible solutions, whilst at the same time support the strategic context of the organization that drives the community.

The innovation community is built on top of a set of baseline features one can expect from any enterprise social media platforms such as user management, integration with user directory services, content management, search and access control, community functions (i.e. profile page, interest groups), communication tools (i.e. chat, comments and messaging) and collaboration tools (i.e. workgroups, task management and file sharing). The more specialized features support different levels of openness (i.e. company/organization, enterprise internal innovation, innovation in networks and public innovation zones). In order to support a good user dialogue it is typically instantiated for the relevant natural language.

The platform supports different innovation practices through customizable processes by providing generic workspaces for innovation and portfolio work. It supports different ways of tracking interest such as voting, evaluations, rating and commenting. It supports different ways of delegation of responsibilities such as dedicated roles for doing certain activities such as evaluating, responding to and following up innovation projects. Finally, it supports reporting such as innovation funnel, focus area matrix, impact estimation and cost/benefit quadrants.

The innovation community support the steps of an innovation process. This way of working with innovation processes acts as scaffolding for innovation projects; ensuring a repeatable, comparable and evolvable approach to running innovation projects. One can choose to have an arbitrary number of stages but map them to a generic innovation process. The purpose of such mapping is to maintain comparability and make consolidated overviews of innovation progress across the different innovation types that are supported (i.e. process, product and service innovation).

In the process of generating or evaluating of ideas, it is possible to create or link to related business models that can be developed from a business model innovation perspective. Community members can contribute challenges and ideas into a social innovation process where the status and progress can be presented and further analysed and progressed. Figure 2 shows the innovation funnel, and shows the progress of ideas through different stages. Ideas can be analysed and refined further through a link to business model innovation with value models in the Business Operations platform (BOP), with potential further process and service innovation support. Maintaining the associations between ideas and business models and the diagrams of these capture important contextual information and support for analysis which is helpful in deciding which ideas to develop further.

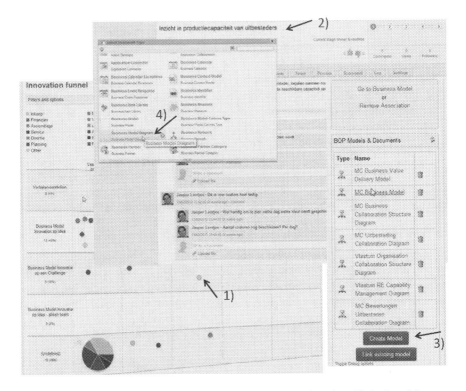

Figure 2. *The Innovation Community with Innovation funnel and linked models*

Figure 2 shows how an idea can be selected from the innovation funnel 1) to open a window with an idea page with relevant discussions 2), from which it is possible to create new models and diagrams, or link to existing one 3), such as a business model diagram 4). It is also possible for an underlying system to generate new ideas or challenges into the innovation community for further innovation management.

3. Business Model Innovation with VDML

The Business Operations Platform (BOP) serves as the integrated component in the NEFFICS platform that supports modelling and model-based management of business and business operations. It is logical to extend modelling support in BOP with support for model-based design and analysis of Business Models (BMs). In

NEFFICS, BMs are considered to have six different views in to one integrated model, conceptually represented as a cube, while other related approaches like [Osterwalder 2012] consist of separate building blocks or dimensions. The six dimensions of the "business model innovation cube (BMI Cube)" [Lindgren, et al. 2011a], [Lindgren, et al. 2011b] are: Customers, Value Propositions, Activities (the "value chain"), Capabilities (or Competences), Network Partners and Value Formulas. This cube, together with an unfolded representation, in this paper referred to as "BM Diagram", is represented in Figure 3.

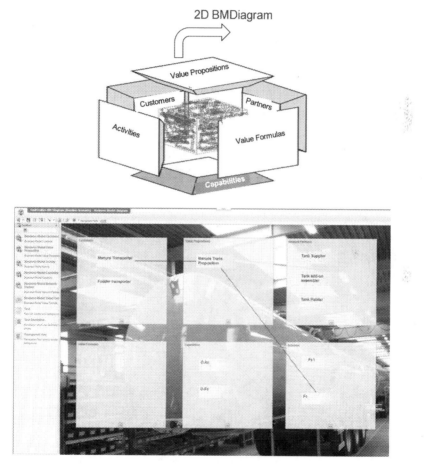

Figure 3. *BMI Cube with BM Diagram as 2D representation for the 6 related dimensions*

Each dimension of a BM is typically associated with one or more "BM items". The main areas and related diagrams of VDML happen to align well with the dimensions of the BMI Cube, as indicated in Figure 4. VDML provides a diagram for each dimension of a BM. Every BM item, as associated with a BM dimension, can also be represented on the corresponding VDML diagram. This allows navigation from the BM diagram to the "underlying" VDML diagrams which represents how the BM item is related to other items. Thus VDML-based models provide a structured and detailed representation of BM items (according to the six dimensions) and their "relationships" (seventh dimension). Note that this integration between the BMI Cube framework and VDML will benefit managers, innovators, and business designers (e.g. analysts and architects):

- It enables managers and innovators to abstract from business design and business architecture details. It will also, and eventually, provides them with a useful context to present measurements, ideas and challenges, that are related to underlying details.

- It will provide a useful way to guide business analysts and architects, whereby the various dimensions of a BM serve as "chapters" of business design "methodology". It will provide them with a broad understanding and context of the business and with a useful means to navigate business designs.

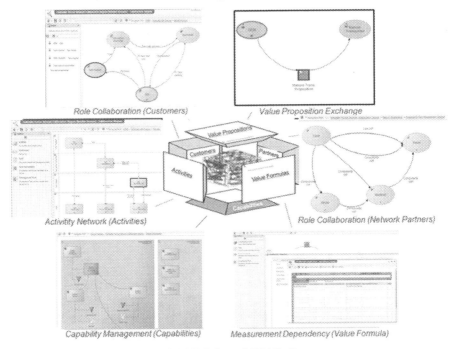

Figure 4. *BMI Cube with VDML diagrams*

It is intended to extend the VDML metamodel and notation with integrated BM metamodel and BM diagram. This will involve integration of both model objects and notation (diagrams), with support for diagram-based navigation from BM Diagram to VDML diagrams (and vice versa), where appropriate. Further details about BM use of each of the VDML diagrams can be found in [Berre 2013a].

4. Process Innovation with VDML

A high-level representation of VDML concepts is represented in Figure 5. The figure clarifies how VDML model elements can identify BM items in the various dimensions of a BM: A "business", typically an enterprise, modelled as organization unit, might fill a role in (a) business network(s), via which it collaborates with customers and network partners, which fill roles in the business network(s) as well. They exchange value propositions, through collaboration. Value propositions that "the business" provides to its customers are the value propositions that are represented in a BM. A "business" collaborates with both customers and network partners, and it may provide and receive value propositions to and from both, which is the basis for "value formulas" in a BM. In order to deliver value, "the business" and its network partners have to perform certain activities, which require certain capabilities that are provided by their organization units. Note that, as far as activities explicitly contribute value, as articulated by value propositions to the customers, these activities, together with the capabilities that they require, are also BM constituents.

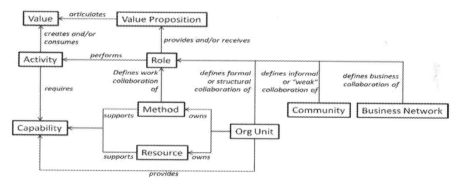

Figure 5. *VDML concepts*

Organization units typically use "capability methods", to provide their capabilities. A capability method is a work collaboration of roles, designed to support and provide a particular capability. As such it also expresses which activities are performed by these roles, to deliver the intended value. Capability methods that are sufficiently structured can be considered "processes". Figure 6 provides a VDML activity network view on a Capability Method. It looks like a "process", but is distinct from "control" oriented representations of process, such as BPMN and CMMN provide.

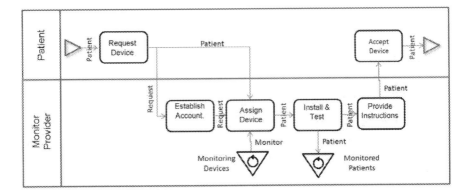

Figure 6. *VDML Activity diagram of Capability Method*

An activity network view in VDML focuses on the flow of deliverables and contributions of value, and is not concerned with control flow. It is possible to transform a Capability Method in VDML, as used in a particular context in VDML, to a BPMN process or Case Management model, so that the work that is represented by a Capability Method, can be enforced by "process automation" in the operations of the business. Figure 7 suggests how value-driven business analysis and design, based on VDML models, is a business-oriented way to "discover" processes, supporting process innovation, in a way, whereby business, using VDML models, and IT, using BPMN and CMMN models, are aligned.

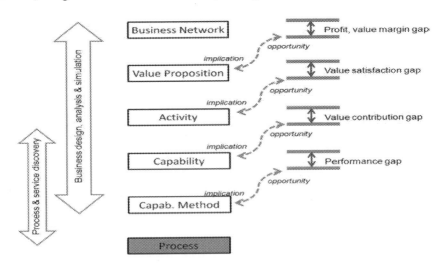

Figure 7. *Value-driven process innovation, with VDML*

5. From Business Model Innovation to Service Innovation with ServiceML

In many cases the value proposition from a Business Model Innovation will be about providing a service. In this case the VDML models will also be able to serve as a foundation for further service innovation. Service innovation provides a holistic approach to the development of innovative services by relying on the way customers experience such services. By integrating design-thinking into the service platform creation, service innovation enables service providers to enhance their service portfolio through improved or innovative services. The concept or role collaboration is the central concept both in VDML and in service design, so VDML also provides a good foundation for service innovation.

5.1. ServiceML Based on the AT-ONE Method

The AT-ONE method [Clatworthy 2008] provides a valuable insight into service innovation by proposing to innovate a service in terms of five distinct lenses, namely (A)ctors, (T)ouch-points, (O)fferings, (N)eeds and (E)xperiences. The ServiceML language has been aligned with AT-ONE and comprises three different packages [Carrez et al. 2012], namely: (1) Business-SoaML, a SoaML variant suited for business people, (2) Light-USDL, a USDL variant for interface descriptions for business-minded people, and (3) Service Journey Maps, an AT-ONE customer journey map variant for describing service experiences.

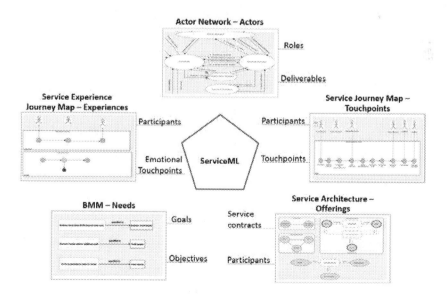

Figure 9. *Summary of ServiceML models for the five AT-ONE lenses*

ServiceML is currently being tested with the cooperation of industry partners. Figure 9 depicts the five ServiceML AT-ONE lenses which are described as follows:

- *Actors*: An actor network represents a collaboration of roles and deliverable flows in a value network [Allee 2002]. We make use of a hybrid notation, namely: 'participants' (roles in a service collaboration) and 'conversations' (BPMN 2.0 [OMG 2011]) to group together a set of flows between roles.

- *Touch-points*: We model touch-points (physical or logical points of contact such as mobile phones and web) using a service journey map which is similar to an AT-ONE customer journey showing the flow of events from both service providers and service users [Schneider and Stickdorn 2011].

- *Offerings*: Service offerings are described as Service Contracts forming part of a Service Architecture (from Business-SoaML). A service contract establishes a service agreement between two participants while a service architecture provides an overview of all participants and proposed services.

- *Needs*: Matching the customer needs to offerings is very important. Needs, in ServiceML, are expressed as goals which are quantified by objectives as explained in the BMM (Business Motivation Model) standard [OMG 2010].

- *Experiences*: In ServiceML, service experiences are modelled as different coloured icons representing various levels of emotional states which a consumer of a service goes through as touch-point events are being carried out. "Bad (Poor)" (represented by red circles), "Average" (represented by yellow circles), "Good (Normal)" (represented by green circles), and "Outstanding" (represented by blue circles).

5.2. *VDML and ServiceML Alignment*

The elements of VDML and ServiceML have been aligned to provide integration support for the various AT-ONE models. Each ServiceML model, which will be discussed in the next section, can be related to its corresponding VDML model(s) across a particular AT-ONE perspective as shown in figure 3. For instance, roles present in a ServiceML Actor network can also be found in VDML role collaboration models.

A ServiceML Service Journey Map typically describes touchpoints or a set of user activities that are also detailed in a VDML Activity network. Services present in a ServiceML Service Architecture diagram can be regarded as providing value propositions to various actors or participants in a VDML Value Proposition Exchange diagram. A ServiceML BMM diagram articulates customer needs that can be regarded as forming part of the VDML Value Proposition Exchange diagram as well as the Measurement Dependency Graph used to express value formulas based on customer interests.

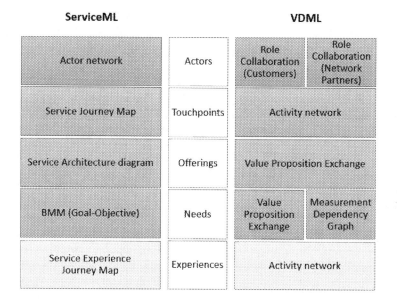

Figure 8. *VDML and ServiceML alignment*

Finally, a ServiceML Service Experience Journey Map can be used to define the set of VDML activities with user emotions based on the level of satisfaction experienced by service consumers. Further details about each of the ServiceML diagrams can be found in [Berre 2013b].

6. Conclusion and Future Work

This paper has presented a platform for Open Business Model, Process and Service Innovation with VDML and ServiceML. The platform is currently being tested and validated in different pilot case scenarios.

Future work is focusing on reflecting the experiences from the platform usage to potential updates to the current VDML standardisation proposal. The approach provides a basis for further development of corresponding executable models and simulation models.

7. Acknowledgements

The research leading to these results has received funding from the European Union Seventh Framework Programme FP7/2007-2013 under grant agreement n° 258076 NEFFICS and the Norwegian program CSI, Center for Service Innovation. The authors would like to thank the members of the NEFFICS project and the CSI program for their contributions.

8. References

Allee V, "A Value Network Approach for Modeling and Measuring Intangibles", White paper, November 2002. http://www.vernaallee.com

Berre A.-J., "An Agile Model- based Framework for Service Innovation for the Future Internet", MDWE' 2012, Berlin, July 2012, in M. Grossniklaus, M. Wimmer (Eds): ICWE: 2012 Workshops, LNCS 7703, pp 1-4, Springer, 2012

Berre A.-J., H. de Man and P. Lindgren "Business Model Innovation with the NEFFICS platform and VDML", NGEBIS'2013 workshop at CAISE'2013, Valencia, June 2013, CEUR Workshop Proceedings, 2013, p. 24-30

Berre A.-J., Y, Lew, B. Elvesæter and H. de Man, "Service Innovation and Service Realisation with VDML and ServiceML", Service-oriented Enterprise Architecture for Enterprise Engineering (SoEA4EE) IEEE workshop at EDOC 2013, Vancouver, BC, Canada, September 2013

Carrez C., B. Elvesæter, and A.-J. Berre, "Unified and Extended Models for Networked Processes and Services (v2)", NEFFICS (FP7-ICT-258076, Collaborative Project, 2010-2013), Deliverable D5.6, 2012., http://neffics.eu

Chang T., A.-J. Berre, C. Carrez, and B. Elvesæter, "Business-SoaML: Service Identification and Specification from a Business Perspective", in Enterprise Interoperability V, Springer, 2012, pp. 379-389. http://dx.doi.org/10.1007/978-1-4471-2819-9_33

Clatworthy S., "Innovations in service experiences: The AT-ONE method", in Proc. of the 6th International Conference on Design and Emotion, 2008.

Lentjes J., "Initial Release of the Virtual Extended Factory", NEFFICS (FP7-ICT-258076, Collaborative Project, 2010-2013), Deliverable D1.3, 2012.

Lindgren P., R. Jørgensen, Y. Taran, and K. F. Saghaug, "Baseline for Networked Innovation Models, Version 1.0", NEFFICS (FP7-ICT-258076, Collaborative Project, 2010-2013), Deliverable D4.1, 11 May 2011, http://neffics.eu

Lindgren P., Y. Taran, and R. Jørgensen, "Open Business, Networked Process, Service and Product Innovation Models, Version 1.0", NEFFICS (FP7-ICT-258076, Collaborative Project, 2010-2013), Deliverable D4.2, 20 September 2011, http://neffics.eu/

OMG, "Business Motivation Model, Version 1.1", Object Management Group (OMG), Document formal/2010-05-01, May 2010. http://www.omg.org/spec/BMM/1.1/PDF/

OMG, "Business Process Model and Notation (BPMN), Version 2.0", Object Management Group (OMG), Document formal/2011-01-03, January 2011. http://www.omg.org/spec/BPMN/2.0/PDF

OMG, "Service oriented architecture Modeling Language (SoaML) Specification, Version 1.0.1", Object Management Group (OMG), Document formal/2012-05-10, May 2012. http://www.omg.org/spec/SoaML/1.0.1/PDF

OMG, "Value Delivery Modeling Language (VDML), Revised submission for November 12, 2012", Object Management Group (OMG), OMG Document bmi/2012-11-06, November 2012. http://www.omg.org/cgi-bin/doc?bmi/12-11-06.pdf (Restricted to OMG members), also available at http://neffics.eu/

OMG, "Case Management Model and Notation (CMMN), FTF Beta 1 ", Object Management Group (OMG), OMG Document dtc/2013-01-01, January 2013. http://www.omg.org/spec/CMMN/1.0/Beta1/PDF/

Osterwalder A., Y. Pigneur, *Business Model Generation: A Handbook for Visionaries, Game Changers, and Challengers*, Wiley, 2012.

Schneider J. and M. Stickdorn, *This is service design thinking*, John Wiley & Sons, Inc., Hoboken, NJ, 2011.

Reference Ontologies for Manufacturing

R. Young* — N. Hastilow* — M. Imran* — N. Chungoora* — Z. Usman* — A.-F. Cutting-Decelle**

* Loughborough University-Wolfson School of Mechanical & Manufacturing Engineering, Loughborough, Leicestershire, UK

** CODATA France, 5, rue A. Vacquerie, F-75016 Paris, France and University of Geneva, CUI, ICLE, CH 1227 Carouge, Switzerland
r.i.young@lboro.ac.uk

ABSTRACT: There is a clear need for improved semantic communication to support information sharing across engineering groups and their systems in manufacturing industry and standards should play a large part in this. However, for standards to be effective in supporting the wide range of information required by manufacturing industry, they too would benefit from an interoperable base upon which they are defined. This paper presents ideas towards the development of a reference ontology for manufacturing which could provide a basis for the validation of the interoperability compliance either between systems or between standards.

KEYWORDS: interoperability, standards, manufacturing, ontologies

1. Introduction

As ICT technologies improve their capabilities, manufacturing companies look to exploit these to improve their business performance so that all aspects of business now rely heavily on ICT to provide information to support decision making throughout the enterprise's activities. A major problem remains however, which is how to effectively share information across the many business domains and across the many software tools that support these business domains.

There have been substantial advances over the years in the ability to exchange information between systems with similar functionality e.g CAD data through the use of ISO 10303. There is also much greater understanding of the scale of problems involved in interoperability and the need for methods to both understand the level of interoperability that may be achievable in a business situation (ISO 11354) and to develop more effective standardisation approaches across industrial automation systems and integration (IDIOM).

The research behind this paper is committed to the belief that the best route to effective systems interoperation should be through the use of standards, as these should provide a shared basis upon which all the parties involved can develop a common understanding. However the use of current standards has critical shortcomings where multiple interpretations of a standard are possible and where multiple standards are needed to cover the range of information to be shared. Typically interoperability between existing standards themselves is not achieved and hence they cannot be expected, in their current form, to support the information sharing requirements of complex multi-system networks.

This paper proposes that the development of a manufacturing reference ontology defined in Common Logic or equivalent will have three important consequences: (i) it will provide a basis upon which new manufacturing system requirements can be automatically checked for compliance against an existing configuration of systems, (ii) new standards can be generated which cannot be inadvertently misinterpreted and hence can provide a base of confidence for effective dynamic inter-system communication (iii) the understanding gained can provide a migration path towards interoperable standards across a broadly based manufacturing scope.

2. Multiple Information Requirements and Multiple Standards

Although much has been learnt in regards to enterprise interoperability (Panetto, Goncalves, & Molina, 2012), and manufacturing interoperability in particular (Borgo & Leitão, 2007) (Young, et al 2007), there is still much to be achieved before information can be seamlessly shared across system and domain boundaries.

The product lifecycle domains of design, production, service and disposal should all, in principle, be able to easily share information. However, this is clearly not the case, even in relation to possibly the four main areas of software support systems in Enterprise Resource Planning (ERP), Product Lifecycle Management (PLM), Customer Relations Management (CRM) and Supply Chain Management (SCM).

Standards in the area of industrial automation and integration (ISO TC184 SC4) have over the years provided a substantial effort into improved methods for information sharing and probably provide the most advanced solutions to date in terms of information sharing where there is a need for data exchange across like systems. However, even though the standards developed here cover a range of domains and are intended to be compatible, it is clear from our investigations that they are insufficiently consistent to be interoperable (Chungoora et al 2011). The range in information needed to support decisions related to the production of designed parts is wide and some of the relevant standards ISO 10303, 13584, 15531, 18629, 13399 and 19439.

It has been recognised that the textual definitions of similar terms across a number of ISO standards in industrial automation can be varied (Michel 2005). As a consequence of this, subjective interpretation of concept meanings can occur and, therefore, there is a need to be able to formally capture the semantics of these terms to enable their verification and to check their consistency. For example the following "resource" concepts and their definitions are represented in specific standards as shown.

- Resource (ISO 15531-1; ISO 18629-1): Any device, tool and means, except raw material and final product components, at the disposal of the enterprise to produce goods or services. This definition includes ISO 10303-49 definition.

- Resource (ISO 10303-49): Something that may be described in terms of a behavior, a capability, or a performance measure that is pertinent to the process.

- Resource (ISO 15704): An enterprise entity that provides some or all of the capabilities required by the execution of an enterprise activity and/or business process.

It is clear from studying these definitions that it is not easy to clearly understand the level of similarity between the definitions and therefore the extent to which they could be used interoperably. Formalising the sematics of the concepts can overcome this problem by offering a single precise definition against which others can be compared. For example the code below specifies potential relationships between "resource", "capability", "enterprise" and "process'; all concepts that are present in the textual definitions above. Significantly the word "may" in the text is very important in the description as it indicates that the relationship can exist but that it does not need to exist.

```
(=> (Core.Resource ?r)
 (exists (?c)
 (and (Core.Capability ?c)
  (Core.hasCapability ?r ?c))))
:IC soft "Every resource may have some capability."

(=> (Core.Resource ?r)
 (exists (?e)
 (and (Core.Enterprise ?e)
  (Core.isHeldBy ?r ?e))))
:IC soft "Every resource may be held by some enterprise."

(=> (Core.Resource ?r)
 (exists (?p)
 (and (Core.Process ?p)
  (Core.isUsedBy ?r ?p))))
:IC soft "Every resource may be used by some process."
```

This sort of formality in definition is fundamental for the interoperability of systems that are developed based on standards-based definitions. This need for improved standardisation approaches has also been recognised through the work of ISO TC184 SC4 on "Industrial Data Integrated Ontologies and Models (IDIOM)" (Price, Leal & Feeney, 2010) and also in the standardisation task force report of the FInES cluster (Pattenden, Young & Zelm, 2012).

3. The Manufacturing Reference Ontology Concept

The idea of a reference ontology is to provide a formal foundation set of concepts against which system specific set of concepts can be aligned or at least checked for incompatibilities. Such a specific system may be a new software tool, database or even a new standard to be aligned with the semantics of the reference ontology.

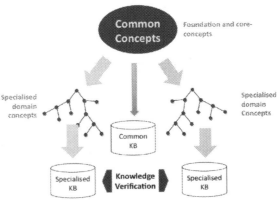

Figure 1. *Formal Concepts and specialisations*

The Interoperable Manufacturing Knowledge Systems (IMKS) project has shown the potential for the exploitation of new formal approaches through their reference ontologies for manufacture (Young et al, 2009) that can flexibly support multi-context understanding through the provision of a stable foundation upon which specialised viewpoints can be constructed. It has demonstrated the importance of the powerful expressivity of Common Logic based approaches in modelling the semantics of complex manufacturing concepts, relationships and constraints (Chungoora et al., 2012) and also how inter-system compliance can be evaluated through the specialisation and merging of production system ontologies. The concept is illustrated simply in figure 1, which can be repeated over many levels of domain decomposition. Such a reference ontology will need to exist with concepts at different levels of specialisation, dependent on how broadly or narrowly applicable these concepts are. So, when concepts are specialised to suit specific domain requirements, there is a need to evaluate the differences in concept specialisations across domains in order to verify the extent to which knowledge across these domain concepts is sharable.

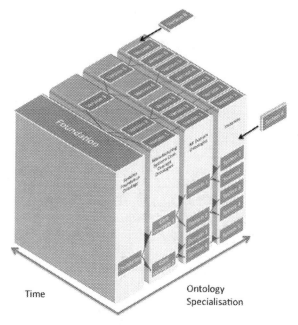

Time   Ontology
                        Specialisation

Figure 2. *Ontologies for system compliance evaluations*

A number of explorations have been undertaken within the IMKS context; in particular in relation to machining (Usman 2012) and assembly knowledge (Imran et al 2012) related to product design and in relation to systems interoperability across manufacturing systems in the context of Manufacturing Intelligence (Hastilow 2012). An extension to the IMKS concept when applied to Manufacturing Intelligence as proposed by Hastilow (Hastilow 2013) is presented in figure 2.

4. Initial explorations of the concept

The process for the development of a manufacturing reference ontology has been to work firstly with our industrial collaborators to understand the concepts of interest to their engineers. Also to exploit the understanding already available from previous research and especially the understanding that is available from existing international standards. Figures 3, 4 and 5 illustrate the concepts, at UML class level, that have been explored following the IMKS concept: respectively in knowledge sharing from machining with product design (figure 3); knowledge sharing from assembly planning with design for assembly (figure 4) and finally core concepts for Manufacturing Intelligence systems (figure 5). Each of the sets of concepts illustrated in these figures have been formally specified, implemented and used in knowledge sharing and interoperability validation experiments. It is important to note that although only a very small example of the formal specification of concepts has been has been shown here, due to its scale and complexity, it is totally essential to the value of the work.

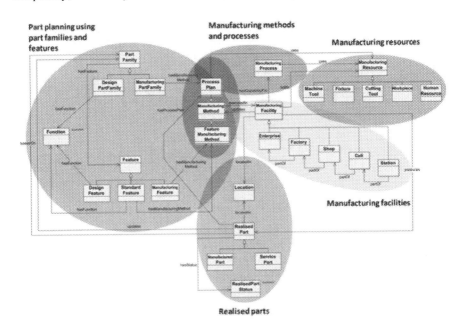

Figure 3. *A UML model of the IMKS reference ontology*

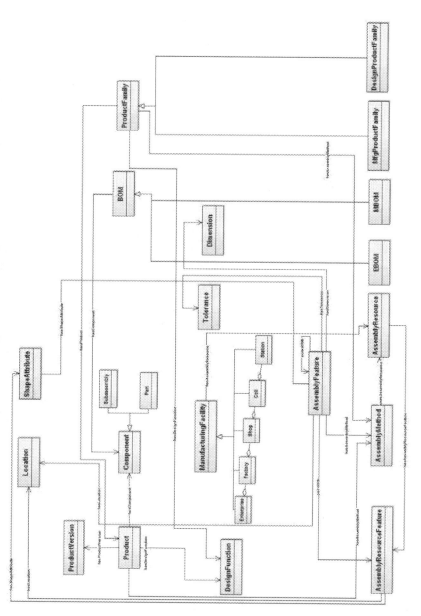

Figure 4. *A UML model of the Assembly reference ontology*

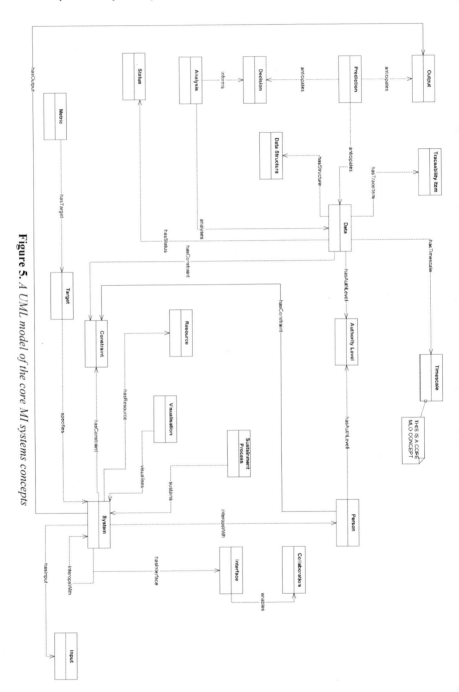

Figure 5. *A UML model of the core MI systems concepts*

5. Discussion

The work that we have done to date on defining a manufacturing reference ontology shows great promise as a route to providing a basis for improved interoperability across systems, or at least as a basis for understanding the potential level of interoperability that could be achieved across systems.

There is much still to be done. The work to date has targeted elements of such a reference ontology but more comprehensive initiatives are required if this approach is to achieve its full potential. One such initiative is the new EU FP7 FLEXINET project due, subject to negotiation, to start in the next few months. It will employ this general approach and explore its applicability to the design of global production networks for dynamically changing product-service systems.

There will also be the need at some point in the future, to agree on a common foundation set of concepts upon which such reference ontologies are to be built. The work presented in this paper has been pragmatic in its approach to this issue and has used the foundation concepts available in the software environment in which we have been exploring the ideas. Future work will continue in this direction in order to build a greater understanding of the real value of the approach. We recognise that there is a substantial overhead in providing a formal basis for all relevant concepts, but cannot see an effective alternative to this if we are to overcome the problems of interoperability across manufacturing systems.

6. Acknowledgements

This research was funded by the EPSRC through the Innovative Manufacturing and Construction Research Centre in Loughborough University (IMCRC project 253).

7. References

Borgo, S, Leitão, P., (2007), Foundations for a core ontology of manufacturing, Laboratory for Applied Ontology, ISTC-CNR, via Solteri 38,38100 Trento, 2Polytechnic Institute of Bragança, Quinta Sta Apolónia, Apartado, Bragança, Portugal.1134,5301-857

Chungoora N., Cutting-Decelle A.-F, Young R.I.M., Gunendran G., Usman Z., Harding J.A. & Case K. (2011): Towards the ontology-based consolidation of production-centric standards, International Journal of Production Research

Chungoora N., Gunendran G., Young R.I.M., Usman Z., Anjum N., Palmer C., Harding J., Case K. & Cutting-Decelle A.-F (2012) Extending product lifecycle management for manufacturing knowledge sharing. Proc IMechE Part B: J Engineering Manufacture 226(12) 2047–2063

Hastilow, N. 2013. An Ontological Approach to Manufacturing Systems Interoperability in Dynamic Change Environments. PhD thesis in preparation. School of Mechanical and Manufacturing Engineering, Loughborough University, UK

Imran M, and Young R., Usman Z. 2012 Formal assembly reference ontology for assembly systems compatibility assessment. Advances in Manufacturing Technology XXVI Tenth International Conference on Manufacturing Research Edited by T. S. Baines, B. Clegg and D. K. Harrison. pp 146 -1 151

Michel, J.J., 2005. Terminology extracted from some manufacturing and modelling related standards. CEN/TC 310 N1119R2.

Oberle, Daniel, et al. (2007), "DOLCE Ergo SUMO: On Foundational and Domain Models in the SmartWeb Integrated Ontology (SWIntO)." Web Semantics: Science, Services and Agents on the World Wide Web 5.3: 156-74.

Panetto, H., Goncalves, R., & Molina, A. (2012). Enterprise Integration and Networking: theory and practice. Annual Reviews in Control, 36(2).

Pattenden, S., Young, R., and Zelm, M. Standardisation Task Force Report to Future Internet Enterprise Systems (2012)

Price, D., Leal, D. and Barnard Feeney, A., 2010. IDIOM architecture specification. Future SC4 Architecture PWI deliverable version 02. This document follows Resolution 785 from the ISO TC184/SC4 meeting in June 2009, Parksville, Canada

Usman Z. "A Manufacturing Core Concepts Ontology to Support Knowledge Sharing" 2012. PhD Thesis, Loughborough University, Loughborough, UK

Young, R., Chungoora, N., Usman, Z., Anjum, N., Gunendran, G., Palmer, C., Harding, J., Case, K., and Cutting-Decelle, A-F., 2010, *An exploration of foundation ontologies and verification methods for manufacturing knowledge sharing*, Interoperability for Enterprise Software and Applications (Proccedings of I-ESA Workshop, 2010), Coventry, UK, Editors. H Panetto & N Boudjlida. Pub. ISTE & J Wiley. pp 83 – 92

Young, R.I.M., Gunendran, G., Chungoora, N., Harding, J.A and Case, K., 2009. Enabling interoperable manufacturing knowledge sharing in PLM. In: McMahon, C., Dutta, D. and Huang, G., eds. Product Lifecycle Management: Supporting the extended enterprise – Proceedings of the 6th International Conference on Product Lifecycle Management (PLM). Bath, UK: University of Bath. July 6-8. pp. 130-138.

Standardisation Tools for Negotiating Interoperability Solutions

Tiago Santos* — Carlos Coutinho* — Adina Cretan**
Miguel Beca* — Ricardo Jardim-Goncalves***

* *Departamento de Engenharia Eletrotécnica, F.C.T. – Universidade Nova de Lisboa*
Lisbon, Portugal
{tj.santos, c.coutinho}@campus.fct.unl.pt

** *Computer Science Department, "Nicolae Titulescu" University of Bucharest*
Bucharest (031046), Romania
badina20@yahoo.com

*** *UNINOVA, F.C.T. – Universidade Nova de Lisboa, Lisbon, Portugal*
{mfb, rg}@uninova.pt

ABSTRACT: *Globalisation is pushing markets and enterprises to abandon their traditional product centrism and focus instead their efforts into their own specialisation fields, maintaining networks of supply chains that are able to fulfil their needs towards the development of complete solutions. In that vision, given the heterogeneity of these global collaborations and the constant demand for change, innovation, and compliance to more exigent rules and the adoption and definition of standards, it becomes very difficult for enterprises to cope with the pace of change. This paper proposes the effort to develop a standard implementation of a framework based on agents and rules to achieve solid and stable integration of solutions using proven standards, via the use of a strong and formal negotiation mechanism. Negotiation will be the basis for increasing enterprise interoperability in the supply chain, proposing this as means for standardising an approach for developing interoperability solutions.*

KEYWORDS: *rules, agents, interoperability, negotiation, standards*

1. Introduction

Enterprises are struggling to remain competitive in a rough economy that is facing serious difficulties, together with a globalised environment (and competition). In order to counter this trend, enterprises and organisations are forced to develop new strategies by searching, facing and acting towards, not just for new business opportunities, but also to new collaboration opportunities. In this economy turbulence, where markets are evolving rapidly, business and collaborative opportunities are transient and insecure. In order to follow this rapid evolution, enterprises must be able to provide best-practices and standard solutions that comply to all needed requirements in a short period, which often is only possible if they are able to collaborate with their peers. In order to develop standard, agile and survival mechanisms to overcome the upcoming difficulties, enterprises should be capable of forming Virtual Organisations (VO) [1].

Despite companies and organisations should try to form VOs to stand out in the current markets, they should have in mind that their systems need to be interoperable, i.e., not only capable of changing all types of information without any constraints, within and across organisations, but also be adaptable to different network environments [2] and [3]. As environments are constantly changing, enterprises and organisations should find a way to adopt standard best-practices and solutions to maintain their interoperability with partners, suppliers and customers.

The advances in the Information Communication Technology (ICT) address new concerns of reliability regarding data exchanges in the advent of a Future Internet that goes beyond being able to interconnect and focus only on the data flow establishment where the involved parties exchange data with no errors, with the correct format and syntax. The new concerns about interoperability relate to deeper knowledge, semantics, models and business flows [4]. These concerns entail the concepts of Sustainable Enterprise Interoperability (SEI), where enterprises can collaborate by creating sustainable environments with collaboration networks in order to maintain their interoperability via standardised, mature solutions even when changes occur in the environment. In order to reach a SEI environment, the framework in Figure 1 the following capabilities must exist [5]:

- Discovery, in order to detect new systems and systems update;

- Learning and adaptability, to learn with the environment changes and the adaptations required;

- Transient analysis, to understand how a network will suffer from transient period;

- Notification, in order to inform the way that the system should react.

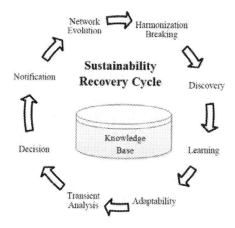

Figure 1. *Sustainable Interoperability Framework (simplified)*

By adding the negotiation factor to the previously presented SEI capabilities, a collaborative framework can be achieved where the systems interoperability can be improved through the enterprises interoperability changes negotiation that occur in the environment with all parties with business-to-business interactions [6], working towards a de facto standardisation about the way to reach these solutions.

Focusing on the most important SEI framework capabilities, we can highlight some of them because of their importance for this prototype, such as the discovery, the learning and the negotiation. Assigning each of these capabilities to some development technologies that we will analyse later, we can think in the Agent technology to perform the discovery task, because they can be autonomous, reactive and proactive, and additionally they can perform all the communications on the environment, creating a Multi-agent System (MaS). For the learning, the Rule Engine technology is the most proper to be used, as it separates the business data from the business logic which is very good as knowledge represents the business data.

The negotiation will be divided between the Agents and the Rules Engine since the negotiation communication will be developed in the Agents side and the negotiation flow will be controlled by the Rules Engine.

Section 2 will explain briefly these two technologies and also will explain more deeply the prototype, from the design to the implementation, and show some results taken from simulations of real world scenarios. In Section 3 we will perform the conclusions and present some ideas to future work on an industrial scenario prototype, as well as the potential of standardisation of the proposed approach.

2. Problem Solutions

2.1. *Rules Engine*

Facing the current needs in software development, too much time and money are being spent in order to fit all software requirements, mainly in terms of complexity and frequent changes in the developed software. To minimise these constraints, Java-based rules engine technology are being improved constantly, aiming the separation of the application code from the logic code [7] and making an efficient matching between the submitted data (the facts) and the business rules [8]. These features ease the changes in the software, leading to effective cost reductions in development.

Regarding this prototype, this technology can be used in the negotiation process and the system knowledge. In the negotiation process, it controls the negotiation flow as a state machine controller, i.e., we represent our negotiation transactions in rules types, where the inputs are the facts, which allow a better control over the state machine flow. In the system knowledge, our system needs to be able to learn from the previous negotiations (knowledge base), in order to be capable of making decision suggestions to the negotiation participants.

From several technologies provided over the Internet, we chose three of them to make an analysis which would determine the technology that is used in our prototype. The criteria used in analysis included the following aspects:

- Cost to obtain the full version;

- The available documentation;

- Ease of understanding the rule language;

- Ease of Java integration;

- Performance of the engine.

The selected rules engines were JESS [9], OpenRules [10] and Drools [11]. After the performed analysis we concluded that only Drools fitted perfectly the used selection criteria [19].

2.2. *Agents*

Agents can be defined as autonomous and interactive entities that live in some environment where they have some responsive, proactive and social-able abilities [12][13]. With this technology, our prototype should be able to create a Multi-agent

System (MaS), where agents can interact with each other and mainly where they work together in order to reach the overall goal of the system [14].

Since agents are able to interact with other agents and they can be responsive and proactive, in our prototype they should be capable not only of making all communications in the environment, but also fire a trigger that will notify the responsible authority in the system that a change occurred in some system.

Agent technology is widespread over the Internet, with numerous implemented solution alternatives. Using the same approach used with the rules engines we also selected some technologies in order to decide which would fit better, using the following selection criteria:

- Cost to obtain the full version;

- Documentation available;

- Preference of use of Java programming language;

- Ease of developing and understanding the programming language;

- Must have an easy way to perform the agent communications over the system.

After the analysis over the Java Development Framework (JADE) [15], JACK framework [16], Open Agent Architecture (OAA) [17] and Jason [18] we concluded that JADE is the one that best fits all the points presented in the selection criteria [19].

2.3. *Prototype Description*

This prototype is focused in proving that the interoperability between two or more systems is much more controllable and stable when we use negotiation to reach an interoperability state between the interoperability participants, ensuring that the participants will spend less time to modify their systems to handle the changes proposed by some participant system.

This approach, in general, produces a better result than having systems where one of them performs changes unilaterally, leading the other ones to adjust its system in order to continue with previous interoperability. This often carries a lot of time and produces poor and immature solutions. With the proposed solution, if a system wants to change something, it will trigger a negotiation, where the involved systems can reach a solution that is probably better for all the systems instead of only one.

The developing process of the prototype was focused on an implementation of a simulation of a real negotiation SEI scenario. We have chosen the Java programming language to develop this prototype allied to the usage of the rules engine and agents technologies integrated also in Java.

The prototype, whose architecture is detailed in [19] consists in a distributed system composed by a central application and various clients connected to it, forming a negotiation SEI environment. This environment has two classes of modules:

- *System Controller*: is the central point in our environment and is responsible to control all interactions between all clients connected to him through the MaS. This application is also responsible to control the negotiations in the environment, not only the negotiation flows, but also to save same negotiation knowledge in order to be capable of helping the clients in the negotiations decisions. These features will be performed by the rules engine situated in the knowledge manager and in the negotiation manager.

- *Trigger Agent*: completes the MaS, as it is connected to the System Controller by its agent. This application, besides performing all communications with the System Controller, also has a task to fire a trigger when a change occurs in the Trigger Agent system. When this happens, the trigger notifies the System Controller that a negotiation round should start to handle the change. The negotiation module is responsible only to notify the user that is necessary to make and action over the current negotiation round.

These will be the basic elements for performing the negotiation part of NEGOSEIO, which is a collaboration framework which is proposed to enable negotiation as central focus of the solution determination to improve Enterprise Interoperability [4]. This framework is making use of several standards and state-of-the-art practices like Model-Driven (Development – MDD, Architectures – MDA, Interoperability – MDI), ISO 10303 STEP data modelling and access [21]. It was also developed in projects which aim to propose standards for concurrent engineering (ECSS-E-TM-10-25A [20]). The whole NEGOSEIO framework is proposed to be set as a standard for dealing with interoperability throughout the whole enterprise product life cycle.

Now we will explain how the knowledge about the negotiations is handled in the environment through the System Controller. The knowledge is acquired from negotiation decisions made by the Trigger Agents to the formularies (questionnaires) created in the negotiation initiator and is stored in the System Controller.

The formularies in the current version of the prototype are static, i.e., the negotiation initiator system is limited to the pre-created formulary that we can see in

Figure 2, but efforts are being made in this research to change them to dynamic surveys.

Each questionnaire is intended to all negotiation participants when a new negotiation round starts and all the answers made by the participants are saved in the System Controller's knowledge base where each answer is saved in form of a rule.

These rules are constituted by key elements, like the name of the agent that made that answer, the elements that constitute the questionnaire, the answers to each question and the decision taken by the Trigger Agent.

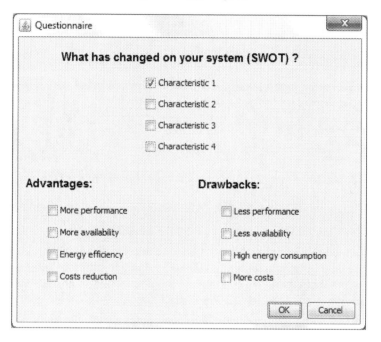

Figure 2. *Questionnaire made by negotiation initiator*

An example of a rule can be viewed in the piece of code showed below and in this rule we can see that when the negotiation initiator creates a questionnaire that has the value "Characteristic 1" selected, the response of the TriggerAgent to this questionnaire will be to reject. Of course that the decision is not direct from this rule, because the knowledge base can contain more rules of this type but with accept result which may influence on the suggestion certain percentage.

Example of a rule written in Drools language that could be saved in the System Controller knowledge base:

```
rule "Rule-Example-Reject"
when
        $map : java.util.HashMap(
        this["Energy efficiency"] == false,
        this["High energy consumption"] == false,
        this["Costs reduction"] == false,
        this["More costs"] == false,
        this["Less availability"] == false,
        this["More availability"] == false,
        this["Less performance"] == false,
        this["More performance"] == false,
        this["Characteristic 1"] == true,
        this["Characteristic 2"] == false,
        this["Characteristic 3"] == false,
        this["Characteristic 4"] == false,
        this["Agent"] == "TriggerAgent-2",
then
        resBean.addReject();
end
```

After focusing on the prototype implementation we will focus on a method to do some tests in order to determine the time that a client needs to change his system to continue to be interoperable with the system that made the interoperability change proposal.

For that we have created a web-service to accommodate some changes, this web-service was created in both Java and C#, but since both showed similar results, in this research we will focus only on the Java web-service. The created web-service consists in one method called "*carPaint*" that takes for input a car and a date of delivery and returns the date that the car will be painted and ready for delivery.

In order to reach the pretended results, we will apply some changes in the previously created web-service that will consume some time that is different depending on the change complexity. The changes and the time consumed are listed below:

- The first change, only the port of the web server has change from 8080 to 8081. This change requires some changes in WSDL file and requires generating the client classes and will consume between thirty seconds and one minute.

- The second change was made in the delivery date that now becomes to be validated in the server side. This change requires a validation in the date returned by the method and requires a rebuild. This will consume about one and a half minute.

- This time was added a new argument to the previous method. A colour variable to determine the colour that we want to paint the car. For that it's necessary some changes in WSDL file, requires generating the client classes and requires a rebuild. This will consume about three minutes.

- The fourth change was in the semantic side. Previously we have a class named *Car* that represents a car but this car can be interpreted differently by different people. So, it's necessary to develop an ontology in order to represent the Car equally for all clients that use this method. Developing an ontology includes some steps, like defining classes in the ontology, arranging the classes in a taxonomic (subclass-superclass) hierarchy, defining and describing allowed values for this slots and filling in the values for slots for instances. This change can be made in about three or four days.

- The fifth change occurs when an entity wants to do a modification in the car ontology used in the previous example. For example, previously the ontology represents a toy car, whereas now, the ontology represents a real car. This change may take very long time to be matched, since the client needs to know exactly what the server are "talking". The changes are the same as in the fourth point adding just one more task before, that is know exactly what has changed. These changes will take five or 6 days to do all the tasks.

- The last change is the most complex, since it's a change in the process of an operation. In this case is a change in the painting process. The previously process of painting was done by spray and now the car is painted by submersion technique. This change seems to be a simple change, but if we analyse more deeply, we discover that this change has a lot of complications in the client side. These complications are the method that the client delivery the car, because now, the client have to delivery only the car body and not the whole car, the car body needs to resist painting temperature which in this case the temperature is very high, all that the submersion process may do to the car body, for example, corrosion, deformation and the screw holes can be covered and finally, changes in the logistics, since it must be delivered only the car body and the rest of the car should be treated separately, which may be cause some problems with other supplier companies. This complex change will consume between fifteen to twenty days.

This analysis is depicted in the chart of the Figure 3 where is outlined the curve that characterises the time that we spend in the client side in terms of the complexity of the change. This time represents the time that the client needs to change his system to continue interoperable with the system that make the change, in other words, represent the system "downtime".

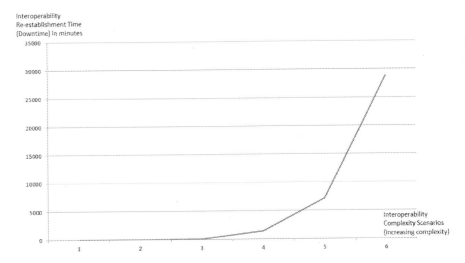

Figure 3. *Re-establishment time without negotiation*
(current scenario)

When we have negotiation between entities, we can see in Figure 4 that although the interoperability complexity grows over time, the downtime raises in a very slower pace with negotiation. In the most complex scenario that was tested, the results that were attained were one-third of the recovery time in the current scenario. This may not seem extraordinary, but has to do with a simple factor which is the negotiation time itself. As can be seen in the same figure, the negotiation time also increases a lot according to the complexity of the scenario. However, these figures do not account some additional factors that are proposed by NEGOSEIO, which are the maturity of the solutions (a solution coming from negotiation has undergone alternatives analysis and hence is considered more mature and less prone to errors and to rework).

These scenarios also improved greatly when we added to this environment one factor which is determinant in this framework, which is knowledge of past negotiations. The negotiation knowledge, empowered by the definition of this knowledge in the shape of rules in the rules engine (see section 2.1) showed great improvement in the negotiation time itself, as the knowledge of previous decisions and their success contributed a lot to speed the taking of new decisions for the forthcoming negotiations, as well as the knowledge of previous solutions for the same scenarios contributed greatly to the immediate proposal of these solutions on forth scenarios.

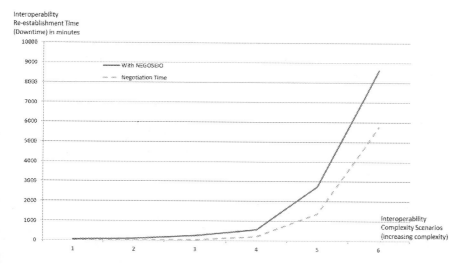

Figure 4. *Re-establishment time with negotiation*

These scenarios are also expected to improve thanks to the adoption of standard negotiation techniques and strategies like Block or Split [4], thus contributing to reduce even further the downtime with negotiation.

3. Conclusions and Future Work

Once finished the prototype where we have developed a system that simulates a SEI environment and after concluding the tests explained in the Section 2.3 we can conclude that it's possible to reduce the time that the enterprises spent in their systems adaptation in order to correspond to other enterprise's needs when the negotiation factor allied to the knowledge is introduced in the SEI environment. This conclusion can be achieved quickly if we are facing enterprises that change their systems frequently, what is common practice nowadays [6], and even more in the future.

3.1. *Potential for Standardisation*

This research work is integrated in the scope of the development of the NEGOSEIO framework. This framework was proposed – and accepted for small-scale integration – for implementation in the European Space Agency's Concurrent Design Facility (ESA-CDF), to complement the work developed in the standardisation Technical Memorandum ECSS-E-TM-10-25A [20] for Concurrent Engineering. The principal intention of these standards is to be used at ESA. Nevertheless, it will contribute to their potential adoption also on other space-related agencies. Despite that, NEGOSEIO may indeed be used also on other domains, but specific plans for its submission in other SDOs will only be considered after additional development of the framework.

The purpose of this framework is to be able to standardise the approach for dealing with interoperability solutions, so that it always includes negotiation as central behaviour. To be able to be set as a reference and standard, this framework makes use of several best-practices and approaches that are being stated as state-of-the art in interoperability.

The development of this framework reuses several concepts, like the already stated the separation of enterprise views in two, each with their MDA-like approach: Technology (with abstraction levels CIM/PIM/PSM), and Business & People (with abstraction levels BOM/TIM/TSM), coming from the Manufacturing SErvices Ecosystem (MSEE), a consortium project of the ICT Work Programme, of the European Community's 7th Framework Programme (FP7) [29].

MSEE targets to pave the way for service development in Europe, with the creation of virtual manufacturing factories (Factories of the Future) which shall make use of extended servitisation for the shift from product-centrism to product-based services, distributed in virtual organisations and ecosystems.

Besides MSEE, the framework also reuses standard access and modelling from ISO 10303 STEP, a reference ontology and best-practices from the state-of-the-art in Service-Oriented Architectures and Cloud Computing.

The purpose of this work, as stated before, is to establish negotiation as a standardised approach for dealing with the determination of solutions for enterprise interoperability, and rules/rules engines in particular as the standard means to develop and establish dynamic knowledge about past negotiation for the future ones.

Standardisation is hence proposed for this framework with respect to negotiation, and all its related aspects: Negotiation-specialised strategies and knowledge from previous negotiations.

3.2. *Future Work*

Focusing in the close future, this prototype has much to improve since there are some points that need more attention, like the negotiation formulary, that we already talked about in the Section 2.3, should be modified to be a dynamic survey to allow enterprises customise their negotiations, because this survey not only can vary from enterprise to enterprise but also varies from negotiation to negotiation. Additional work foreseen in a near future is the improvement in the knowledge acquired by System Controller that should be focus on improving the accuracy of the System Controller suggestions to Trigger Agents about the negotiation decisions.

4. Acknowledgments

The authors wish to acknowledge the support of the European Commission through the funding of the FP7 ENSEMBLE, UNITE, MSEE and IMAGINE projects, and the ESA-CDF for the help in the business case.

5. References

1. Oliveira, A.I., Camarinha-Matos, L.M.: Electronic Negotiation Support Environment in Collaborative Networks. In: *Advances in Information and Communication Technology*, vol. 372, pp. 21-32 (2012)

2. Ray, S. R., Jones, A. T.: Manufacturing interoperability. In: *Journal of Intelligent Manufacturing*, vol. 17, pp. 681-688 (2006)

3. Jardim-Goncalves, R., Agostinho, C., Malo, P., Steiger-Garcao, A.: Harmonising technologies in conceptual models representation. In: *Int. Journal of Product Lifecycle Management*, vol. 2, pp. 187-205 (2007)

4. Cretan, A., Coutinho, C., Bratu, B., Jardim-Goncalves, R.: NEGOSEIO: A Framework for Negotiations toward Sustainable Enterprise Interoperability. In: *IFAC Journal Annual Reviews In Control* (2012)

5. Jardim-Goncalves, R., Agostinho, C., Steiger-Garcao, A.: Sustainable Systems' Interoperability: A reference model for seamless networked business. In: *Systems Man and Cybernetics* (SMC), pp. 1785-1792 (2010)

6. Coutinho, C., Cretan, A., Jardim-Goncalves, R.: Cloud-based negotiation for sustainable Enterprise Interoperability. In: *Engineering, Technology and Innovation* (ICE), pp. 1-10 (2012)

7. Zhang, G., Shan, W., Wang, F.: Research on the Promotion of Rule Engine Performance. In: *Intelligent Systems and Applications* (ISA), pp. 1-3 (2010)

8. Liu, D., Gu, T., Xue, J.: Rule Engine based on improvement Rete algorithm. In: The 2010 International Conference on Apperceiving Computing and Intelligence Analysis Proceeding, pp. 346-349 (2010)

9. JESS Rule Engine, http://www.jessrules.com [accessed in 2012-08-10]

10. OpenRules Rule Engine, http://openrules.com [accessed in 2012-08-12]

11. Drools Rule Engine, http://www.jboss.org/drools [accessed in 2012-08-14]

12. Jennings, N.R., Sycara, K., Wooldridge, M.: A Roadmap of Agent Research and Development. In: *Autonomous Agents and Multi-Agent Systems*, vol. 1, pp. 7-38 (1998)

13. Alonso, E.: AI and Agents. In: *AI Magazine*, vol. 23, pp. 25-29 (2002)

14. Leeton, U., Kulworawanichpong, T.: Multi-Agent Based Optimal Power Flow Solution. In: Power and Energy Engineering Conference (APPEEC), pp. 1-4 (2012)

15. JADE Agent Framework, http://jade.tilab.com [accessed in 2012-09-10]

16. JACK Agent Framework, http://aosgrp.com/products/jack [accessed in 2012-09-12]

17. Open Agent Architecture, http://www.ai.sri.com/~oaa [accessed in 2012-09-14]

18. Jason Agent Framework, http://jason.sourceforge.net/wp [accessed in 2012-09-16]

19. Santos, T, Coutinho, C., Jardim-Goncalves, R., Cretan, A.: Negotiation Environment for Enterprise Interoperability Sustainability. Paper submitted to 17th IEEE International Conference on Computer Supported Cooperative Work in Design (CSCWD 2013).

20. ESA/ECSS WG: ECSS-E-TM-10-25A Technical Memorandum, 2010.

21. Jardim-Goncalves, R., Figay, N., Steiger-Garcao, A.: Enabling interoperability of STEP Application Protocols at metadata and knowledge level. In *International Journal of Technology Management*, vol. 36, no. 4, pp. 402–421(20), 2006.

22. MSEE Project 2012: http://www.msee-ip.eu/project-overview. [Accessed: 10-Jan-2013]

Workshop 4

Case Studies on Enterprise Interoperability: How IT Managers Profit from EI Research

Report Workshop 4

Stephan Kassel

University of Applied Sciences
PFS 201037, 08012 Zwickau, Germany
Stephan.Kassel@fh-zwickau.de

1. Introduction

The workshop was aiming to develop a draft for an industry-oriented use-case template for enterprise interoperability. This template should describe practical experiences with the development of enterprise interoperability solutions. Interested IT managers respectively strategic decisions-makers should be provided with the latest scientific approaches and latest industrial experiences of Enterprise Interoperability.

From a business perspectice, a template should provide two main chunks of information. First of all, readers should easily identify business indicators and the business field of the described enterprise. This has to be combined with a short problem description together with the main solution idea. For these information, a template has to make a simple comparison available by using an easily understandable classification.

This information, which should be provided in a public or semi-public database, supports interested enterprises to find use cases available to solve their own interoperability problems in the best way. The second part, describing the theoretical approach, should provide information about the theories and methods applied to build a solution. It should detail, in which way the Enterprise Interoperabilty approach was used to develop a solution for problems of a complex IT environment.

2. Presenting the Topics of the Workshop

In the beginning, the situation of enterprise interoperability research was described, which can be characterized by a series of large funded research projects (funded by the European Union) which produced a significant number of academic results (e.g. in the area of interoperability infrastructures, model-driven interoperability, ontologies and taxonomies, standardization of terms and definitions) and an extensive research agenda for the future (mainly in the same areas, but also in servitization, semantic foundations, and standards). But from outside of the academic culture the impact of the research is still rather limited. Only a small number of companies were involved in the big research projects, and it is hard to roll out the ideas to other companies, even if they can be characterized by interoperability problems in different areas. If the situation is analyzed, one can see a lack of existing approaches to directly address companies with the results of the research work done in the last decade of research. Industry has to concentrate on "quick wins" with every new technology to attract some early adaptors for utilizing new methods. Some small solutions with a positive return on investment (ROI) have to be developed to gain interest of industry. No company wants to start very innovative projects with a high pre-investment and a high risk without clearly seeing the chances for improving their respective businesses.

The situation needs to be improved by collecting best practices from different industries as well as collecting open problem from these industries which can be solved with methods of interoperability. There should be a guideline for achieving interoperability which could be easily adopted by companies. So the discussion should concentrate on several important questions concerning the provision of the use cases. Who are the addressees of the use cases, which cases are the important ones, and how should these cases be collected?

3. Presentation of a Few Case Studies

To be able to discuss different approaches for the collection of industrial case studies for interoperability, several specific cases were presented, which are partly included in these proceeding. The cases came from different domains, and they are not conforming to some standardized format, which helped to see the diversity of cases and of case descriptions currently in use in the academic community. There are nearly no standards, and the limited ones are very elaborate and maybe are too verbose to be used for the descriptions of the cases.

4. Discussion

After the presentation of the cases, and provoked by the introduction to the workshop, a vital and very constructive discussion on the purpose of the case studies, on the way how to collect them and the addressees came up. It ended in the collection of three objectives for the collection of use cases and some action points to make progress towards the objectives.

The objectives for collecting case studies of enterprise interoperability are:

– Get credibility in front of enterprises and in front of stakeholders of the domain

– Use significant cases as examples "what can we do today"

– Use significant cases as examples "what are the drivers for tomorrow?"

The next steps will be to evolve a template conforming to the 3d framework of interoperability provided by David Chen and colleagues, to provide action points for reaching the objectives, and to organize a telephone meeting of the participants of the workshop to further discuss the ideas.

Experiences of Transferring Approaches of Interoperability into SMEs

Florian Gruner — Stephan Kassel

University of Applied Science
Dr.-Friedrichs-Ring 2a
08056 Zwickau
florian.gruner@fh-zwickau.de
stephan.kassel@fh-zwickau.de

ABSTRACT: This workshop contribution illustrates the utilization of our Business Case Template. Therefore the authors transformed an already existing business case into this template. Such a shortened version of business cases should help readers and practitioners to identify and select useful cases for their own initial situation.

KEYWORDS: business case template, enterprise interoperability, enterprise classification and identification

1. Introduction

This document provides an example of a Business Cases by utilizing our template. It is designed to simplify identification and categorization of interoperability business cases. In the first section "Management Summary" authors are encouraged to supply readers with some basic information about the use case. This information should support practitioners to select interesting and appropriate studies of interoperability challenges. The following sections provide readers with technical details of an interoperability project. Interested IT managers and strategic decisions-makers are getting information about the latest scientific approaches and latest industrial experiences of Enterprise Interoperability (EI). Following this idea, practitioners will be enabled for a better evaluation of scientific approaches of technology and methodology conforming to the theories of EI.

2. Details of the Business Case Template

2.1. *Management Summary*

2.1.1. *Enterprise Information and Classification*

This section provides the reader with some basic information to classify the enterprise of the use case. In our case it is a regionally based small and medium based enterprise. Figures in brackets are further details to classify an enterprise.

- Name of Enterprise: BÄKO Ost eG

- Size of Enterprise (employees): 11 to 500 (up to 10 or more than 500)

- Enterprise Turnover (in million €): more than 50 (up to 2, up to 10 or up to 50)

- Enterprise Classification (according to the "UK Standard Industrial Classification of Economic Activities 2008): Main Business G 46; Further Business S 94 and C 33 (characters represents the section, numbers represents the division)

- Business Relations: B2B (B2C)

- Selected Department: Customer Service (Controlling, Financial/Accounting, Logistics, IT, Marketing, Research and Development or other departments)

2.1.2. *Use Case Classification*

This section contains a brief summary of the use case content. Readers should be supported to select an appropriate use case, fitting to the own questions and challenges of business and IT transformation.

- *Interoperability Efforts*: company wide (cross-company)

- *Reasons for Interoperability Efforts*: Raise in Effectiveness, Raise in Flexibility and Cost Savings (Expansion, Outsourcing, Bought Skills, Extension of Offering, Entering New Locations/Countries, Leaner Administration or other reasons)

- *Expected Effects of Interoperability Efforts:* Service and Flexibility (Production, Innovation, Productivity, Product Range, Price Structure, Consumer Topology, Quality, Quantity or other efforts)

- *Supported Key Areas*: Technical Customer Service on affiliated bakeries (SCM, Corporate Integration, R&D Cooperation, Corporate Networks, eBusiness, Mergersor other key areas)

- *Supported Business Process*: Core Process (Support or Management Process)

- *Most Critical Task of the Project*: Technical Change, Administrative Effort, Motivation/Training of Employees (Reorganisation of Employees, Project Management Issues, Reorganisation of Management, Logistic Effort or other critical tasks)

2.1.3. General Use Case Information

In this section readers should be provided with some basic information about the state of the BÄKO Ost eG business case. Furthermore project participants are encouraged to offer their business contact details.

- *State of Development:* Project Execution (Brief Idea, Idea Accepted, Project Finished)

- *Date:* 06.12.2012

- *Version:* 1.0

- *Contact Details Enterprise:* Boden H. and Schreiber B

- *Contact Details Author:* Kassel S., University of Applied Science Zwickau, stephan.kassel@fh-zwickau, +49-375-536-3492 and Gruner F., University of Applied Science Zwickau, florian.gruner@fh-zwickau.de, +49-375-536-3465

- Contact Details Details Implementation Partner: AGETO

2.2. *Initial Position and Kick-off for this Interoperability Project*

2.2.1. Background of Enterprise

BÄKO as a medium sized trading company is primarily interested in enhancing their relationship to nearly 700 regionally based crafts. Caused by ongoing structural changes in the market BÄKO has to develop their business focus from a conventional trading company to a full service provider to sustain their own success and even the success of affiliated bakeries.

2.2.2. Technical and Process Background

This transformation is not supported by their legacy system (ERP-System). There exist no standard functionalities to make this system interoperable with other information systems at low costs and low personal interventions. In summary, the change of the business model is causing a gap between new requirements and the provided functionalities of the ERP system. In consequence a solution is needed, allowing us to integrate new business processes and the supporting IT systems to fulfill daily needs. An integration system should manage transformation and transportation tasks between integrated applications. It should further simplify the exchange of any application in order to meet changing market requirements.

2.2.3. Difficulties and Problems to be Solved

In this section readers should be provided with an all-embracing description of the difficulties, problems and core issues of the process.

2.2.4. Expected Improvements and Major Objective

Considering the business objectives of BÄKO IT managers should be enabled to follow the principles of the best-of-breed strategy by choosing specialized software systems in order to fulfill the requirements of the involved business departments in charge of their business processes. In a technical view it is easier for a SME to abstract from the SOA philosophy and its focus on coarse-grained services to complete applications, offering needed business processes. This property of the developed prototypical integration system leads to the possibility that the decision for a software system is no longer concentrating on provided interfaces, exchange file formats, programming languages and the question of in-house installation or on-demand SAAS-offers. The criteria catalogue for the decision towards a specialized software system has to be focusing on one single question – the capability to fulfill the business requirements. This is chosen to simplify the selection process, but mainly to increase the degree of flexibility and agility

2.3. Solution and Details of Implementation

2.3.1. Technical Description

In cooperation with AGETO Holding AG, the Service-Integration-System (SIS) was developed to simplify the efforts of interoperating with further software modules of different technical characteristics, such as interfaces, file format or programming languages. The SIS serves as an independent and intelligent integration platform with interfaces to the existing ERP and future service systems to be installed, comparable with an Enterprise Service Bus, because both bridge the massive disadvantages of conventional point-to-point connections by introducing a hub-and-spoke architecture. This is the basis for an easier integration of new software systems, leading to a massive reduction of the efforts to code the interfaces and provide the data mappings. The SIS is acting as a mediator in a heterogeneous application environment, which will grow in future according to the entrepreneurial changes of the business of BÄKO. For this purpose the SIS provides a variety of functionalities for the intelligent management of interfaces for business process management and data management.

2.3.2. Process

The approach of the SIS lies in the orchestrating of complex sub-processes, which can be performed by using the specialized services only. Thus, the overall business process has to be carried out by using several IT systems, but most steps can be done using the standard functionality of the specialized modules without company-specific programming. The aim is to develop an integrated enterprise information system out of (nearly) uncustomized standard software systems, thus reducing costs and risks for the SME resulting from extensive customizations. On the other hand, it reduces the danger of implementing software modules as isolated applications without any connections to surrounding systems. Avoiding this, the SIS will provide supporting tasks of data management, such as transportation and transformation, between the affected components. Therefore, IT managers have to define the processes to ensure data exchange to supply each single system with a consistent database. Especially the fact of data management will be interesting for SME. In the first stage, a module pushes data into the SIS, which should be transferred to target systems. The SIS is additionally storing these data in order to just push the changed data to the target system. Beside that, this database will be used to build up a cross-module data warehouse later.

2.4. *Experiences*

In the next steps, IT managers have to define the management processes for the independence of different sets of data. Every single system will be in charge for their own set of information and data required for the supported business processes. Thus the ERP system still has an important role in this architecture. Major data, such as financial data and customer related data are mainly managed in this system. Without a consistent database of these information a sound enterprise information system cannot be guaranteed. But other kind of data, such as technical customer service related data (customer machine data, customer service contracts) are managed by the corresponding software systems, reducing the need to change the ERP system in order to be able to handle these kinds of data as well.

In our case study an ongoing exchange has been illustrated between the ERP and the technical customer service supporting system (service system). This could not be done without focusing on the required data mapping processes. Because of the leading role of the ERP system for the customer data debtors data (customer data), creditor data and machine or rather spare part data has been exported from the ERP system to the service system. Because of the importance of these data they can only be updated in the ERP system. From the service system service reports are exported, being the base for accounting. In the next step, there will be a real-time query of spare parts from the service system to the ERP system to give an actual overview of parts in stock, in order to provide a better technical service to the customer.

2.5. *Conclusion*

The main difference between SIS and SOA/ESB is the possible integration of independent standardized software modules, supporting a department with integral standardized business processes. Any aspect of entrepreneurial tasks may be covered by self-contained and specialized software modules, which can be intelligently connected and integrated with each other. That means basically that the mainly technical approach of SOA and its implementation with ESB is further simplified by changing the focus from primarily encapsulated, self-contained and fine-grained services, which can be freely combined to generate any possible business processes to integrated service-providing applications which are combined on a higher level.

3. References

Gruner F., Kassel S., "Experiences of Transferring Approaches of Interoperability into SMEs: A Case-Study of Implementing an Integration Platform", *Enterprise Interoperability V*, 2012, p. 441–451.

Gruner F., Kassel, S., "Extending Lifecycle of Legacy Systems - An Approach for SME to Enhance Their Supported Business Processes through a Service-Integration-System". *IFIP Advances in Information and Communication Technology*, 2012, p. 43–50.

Prosser L., UK Standard Industrial Classification of Economic Activities 2007, 2009.

Schubert P., Wölfle R., The eXperience methodology for writing IS case studies. Proceedings of the Thirteenth Americas Conference on Information Systems (AMCIS), 2007.

Wölfle, R. et al.: eXperience Handbuch für Autoren, 2007.

Workshop 5

Selected New Applications
of Enterprise Interoperability

Report Workshop 5

Luís Ferreira Pires* — Pontus Johnson**

*University of Twente
PO Box 217, 7500 AE Enschede, The Netherlands
l.ferreirapires@utwente.nl

**KTH Royal Institute of Technology
Osquldas v. 12, 100 44 Stockholm, Sweden
pontusj@kth.se

1. Paper Presentations

This is the report on the 'Workshop on Selected applications and methods for Enterprise Interoperability, which has been organized in conjunction with the IWEI Conference 2013 (Enschede, the Netherlands). This workshop has taken place on 26 March 2013 and was attended by around 15 people

Five papers were presented during the workshop:

– *Wout Hofman* presented his paper entitled "Service-Oriented enterprise interoperability in logistics". The main purpose of this work has been to develop an approach to move from goals to choreographies of business services. In this work ontologies are used to define the concepts of the logistics domain and BPMN is used to define choreographies. During questioning there was a discussion on the use of a registry for storing information on business services in a certain region, which happens to be a good idea. Another question was whether the ontologies in this work are being used for reasoning, which is not the case now, but is a long-term goal in this work.

– *Laura Daniele* presented her paper entitled "An ontological approach to logistics". She motivated the used of ontologies in logistics, especially by pointing out problems related to terminology mismatch. The main purposes of using ontologies in logistics are to improve communication, interoperability and software development. In her work, a core ontology was developed to serve as the starting point for all the purposes mentioned above. During questioning there was a question concerning reasoning, and the presenter answered that this is enabled by the use of a logics-based language (OWL) to describe the core ontology. Another question concerned the collaborative development of ontologies, which is surely a challenge to be taken up in future.

– *Aurelie Montarnal* presented her paper entitled "Social vision of collaboration of organizations on a cloud platform". The work has been targeted to the development of OpenPaaS, which is an environment that is capable of choosing process cartographies that can match the goals of the business. This work builds upon MISE (Mediation Information System Engineering). Special attention has been given to the proper representation of collaborative situations. During questioning there was a question about the target domains of this environment, and the answer was that this environment is quite generic and can be used in many different domains.

– *Erwin Folmer* presented his paper entitled "Semantic standards quality measured for achieving enterprise interoperability: The case of the SETU standard for flexible staffing". The purpose of his work has been to develop an instrument to measure the quality of semantic standards. He developed quality models for standards, and applied these models to a standard used by employment agencies in order to validate these models. During questioning there was a discussion on the possibility of deriving guidelines for using ontology development techniques from these quality models, and this should be further investigated.

– *Nicolas Daclin* presented his paper entitled "Requirements formalization for systems engineering: an approach for interoperability analysis in collaborative process model". The works tackles interoperability problems of a collaborative process before runtime, and it aims at facilitating the (re-)writing of interoperability requirements. During questioning there was a discussion concerning the generality of the approach.

2. Discussion Session

After the presentation of the papers there was a discussion session. The following statements have been made:

– Ontologies can be very beneficial for interoperability, but techniques for ontology engineering should be improved in order to facilitate the development of ontologies that are appropriate for this purpose.

– There is a gap between theoreticians and practitioners concerning ontologies, which has to be bridged.

– We should look for ways to offer simple and consistent system interfaces to users, and ontologies can also be useful in this respect.

– Standards should in principle be aligned, but this is even a bigger problem when these standards are actually ontologies.

– Business people do not care for ontologies. Business components are therefore still necessary, and ontologies should make sure these components are consistent and interoperable.

Service-Oriented Enterprise Interoperability in Logistics

Wout Hofman

TNO
P.O. Box 5050
2600 GB Delft, the Netherlands
Wout.hofman@tno.nl

ABSTRACT: *There are many initiatives to improve interoperability in logistics. The EC DG Move has launched the e-Freight initiative to stimulate multi-modal logistics, the Dutch government has initiated the NLIP (Neutral Logistics Information Platform) with the objective to construct a Logistics Information Gateway to Europe, and the Rotterdam Port Authority stimulates the multi modal shift to deal with an ever increase logistics flow. In the past, bilateral or community agreements were implemented by a limited number of stakeholders, leading to closed communities and a relative slow adoption based on for instance long implementation times. To achieve the aforementioned goals and to create an open environment, this paper presents an approach based on a classification of logistics services supported by a semantic model and a business choreography. Once a company has implemented the complete model and the choreography, it will be able to do business with customers and logistic service. Possibly, transformation functions have to be put in place in case two business partners use a different (version of a) semantic model.*

KEYWORDS: *business services, value exchange, interoperability ontology, business process choreography*

1. Introduction

Interoperability of businesses amongst each other and with government agencies, requires agreements on several levels [1]. Communication is in most cases solved by implementing Internet protocols. Semantics and syntax has been combined in for instance Electronic Data Interchange (EDI), XML Schema Definitions (XSDs) and web services for a Service Oriented Architecture [2], although there are also UML (Unified Modeling Language) class diagrams developed to support different syntaxes for data sharing [3]. Moreover, there is also technology available for explicitly referring to semantic models when using web services, e.g. in Semantic Annotations for Web Service Definition Language [4]. Also conceptual approaches have been developed based on Abstract State Machines [5] like Web Service Modeling Ontology [6]. Whereas WSMO allows to model not only web services, which are of a technical nature, but also business services, SA-WSDL enhances web services with semantics and does not support business services. However, WSMO has never been taken up due to various reasons [7]. There are also other approaches that tackle the aspects of dynamic service composition, e.g Dynamicos [8].

There have been other approaches to interoperability in the past, e.g. electronic business XML [9]. ebXML both took a process approach to either bilateral - or multilateral collaboration by modeling activity diagrams for interactions between actors, and developed a secure messaging protocol, ebMS (ebXML Messaging Service). The process modeling approach has been taken up and further refined by the United Nations/CEFACT by developing the UN Modeling Method [10]. It has been applied in for instance the Beer Living Lab of the EC FP6 ITAIDE project [11]. Both ebXML and UMM have not been widely applied and accepted, due to potential complex process models that could only serve as reference models.

More recent approaches introduce the concept of (business) transaction [12] as all interactions between all actors to fulfill a commercial sales, delivery, and payment process, which is internationally also known as the Buy-Ship-Pay model [13]. In this context, a business transaction has a (potential) long duration and spans complete logistic chains that can be complex [14]. Like in ebXML, it leads to types of reference models. Yet another approach is to model the choreography between actors participating in a bilateral collaboration [15]. The choreography of events, semantics of shared data, the syntax, and communication protocols have to be implemented by these two collaborating actors. In this paper, we propose to take this latter approach and enhance with the concepts 'business service' or 'value proposition' taken from service science [16]. We will apply these concepts to logistics to address issues like multi-modal shift to increase sustainability that require interoperability [17]. Since syntax and communication protocols are fairly stable, we will only address semantics and choreography for logistic services in this paper.

First of all, the concept of logistic service is introduced, linked to logistic semantic concepts, and illustrated by examples. Secondly, the choreography for bilateral collaborations to support data sharing for logistic services is specified, and thirdly, the application of these concepts by a customer and logistic service provider are given. Finally, conclusions and future work will be identified.

2. Logistic Services

This section introduces logistic services as a specialization of business services for logistics. First of all, general concepts are introduced and secondly, two examples of a logistic service is modeled, namely transport and transship.

2.1. *Business Services*

Business services relate to actions that can be performed by one actor that have value for another actor, implying that another actor is willing to pay for the execution of that actions. We will call an action at business level 'business activity'. A 'value proposition' can be described as the offer of an actor to perform a particular action [2]. As value propositions are specific to a particular actor, more than one actor can perform the same business activity, e.g. there are several actors offering transport with specific prices and conditions. Thus, in our approach the concept 'business activity' is generic to a particular application area like 'transport', 'finance', and 'government'. A business activity can be seen as an atomic unit that is offered as a value proposition by an actor to its business environment. An enterprise system supports the execution of a business activity.

Whenever a value proposition is performed, value is exchanged between a customer and provider [18]. Accounting learns that value is exchanged by exchange of resources like products, rights or services [6]. To be able to exchange value, certain internal resources need to be allocated and utilized, e.g. transport means and personnel [19]. Resource allocation can be defined as an internal process of an actor to assign its particular resources for one or more value exchanges. Information needs to be shared amongst actors to allow resource allocation, for instance by business document that we will call 'interaction types'. According to [20] and [19] three phases of information sharing can be distinguished: prepare value exchange by resource allocation of a provider and agreement on conditions/prices between customer and provider, actual value exchange, and a rollback in case no agreement can be reached or real world conditions change (a planned event can not take place, for instance because the goods have been stolen). These phases imply that value will either be exchanged or not at all. Each business activity will have its particular choreography and the aforementioned value exchange phases can be applied to more than one business activity.

Adding these notions of 'resource', 'choreography', and 'interaction type' to 'action' and renaming 'action' to business activity gives the following shared concepts for business services (see figure 1):

- *Business activity* (or action): an action provided by one or more actors. 'Capability' [16] and, based on computational theory, 'state transition' [21] are synonyms for business activity.

- *Provider*: an actor providing a particular business activity. Provider is a role of an actor.

- *Customer*: an actor requesting the execution of a business activity by a provider. Customer is a role of an actor.

- *Resources*: persons and/or real world objects required by or exchanged as part of a value proposition. Resources can have different roles in a value proposition that are specified at instance level, e.g. they might be actually exchanged or are required for value exchange [2].

- *Business transaction*: all information shared between a customer and provider for the execution of a business activity according to its particular choreography.

- *Interaction type*: a means to share data between a customer and provider within the context of a business transaction. Interaction type is a synonym of the concept event type in REA [22] and is more common known as 'business document' [23].

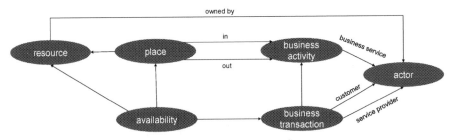

Figure 1. *Ontology of shared business concepts*

2.2. *Logistic Services*

The previous part presents the generic concepts for business service that need further specialization for logistics. A business activity has a number of properties (also called attributes) that will have a particular value for a logistic service. These properties differ per business activity, e.g. transport has different properties than transship. We distinguish the following business activities: physical activities (transport, transshipment, (temporary) storage, and value added services like re-packing, unpacking, ironing (of textile)), supporting physical activities (e.g. vessel waste management, container cleaning), administrative activities (production of transport accompanying documentation (certificate of origin, Bill of Lading) and formal procedures (financial (VAT), (food or product) safety, security)), and financial activities (insurance and logistics financing).

Defining the properties of all business activities is out of scope for this paper; we will only discuss transport and transshipment respectively. To transport has the following properties:

- Type of Cargo: the particular type of cargo that can be transported, e.g. containers, dry bulk, packages, pallets, etc. Additionally, more specifics of the type of cargo can be given, e.g. 20-feet containers, dry bulk containers, liquid bulk containers, reefer containers, etc. This particular parameter refers to other capabilities of a service provider, e.g. characteristics of a means of transport. In principle, a set of potential types of cargo is specified in UN Recommendations on packaging and container types.

- Ranges of physical characteristics of the cargo. Physical characteristics are the weight (gross weight, net weight, tare weight) and the dimensions (length/width/height, volume, over-dimension). Basically, a lower and upper boundary of physical characteristics can be given, e.g. the weight must be within a specific range. Physical characteristics need to be accompanied with a measure unit specifier, e.g. 'kg' for weights.

- Specifics of the cargo: these refer to stowage and transport conditions, e.g. temperature setting (reefer cargo) and dangerous cargo, and any specifics requiring special handling or related to the value of the cargo. In this particular case, a logistic service provider only needs to indicate whether or not reefer or dangerous cargo can be handled, including for which mode in case of dangerous cargo (each mode has its own specifics).

- From-to. The from-to combination can have different values, e.g. a particular location/city, postal code ranges, a region, a state, etc. Values for this particular property can possibly be picked from predefined lists, e.g. there are lists with city, state and country names. Possibly, there are also lists with regions. Postal codes differ per country, so they need to be accompanied probably with an indication of the country and city.

- Duration (min-max, average). This is the estimated duration of the service. Possibly, a logistic service provider wants to indicate a range showing that transport can be faster or later, depending on external conditions.

To transship basically considers the same parameters like type of cargo, physical characteristics, specifics of the cargo, and duration (min-max, average). The 'duration' may have a relation with a temporary storage service, e.g. if the maximum duration is exceeded and the cargo is not collected by a consignee or his representative, the cargo is automatically stored and other rates apply. Additionally, the following properties need to be given by a service provider:

- Type of means of transport. It indicates which types of means of transport can call at a certain transshipment location. It can include any specifics of a means of transport, e.g. a maximum length, maximum weight, draught, etc.

- Transshipment location. This can be a physical location with a decomposition in for instance specific gates, docks or quays at which cargo can be accepted or delivered.

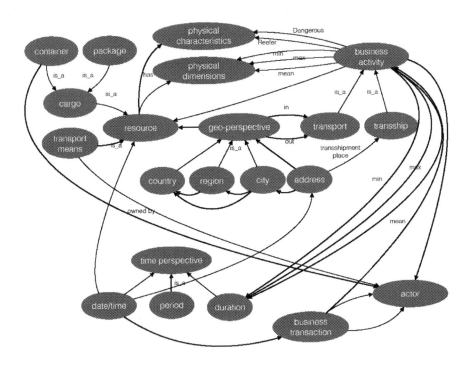

Figure 2. *Ontology for transport and transshipment services and their transactions*

The gate at which the cargo can be accepted (or discharged from for instance a vessel), can be at another location than the gate at which the cargo is loaded on another means of transport. This is called the 'extended gate', by which the actor offering transshipment services arranges internal transport between these different locations.

The previous figure shows the specialization for the generic business service ontology applied to logistics. The concepts 'place' and 'availability' have been transformed into 'geo-perspective' and 'time perspective' respectively to cater with different abstractions of locations used in logistic services and different time perspectives. The geo-perspective is used to list different abstraction levels for transport services. The in and out relation is normally a two way relation, meaning that the values for the 'in' associations are at the same time also 'out' in the same transport service. The time perspective includes for instance the actual date and time in which a resource is in a particular place represented by an address. Duration is relevant for a logistic service to represent the time it takes for performing a particular service, it needs to be refined to represent for instance maximum, minimum and possibly mean duration. We have specialized resources into cargo representing resources that cannot move on their own, and transport means as resources that can. Cargo is decomposed in what could be called re-usable resources (containers) and non re-usable ones (packages). Transport means and containers are the resources owned by a particular actor.

	National parcel service	European parcel service	Rotterdam hinterland container service
Resource	package	package	container
Physical characteristics	max. weight = 5 kg	max. weight = 5 kg	
Dangerous	0	0	1
Reefer	0	0	1
Minimum duration	-	-	12 hours
Maximum duration	24 hours	48 hours	36 hours
Average duration	-	-	-
In	Netherlands	Netherlands	Rotterdam
Out	Netherlands	Western European countries	Bayern region Germany

Table 1. *Examples of transport services*

The ontology can support various different logistic services. Table 1 shows some examples of a national parcel service, a European one and a container service between the port of Rotterdam and the hinterland. The table illustrates that a number of associations results in different entries representing attributes of a logistic service (to limit the number of rows, the physical characteristics have not been detailed but are given in a cell). The 0 or 1 indicates that the dangerous or reefer association exists (1) or not (0). The examples are illustrative, they do not represent actual transport services.

2.3. *Business Service Choreography*

Delivery of a logistic service will adhere to a certain behavior that has to be implemented by both customer and logistic service provider. This section models the requirements for logistic service delivery by a BPMN choreography for information sharing between any two organizations in a so-called binary collaboration [15]. Whenever an organization has outsourced part of its logistic services to other organizations, they participate in a so-called multi-party collaboration. Each organization will have its particular orchestration in such a multi-party collaboration, whilst still supporting binary collaborations with others.

The objective of information sharing in a binary collaboration is logistic service delivery, e.g. a transport service is provided by a carrier to a forwarder. In this respect, the actual delivery of a logistic service is called a business transaction. As such, it consists of one or more interactions or business documents. The next figure shows the choreography of business documents, interactions, or events for delivery of a logistic service. We will call the set of related business documents or interactions a business transaction (see before). The logistic service delivered is atomic, meaning that it is either completely delivered or not at all. Atomicity implies that in case a composed service is required, either all components of that service are delivered or non at all, e.g. in case a transport service is required and documents have to be produced by a service provider in one business transaction, it is of no use to only produce the documents and not deliver the transport service.

A business transaction consists of a booking phase, execution planning, execution which is the reporting on the delivery of a service, and a cancellation phase. The booking and execution planning phase are initiated by a customer, the execution phase by a service provider, and the cancellation phase can be initiated by both a customer or service provider as formulated by the requirements. All phases of the choreography support certain requirements of multi-party collaboration, except the booking phase. This phase considers reaching agreement between a customer and service provider on the delivery of a service. Support of multi-party collaboration requirements in a binary collaboration are:

- Cancellation of a booking: a customer can request bookings for the same service from different providers and actually require one. The others need to be cancelled.

- Changes in places and time. For instance, if cargo is delivered later than expected on a certain location, a customer needs to be informed with an update of a plan and possibly that customer needs to inform the next link in the chain of late arrival with an updated instruction.

- Reports can be given for different physical events which can add detail to an already received plan that might be forwarded to a next link in the physical chain with an updated instruction or a customer with an updated plan. For instance, if actual loading information is known, the estimation of reception at a final destination may be improved.

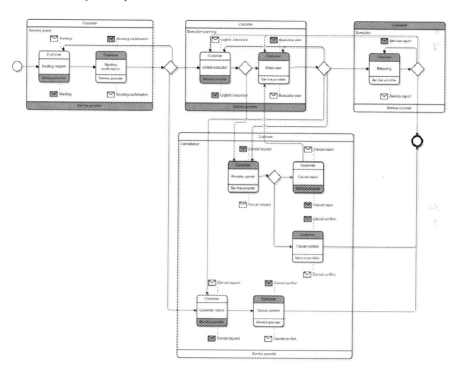

Figure 3. *Choreography for logistics transactions*

The choreography still needs to be refined on three aspects. In the execution planning phase, a first instruction will not lead to a cancel request by a service provider because nothing has been done yet, whereas an update of an instruction may lead to drastic differences in agreed conditions, causing a provider initiated cancellation if the execution did not yet start. In the execution phase, the choreography does not yet differ between one report for execution or reports of two or more events that can lead to an update of the planning, e.g. by giving an update on the estimated time of arrival. In the cancellation phase, customer initiated cancellation after the booking phase will not have financial consequences, whereas it may have after completion of the execution planning phase, since a customer and service provider have a contractual agreement after that phase. However, if an update of a planning submitted by a service provider gives deviations from this contract, a customer might be able to cancel the execution. In both cases, a customer is only allowed to initiate cancellation if execution has not yet been started. Additionally, a service provider can initiate a cancellation in case of for instance incidents or accidents or deviations from a contractual agreement caused by an update of the instruction, only if execution did not yet start.

3. Implementation of the Concepts from an Interoperability Perspective

The concepts can be applied in different ways from both a business – and technical perspective. One example is the application in framework contracts where one can distinguish between a contract concluded with the booking phase, periodic alignment of forecasts by the execution planning phase, and operational transactions representing for instance shipments with an execution planning and execution phase. Another example is a transactional approach [24] in which all phases are implemented for each individual business transaction. This section takes the technical perspective for applying the concepts to achieve interoperability. The concepts of logistic services with their underlying ontology and its choreography can be implemented by both customer and logistic service provider. This section discusses implementation options for both roles, first for a customer and secondly for a logistic service provider.

3.1. *Implementation by a Customer*

A customer will request logistic services supplied by one or more service providers. The common elements of these logistic services are specified as associations to concepts for business activities. Thus, whereas a service provider takes a service perspective, a customer takes the perspective of business activities and provides instances of relevant concepts associated to one or more required business activities. This perspective allows a customer to formulate its goals independent of service composition by service providers:

- To implement those business activities for which it potentially outsources logistic services. From a customer perspective, all associated concepts for required services and the choreography for information sharing need to be known and supported in their IT systems.

- By implementing these concepts and the choreography, a customer is not aware of the way service providers have organized their logistic services. The combination of associated concepts of relevant business activities and the choreography allows a customer to request composite logistic services, without actually being aware of this composition. It also allows a customer to request different services from different service providers.

- Based on values for these associated concepts, a customer is able to specify its goal and discover a service provider with one or more logistic services that meet particular requirements. A goal is formulated by instances of associated concepts that are either submitted to an (distributed) index or to potential service providers. A multi-modal booking site can serve as an index. Thus, potential service providers are discovered based on the formulated goal; to actually book for a customer requirement, a customer has to submit a booking to one or more of these service providers according the specified choreography. Such a booking is considered to be an event with reference to or actually containing relevant data.

This perspective also allows a customer to prepare its implementation at design time for business transactions with all service providers implementing business activities with their associated concepts. To be able to perform a (composite) service request, a customer furthermore needs to know the transport protocol and its address, and the semantic model with its physical representation, that are implemented by one or more service providers. In case the semantic model and its physical representation of a customer differs from the one implemented by one or more service providers, a customer could use a transformation function offered by a particular IT provider or download and implement these transformations in its own software (gateway, access point or ESB (Enterprise Service Bus)).

3.2. *Implementation by a Service Provider*

A Logistic Service Provider takes the perspective of logistic services. It allows him to make its services explicit, publish these services, and select the proper set of services to meet customer requirements:

- Service mediation. By specifying its logistic services internally according to the defined business activities, a service provider can automatically select one or more logistic services meeting customer requirements. Since these customer requirements are formulated in terms of instances of concepts of one or more business activities, service mediation is firstly by selecting the proper business activities and secondly by logistic services for those business activities meeting customer requirements.

- By publishing its logistic services, all potential customers are able to do business with a service provider; the services of a service provider can be found. Like in travel, there can also be an appreciation mechanism linked to these services like done with for instance Zoover.

- By publishing its logistic services, a service provider can potentially enlarge its market and thus increase its turnover and profit to customers that were not yet aware of its services. Logistic services can be published at a central index, e.g. a booking site, or on a web server of the service provider itself. In the latter case, these logistic services can be indexed by customers or external parties providing services. A similar approach is taken in the travel industry where booking sites index services of providers.

There is also an internal and more technical aspect that relates to business activities for which services are provided:

- A business activity is supported by or part of a semantic model and has a choreography. By implementing this semantic model(s) and their choreography for those business activities for which a service provider has specified its logistic services, a service provider can communicate with all its potential customers. By decoupling technology from business, it offers a service provider (and also a customer) more flexibility at business level.

- In case a customer has implemented another (version of a) semantic model and its physical representation, a service provider can either automatically download and implement required transformations at runtime or can assess external provided services that support the required transformation.

4. Conclusions and Further Work

We conclude that the introduction of the concept 'business activity' and its associations to other concepts in logistics provides an open infrastructure that allows business to construct relations for individual business transactions [24]. By implementing the (relevant parts) of the semantic model, the choreography, and the associated concepts for relevant business activities, customers and service providers can optimize their business, improve load factors and thus increase sustainability. In this respect, there is always a discussion on a business case for introducing these concepts. In fact, the business case should be on logistics level, i.e. under the assumption that everyone is interconnected in an open environment and able to share data electronically, the potential improvements at business level should be calculated, e.g. improvement of load factors and reduction of empty kilometers. Such a business case is not just on the concepts and the creation of an open environment, although also costs for interconnections can be reduced.

Another aspect for further study is in dynamic service composition by a service provider, in which that service provider also has outsourced part(s) of the requested service to other service providers. The confirmation of a booking of a customer will thus be based on the results of booking confirmations received from other service providers. Also, the orchestration of the requested and the outsourced services needs to be specified and executed, also including events received from sensors and integration of the business process orchestration with internal processes. Possibly, business process orchestration templates need to be constructed to support composite logistic services that include outsourced services.

A final aspect is the specification of the patterns used in the choreography. These patterns act on concepts specified in the semantic model, e.g. they specify how a booking is composed by a customer and what data is required by a customer in a booking confirmation. Identical patterns need to be implemented by a service provider. These patterns could be specified as a set of rules on an ontology.

5. References

[1] B. v. Lier, "Luhman meets "The Matrix' (in Dutch)," Erasmus University, Rotterdam, 2009.

[2] T. Erl, *Service Oriented Architecture - concepts, technology and design*, Prentice-Hall, 2005.

[3] World Customs Organization, "WCO Data model - cross border transactions on the fast track," World Customs Organization, 2010.

[4] World Wide Web Consortium, "Semantic Annotations for WSDL and XML Schema," W3C, 2008.

[5] E. Borger, "High level systems design and analysis using Abstract State Machines," in *The International Workshop on Current Trends in Applied Formal Method: Applied Formal Methods*, 1998.

[6] D. Fensel, M. Kerrigan and M. Zaremba, *Implementing Web Services - The SESA Framework*, Springer-Verlag, 2008.

[7] W. Hofman, M. Holtkamp and M. v. Bekkum, "Specification of SETU with WSMO," in *IESA2010*, 2010.

[8] E. Goncalves da Silva and e. al., "Supporting Dynamic Service Composition at Runtime based on End-user requirements," in *User generated services workshop, International Conference on Service Oriented Computing (ICSOC)*, Stockholm, Sweden, 2009.

[9] A. Kotok and D. Webber, ebXML - the new global standard for doing business over the Internet, New Riders, 2002.

[10] C. Huemer, P. Liegl, T. Motal, R. Schuster and M. Zapletal, "The development process of the UN/CEFACT modeling methodology," in *Proceedings of the 10th International Conference on Electronic Commerce*, 2008.

[11] Y.-H. Tan, N. Bjorn-Andersen, S. Klein and B. Rukanova, *Accelerating Global Supply Chains with IT-innovations*, Springer-Verlag, 2011.

[12] W.-J. v. d. Heuvel and M. P. Papazoglou, "Towards Business Transaction Management in Smart Networks," *IEEE Computing Society*, 2010.

[13] United Nations Economic Commission for Europe, "Description of the Buy-Ship-Pay model - version 2010A," 2010.

[14] J. Hintsa, J. Ahokas, K. Zaghbour, T. Mannisto, A. Hameri and H. J., "Conceptual model for assessign cost of security in global supply chains," in *17th International Annual EuroOMA Conference*, Porto, 2010.

[15] A. Schonberger, C. Wilms and G. Wirtz, "A requirements analysis of Business-to-Business integration," Fakultat Wirschaftsinformatik und angewandte Informatik Otto-Friedrich-Universitat, Bamberg, 2009.

[16] J. K. S. Spohrer, "Service Science, Management, Engineering, and Design (SSMED) - An emerging discipline - Outline and References," *International Journal on Information Systems in the Service Sector*, May 2009.

[17] J. T. Pedersen, P. Paganelli and H. Westerheim, "A Common Framework Freightwise, Euridice and Smartfreight," 2011. [Online]. Available: www.efreightproject.eu. [Accessed 12 November 2012].

[18] M. Bratman, *Faces of intention*, Cambridge University Press, 1999.

[19] J. Dietz, *Enterprise Ontology, Theory and methodology*, Springer-Verlag, 2006.

[20] W. Hofman and M. v. Staalduinen, "Dynamic Service Mediation," in *eGov2010*, Lausanne, 2010.

[21] "Business Process Modeling notation (BPMn), version 1.2," 2009.

[22] P. Hruby, *Model-Driven Design using Business Patterns*, Springer-Verlag, 2006.

[23] J. Gordijn and H. Akkermans, "Value based requirements engineering: exploring innovative e-commerce ideas," *Requirements Engineering Journal, 8(2)*, pp. 114-134, 2003.

[24] O. Williamson, *Markets and Hierarchies: analysis and antitrust implications*, New York: Free Press, 1975.

An Ontological Approach to Logistics

Laura Daniele* — Luís Ferreira Pires**

*TNO - Netherlands Organization for Applied Scientific Research
2600 GB Delft, The Netherlands
laura.daniele@tno.nl

**University of Twente
7500 AE Enschede, The Netherlands
l.ferreirapires@utwente.nl

ABSTRACT: In today's global market, the competitiveness of enterprises is strongly dictated by their ability to collaborate with other enterprises. Ontologies enable common understanding of concepts and have been acknowledged as a powerful means to foster collaboration, both within the boundaries of an individual enterprise (intra-enterprise) as outside these boundaries (inter-enterprise). This paper argues that the use of ontologies can be beneficial for enterprise interoperability in the logistics domain, to improve communication and foster knowledge reuse, to facilitate the integration of existing systems and to support the development process of software solutions. Our experience shows that the development of ontologies for logistics is not a trivial task, and guidelines and best practices are necessary in this domain, especially to bridge the gap between theory and practice. On the one hand, proper theoretical and methodological support for ontology engineering is necessary in order to deliver precise, consistent and well-founded solutions to the market. On the other hand, solutions to practical issues should be provided and not take too long to be produced in order not to be detached from the original real market needs. This paper proposes an ontological approach for logistics that balances the trade-off between precision and pragmatism, by combining top-down and bottom-up practices for ontology engineering. From a top-down perspective, we promote the reuse of existing general-purpose (upper) ontologies and specialize them for the purpose of logistics. From a bottom-up perspective, we reuse code lists and classifications that already exist in logistics to support the creation of instances of our upper level concepts. The paper also presents a representative fragment of our core ontology for logistics and identifies areas for further work in ontology engineering for logistics.

KEYWORDS: logistics, ontologies, semantic models, interoperability

1. Introduction

In today's global market, the competitiveness of enterprises is strongly dictated by their ability to collaborate with other enterprises. This collaboration allows enterprises to discover new opportunities or joint efforts with other enterprises in order to strengthen their competitive position (Doumeingts *et al.*, 2007, Li 2007). Ontologies enable common understanding of concepts, and have been acknowledged as a powerful means to foster collaboration, both within the boundaries of an individual enterprise (intra-enterprise) as outside these boundaries (inter-enterprise) (Fox 1998, Grubic *et al.*, 2007, Uschold *et al.*, 1996).

In relation to enterprise interoperability, ontologies are potentially beneficial for the following three main purposes: (i) *improve communication and re-use of knowledge*, by providing a shared understanding that reduces ambiguities and misunderstanding in the terminology adopted in a certain domain; (ii) *facilitate the integration of existing systems*, by providing a reference model that allows translation and matching, possibly automatically, among multiple heterogeneous systems that have been developed based on different semantic representations; and (iii) *support the engineering process of software solutions*, by providing a basis for automated specification, analysis and consistency checking of software under development.

In the past decades, logistics companies have grown individually with the goals of increasing efficiency, cutting costs and improving service offers for their customers. Currently, logistics companies still have the same goals, but with the additional aim of becoming more collaborative, especially at the inter-enterprise level. Logistics organizations should now be able to share and reuse data across other organizations (enterprises, authorities, etc.), instead of keeping proprietary data in several and, often, inconsistent versions. Therefore, not only a logistics organization may want to be able to expose its own data outside its boundaries, but also needs that the meaning of this data, or semantics, is correctly interpreted by others, otherwise the collaboration among organizations may lead to ambiguities and serious mistakes. In other words, there is a need for semantic interoperability among logistics organizations.

In this paper we argue that the use of ontologies can be beneficial for enterprise interoperability in the logistics domain. Although some efforts to apply ontologies to this domain have been reported before (Scheuermann *et al.*, 2012), the work on ontologies for logistics is still immature (Grubic *et al.*, 2007). This paper presents an ontological approach to logistics based on the methodology defined in (Uschold *et al.*, 1996). Our approach proposes a core ontology that specifies the main concepts commonly used in logistics operations. This core ontology can be further extended for the purpose of specific logistics applications. The ontology presented is being developed in the context of the iCargo (www.i-cargo.eu) and CASSANDRA (www.cassandra-project.eu) projects, which are both co-funded by the European Union under the Seventh Framework Programme for ICT.

The remainder of the paper is structured as follows: Section 2 presents some examples of semantic interoperability issues in logistics. Section 3 gives some background information on ontologies. Section 4 discusses possible applications of ontologies in the logistics domain. Section 5 presents our ontological approach for logistics. Section 6 presents a representative fragment of our core ontology for logistics. Section 7 discusses some related work in the area of ontologies. Finally, Section 8 presents our conclusions and future work.

2. Motivation

In order to motivate the need of an ontology for logistics, we have analysed some applications1 on the Internet that aim at integrating the offer and demand of logistics services and resources. The terminology used by these applications describes relevant objects for logistics such as, for example, the kind of goods that are transported, the possible mode of transport and the type of equipment used to facilitate the transport, among others. Table 1 shows how these concepts are represented across the different solutions we have analysed.

Table 1 shows that the terminology used is rather domain specific and, in order to be properly interpreted, it requires some expertise (domain knowledge) from the people processing the information. Moreover, this terminology differs across the different solutions, and it is sometimes ambiguous or inconsistent (or both). This may lead to a semantic interoperability issue due to misinterpretation, creating difficulties for a potential customer who wants to make use of the services offered by multiple systems. For example, if a customer wants to transport flammable liquids and compare different solutions, what cargo/load should be selected and what type of container/equipment serves this purpose?

In the current situation, the customer should use his domain knowledge in order to understand the options offered by the solutions, and should also get acquainted with the different terminology adopted in the different solutions.

---

1 Disclaimer: These applications were not originally devised to be interoperable, so in our comparison we do not judge them for that. This example only aims at stressing that disparity arises whenever common agreements are missing.

	Container/Equipment	Cargo/Load
FreightCity (www.freight city.com)	*Container type:* refrigerated container, hazardous cargo, special container, LCL (Less than Container Load), tank container, bulk cargo, breakbulk, roro container	*Cargo type:* mechanics, precision instrument, exhibitions, fresh & live, garment, primary materials, electronics, chemicals, ironware, minerals, junks, personal belongings, grain, steel, food
Transport Marketplace (www.transport marketplace.com)	*Type:* container (dry, flat, HC, open top, refeer), bulk liquid, bulk solid, less than truckload, FCL (Full Container Load), LCL (Less than Container Load)	*Load:* general cargo, controlled temperature, heavy lift, oversized, dangerous (flammable gases, toxic substances, flammable liquids, organic peroxides, radioactive material, etc.)
Shipping Containers24 (www.shipping containers24.com)	*Shipping container type:* dry cargo container (open top, platform or flat rack, closed ventilator), specific-purpose container (thermal shipping container or refeers, named cargo, dry bulk, tank container, etc.)	*Item:* heavy item, bulky item, fragile item, wood, heavy and difficult to manage object, food, frozen goods, perishable goods, cold goods, cars, other vehicles, livestock, poultry, grains, dry foodstuffs, chemicals, gases, hazardous liquids
JCtrans (www.jctrans.net)	*Equipment:* van, reefer, container, straight truck, step deck, flatbed, tanker, walking floor, cargo van, stretch trailer, etc.	*Load:* full truckload freight, less than truckload freight, shipping container, livestock/pets, vehicles, tanker/liquids

Table 1. *Terminology used by different applications on the Internet to denote container/equipment used to transport some cargo/load*

The semantic interoperability issue becomes even more relevant in case automated systems are expected to interpret the information without human intervention, in case different solutions, such as the ones shown in Table 1, have to be integrated in order to automatically interoperate. For example, consider the case of information exchange between two companies, each with its own IT system built based on a certain semantic model. The first company, which provides transportation services and operates trucks, regards a truck as the *transportation means used to move products from a place of origin to a final destination*. The second company, which is a factory that produces trucks, regards a truck as *the product that is moved from a place of origin to a final destination using a ship as transportation means*. Although the two companies seem to adopt the same terminology, they do not share the same meaning, and their information exchange may lead to serious mistakes when talking about products, transport means and their mutual relationships. In this case, the so-called *false agreement problem* (Guarino *et al.*, 2009, Guizzardi 2005) arises, in which the same terminology is adopted, but with different meaning.

3. Ontologies

The term *ontology* has been used in many different ways in the literature (Borst 1997, Gruber 1993, Guarino 1998, Guarino *et al.*, 2009, Guizzardi 2005, Studer *et al.*, 1998, Uschold *et al.*, 1996), so in this section we characterize ontologies for the purpose of this work.

According to its original meaning in Philosophy, an ontology concerns the study of being or existence (Gruber 1993, Guarino *et al.*, 2009), so it concerns things that exist in the real world. In our work, we use ontologies to capture mental images of the real world, the so-called *conceptualizations*. However, such a conceptualization has to be based on concepts, which can be instantiated for each real world situation that we may have to conceptualize. For example, a "container" can be a concept in logistics, which can be instantiated to represent specific containers used in certain logistics operations. Conceptualizations exist in principle in the mind of those whose produce them, but they have to be unambiguously communicated to others. Therefore, an ontology as an engineering artefact requires a language that allows the conceptualizations to be represented and communicated as concrete descriptions (specifications). This language should be suitable to represent instances of the ontology concepts and should have a formal semantics, which allows not only unambiguous interpretation but also rigorous analysis and reasoning.

Figure 1 shows that a conceptualization with respect to (a certain portion of) the real world exists a priori in one's mind and is based on a set of concepts (Guarino 1998, Guizzardi 2005). Since, we as humans need artefacts that allow us to represent things in the real world, we have to capture an abstract conceptualization that exists in the mind of users and practitioners in terms of a concrete specification that can be processed by machines. Figure 1 shows that an ontology should be explicitly represented as a specification of a conceptualization (Gruber 1993). The conceptualization underlining an ontology should be shared (Borst 1997, Studer *et al.*, 1998), otherwise we may run in the *false agreement problem* mentioned above.

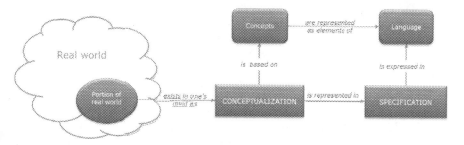

Figure 1. *Ontology as explicit specification of a conceptualization*

Figure 1 also shows that an ontology needs a language for its representation. More precisely, the concepts underlying a certain conceptualization need to be mapped onto elements of a suitable language. For example, the concept of a motor vehicle as a kind of object that moves on its own for the purpose of transporting goods, can be referred to by using the term *truck* (US English), *lorry* (UK English), *autocarro* (Italian), or *vrachtwagen* (Dutch). Depending on the language used to represent them, ontologies range from being *highly informal*, namely loosely expressed in natural language, to *rigorously formal*, namely strictly expressed using formal semantics, theorems and proofs (Uschold *et al.*, 1996).

Informal ontologies may lead to ambiguities, and systems that are based on such ontologies are more error-prone than systems based on formal ontologies, which, in contrast, allow automated reasoning and consistency checking. Several ontology forms are currently used in information systems and on the Internet, with varying expressiveness and complexity. These ontologies span from taxonomies of concepts related by subsumption relationships, to complete representations of concepts related by complex relationships, including axioms to constrain their intended interpretation. We regard a proper ontology as an engineering artefact that consists of a set of concepts and definitions used to describe a certain reality, relations among these concepts, plus a set of axioms to constrain the intended meaning of these concepts (Guarino 1998).

4. Applications in Logistics

We acknowledge that a single common ontology to improve communication and facilitate system integration for all possible applications in logistics is not feasible, since this ontology would get too complex and difficult to maintain. Therefore, we propose an approach of networked ontologies that is based on a *core ontology*, which explicitly specifies the main concepts adopted in the logistics domain. This core ontology can be further extended by creating new ontologies for the specific purpose of individual applications. The development of a core ontology (i.e. the identification of the main concepts) in logistics is not trivial task. Nevertheless, virtually all practitioners in the logistics domain informally say that "logistics is all about transporting something from a place of origin to a destination in a certain time and under certain conditions", so the key words "transport", "something", "place of origin", "destination", "time" and "conditions" are already hints to what type of concepts can be included in such a core ontology, regardless of its specific application in logistics.

4.1. Communication Purpose

A core ontology can be used as the basis to foster communication, by facilitating interoperability among people and organizations that use different standards. Examples of standards in logistics are the following: (i) the EDIFACT standard from the United Nations, which is predominant elsewhere than North America and is based on EDI messages; and (ii) the UBL standard from OASIS, which is mostly used in Scandinavian countries and is based on XML messages. Some relevant work is based on these standards, such as, for example, the World Customs Organization (WCO) data model (www.wcoomd.org), which is aligned with the EDIFACT standard, and the Common Framework (CF) reference model (www.its.sintef 9013.com/CF/v01), which is aligned with the UBL standard.

Our experience shows that each organization in logistics keeps its own standards, models and terminology. Moreover, this terminology often does not have a precise semantics, and its interpretation strongly relies on people's expertise and knowledge. Therefore, communication between people from these organizations would profit from a bottom-up process that raises the level of communication from models based on specific technical standards to an ontology that is neutral with respect to these standards.

This ontology should explicitly and unambiguously specify recurring core concepts in logistics, the relationships between these concepts, and, possibly, mappings of these concepts to synonyms used by different standards. These mappings could be further applied in the development of tools that allow automatic translation from the core ontology to specific standard-based models. This would be beneficial also to reduce the effort of translating from one standard to another, since the ontology could be used as reference model that requires one set of mappings to each standard, instead of a dedicated set of mappings for each pair of standards (Uschold et al., 1996).

4.2. Integration Purpose

A core ontology can be used as the basis for system integration, to facilitate the interoperability among different organizations that use various and heterogeneous IT systems with different representations of logistic concepts. Integration is especially relevant for small or medium-scale providers specialized in a specific segment of the logistic process that cannot provide door-to-door transportation services to their customer and, therefore, need to collaborate with other parties. Currently, the activity of coordinating transport providers that operate in different segments of the logistic process, such as, for example, truckers and barge operators, is supported by centralized planning systems. These systems often rely on humans that make phone calls, exchange e-mails and make use of the IT solutions offered by specific parties. However, this solution is highly dependent of the specific knowledge and expertise of people, and it is also costly and error-prone. Therefore, organizations would benefit from an integrated environment that facilitates the discovery, matching and composition of transport services, possibly by (partially) automating the error-prone activities that are currently carried out by humans.

In order to achieve this integration purpose, individual organizations could keep their own IT solutions that use different terminology for similar logistics concepts, but they should provide interfaces that specify the information necessary for interoperability. These interfaces may describe, for example, the goal and functionality of the service that they offer, the mode of transport, the area and time interval for operation, the type of resources available, i.e., the transport means and type of containers, and so forth. These interfaces should be built upon a common vocabulary, which should be derived from a common core ontology.

4.3. *Engineering Purpose*

A core ontology can be used as basis for engineering purposes, by providing support for the development of software solutions, such as the Transport Management Systems (TMSs) employed in logistics for managing the transportation operations that characterize supply chains. An ontology that specifies consistently and unambiguously the resources commonly used by transport services, their conditions of usage, and the events that can possibly have an impact on these resources, provides a basis to develop a variety of tools. For example, analysis and simulation tools can be developed to facilitate planning and booking of the transport services and resources represented in the ontology, as well as their real-time monitoring and possibly re-planning in case of unexpected events and situations.

Another application of the core ontology for engineering purposes consists of the development of a Domain Specific Language (DSL) for logistics. Once the specific logistic domain concepts are explicitly specified in an ontology using an existing (general purpose) language, such as, for example UML and OWL DL, the same concepts can be used as building blocks to define the syntax of a dedicated language for logistics. In other words, the ontology can be used to generate a metamodel for a DSL for logistics. This DSL would allow the development of textual and (possibly) visual editors, for example, to describe logistic processes and tools to validate their correctness, as a means to facilitate supply chain management, especially for transportation operations.

5. Approach

In order to build an ontology that fosters semantic interoperability among logistics organizations and people, we have followed an approach based on the methodology defined in (Uschold *et al.*, 1996) that combines top-down and bottom-up practices for ontology engineering. Our ontological approach for logistics promotes reuse, modularity, extensibility, maintainability and flexibility as follows:

– *Reuse* of foundational concepts that are defined in existing upper ontologies (Mascardi *et al.*, 2007) and are logistics independent, since they can be in principle used across domains. From a top-down perspective, we have specialized the upper level concepts defined in the *DOLCE+DnS Ultralite* ontology (www.ontologydesignpatterns.org/wiki/Ontology:DOLCE+DnS_Ultralite) for the purpose of logistics. In this way, we could provide a classification of the most relevant objects that are involved in logistics operations, such as, for example, actors, facilities, product classes, packages, pieces of equipment and transport means, and the relationships among these objects. From a bottom-up perspective, since a large amount of work has being done in logistics concerning code lists and classifications that characterize specific logistics objects, we have reused existing work so that we did not need to define from scratch classifications of transport means, packages and dangerous goods, among others.

– *Modularity* to allow separation and recombination of different parts of the ontology depending on specific needs, instead of creating a single common ontology for all applications in logistics, which may not be feasible, since this ontology may get too complex, and may not even be necessary. Towards this aim, we promote a *network ontology* approach, which is based on a *logistics core ontology* that specifies the main concepts commonly used in logistics operations.

– *Extensibility* to allow further growth of the ontology for the purpose of specific logistics applications. For example, we have extended our core ontology with a *logistics services ontology* that describes the main activities and events related to logistics operations. This extension is the basis for building an environment for service discovery and composition, in which logistics providers can publish their services, and consumers can discover services that fulfil their needs. Analogously, we could extend our core ontology with a *logistics documents ontology* that represents all the documents exchanged in the logistics operations, a *port ontology* that extends the concept of port defined as a facility area in our core ontology, and so forth.

– *Maintainability* to facilitate the process of identifying and correcting defects, accommodate new requirements, and cope with changes in (parts of) our logistics ontology. The minimum requirement is that a new module in the network of ontologies must comply with our core ontology. This new module can further extend concepts of the core ontology and the creator of the module is responsible for its maintenance and versioning, independently from the core ontology.

– *Flexibility* to changes in the specific technology for ontology development, enabled by the separation of design and implementation concerns. In our approach, we separated the design of the ontology from its implementation. In the design phase, we defined the concepts of the ontology using natural language, we specified these concepts and their relations using UML class diagrams, and we defined formal axioms that capture the intended meaning of these concepts. We applied UML to represent our ontology in the design phase, since UML is a popular general-purpose language that allowed us to represent our ontology at a high abstraction level, i.e., abstracting from the ways the ontology might be implemented in actual applications. In this way we could focus on the concepts, relations and axioms that we wanted to specify, ignoring the issue of selecting the most suitable language to express them. In the implementation phase, we have specified our ontology using OWL DL, which allows automated reasoning to validate the correct use of axioms and relations, and make queries against our ontology. Due to space limitations we do not present in this paper the OWL DL version of the ontology.

6. An Ontology for Logistics

We consider logistics as the set of activities that take place among several actors in order to deliver certain products at the right time, right place and under the right conditions, by using suitable resources. Therefore, our logistics ontology has been built on top of some foundational (upper level) concepts, such as the following:

– *Activity*, which denotes some action that is relevant for the purpose of logistics and provides value for a potential customer. Activities are, for example, transport, transshipment, load, discharge, storage, consolidation and deconsolidation. These activities are atomic and can be used to compose more complex activities.

– *Actor*, which represents companies, authorities or individuals that provide or request activities and operate on resources related to these activities.

– *Physical Resource*, which represents physical objects that are used in the logistics activities, such as, for example, the moveable resources used during the activity of transport, i.e., the transport means and equipment used to move items to their destination.

– *Location*, which represents the geographical area or geographical point used to define the place(s) relevant for logistics activities. Location can be coarse-grained for scheduling, since in long term planning it is sufficient to specify approximately the place of origin and destination, such as, for example, the Netherlands or the port of Rotterdam. However, location needs to be fine-grained for delivery, since one has to specify the precise address to which a certain item must be delivered.

– *Time*, which represents the start time, end time or time interval associated to activities. Since time is a basic (foundational) concept relevant for logistics, but common to other domains, we have re-used the representation of time proposed in the Time Ontology (http://www.w3.org/TR/owl-time), instead of specifying it from scratch.

In this paper, we cannot elaborate on all the concepts of the ontology due to space restrictions. Therefore, Figure 3 shows only an excerpt of our ontology, which focuses on the specialization of the concept of *Physical Resource*.

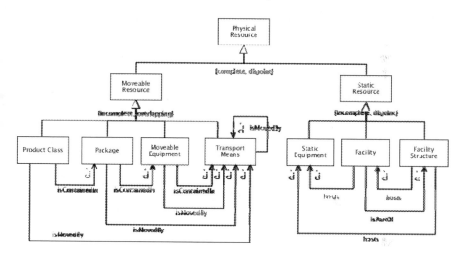

Figure 3. *Core ontology for logistics focusing on the concept of Physical Resource*

In Figure 3, we focus on the concept of Physical Resource, which represents tangible objects used in logistics operations, such as a piece of equipment or a facility. A Physical Resource is further specialized in a Moveable Resource, which is characterized by the capability of moving on its own or being contained for the purpose of transportation, and a Static Resource, which is used to handle moveable objects in a facility prior to their transportation.

Table 2 clarifies and complements Figure 3.

	Definition	Properties
Product class	Object used to select proper package, moveable equipment and transport means for several logistics activities, especially for transport. The selection is based on relevant properties of the product class, such as its physical state (solid, liquid, gas), required temperature, dangerousness, etc.	- Type (regular, perishable, flammable, organic, toxic, heavy machinery, bulk, etc.) - State (solid, liquid, gas) - isRefeer (Boolean value) - isDangerous (Boolean value) - isOversized (Boolean value)
Package	Material used for containment, protection and movement of product classes	- Type (carton, box, crate, barrel, pallet, container, etc.) - Quantity - Volume
Moveable equipment	Reusable resource used for containment, protection and movement of product classes with or without package. A moveable equipment cannot move on its own (unpowered vehicle), but can be pulled or contained in a transport means	- Type (container, pallet, railway wagon, trailer, etc.) - ID - Volume - Quantity
Transport means	Reusable resource that facilitates the activity of transport and moves on its own (powered vehicle)	- Type (aircraft, vessel, truck, train) - Capacity
Static equipment	Reusable resource that is used in a facility to handle moveable resources	- Type (crane, etc.) - Facility
Facility	Static resource (usually a building) built, installed or established to facilitate related activities in a point location. A facility can be part of a facility structure (for example, a terminal is part of a port)	- Type (terminal, warehouse, etc.) - Location - FacilityStructure
Facility structure	Static resource built, installed or established to facilitate related activities in a geographical area. A facility structure may host several facilities	- Type (port, airport, etc.) - Location (GeoArea) - Facility

Table 2. *Definitions and properties*

Some axioms that apply to the ontology fragment in Figure 3 are the following:

– If a moveable equipment *e isMoved* by a transport means *tm*, then *tm moves e* (i.e., the relation *moves* is the inverse of *isMoved*);

– If a product class *pc isContained* in a package *p*, and *p isContained* in a moveable equipment *e*, then *pc isContained* in *e* (i.e., the relation *isContained* is transitive);

– If a product class pc is dangerous (property *isDangerous* is *true*), and *pc isContained* in a moveable equipment *e*, then *e* is dangerous (property *isDangerous* is *true)*. This means that property *isDangerous* is transitive;

– If a product class *pc isContained* in a package *p*, then *p isContained* in *pc* does not hold (i.e., the relation *isContained* is asymmetric);

– If a product class *pc* is of type *perishable*, and its physical state is *solid*, then its property *isRefeer* is *true* and *pc isContained* in a moveable equipment *e*, such that *e* is a refeer container.

7. Related Work

The application of ontologies in logistics is still limited, however, the awareness that ontologies provide a means to foster information sharing and system interoperability and, consequently, strengthen the competitive position of enterprises, is gradually increasing. Although the work reported in (Grubic *et al.*, 2010) targets supply chain ontologies, namely a broader domain than the logistics domain addressed in this paper, we have used some of the conclusions of (Grubic *et al.*, 2010) as input for our work, especially concerning the following needs: (i) combining theoretical support with empirical and field based research when creating supply chains ontologies, addressing the importance of the concept of time that is often neglected, and creating a proper ontology that is more expressive than a simple taxonomy. The ontology presented in this paper addresses the mentioned issues since it combines a top-down approach, which gives theoretical support for ontology engineering, with a bottom-up approach that considers the needs of the market and the expertise of the practitioners in the field, and explicitly addresses the concepts of time. Moreover, our ontology is not a simple taxonomy, but specifies concepts, definitions of these concepts, relations and axioms.

Although some relevant work has dealt with general-purpose ontologies that can be used across different domains (Fox *et al.*, 1998, Madni *et al.*, 2001, Uschold *et al.*, 1998), we observed that these ontologies have limited applicability in logistics since they do not capture the specific issues of this domain. For example, the Enterprise Ontology of (Uschold *et al.*, 1998) specifies concepts and relations that are relevant to business enterprises, but are too abstract to represent specific needs of the logistic domain. Furthermore, the work reported in (Fox *et al.*, 1998) proposes a set of generic and reusable ontologies for enterprises, the so-called TOVE ontologies. Although the TOVE ontology for resources (Fadel *et al.*, 1996) includes some concepts that can be aligned with the *Moveable Resource* and *Static Resource* concepts presented in this paper, the TOVE ontology targets a manufacturing enterprise environment that is quite different from the logistics represented in our core ontology.

8. Conclusions

Our experience shows that the development of ontologies for logistics is not a trivial task, and guidelines and best practices are necessary in this domain, especially to bridge the gap between theory and practice. On the one hand, proper theoretical and methodological support for ontology engineering is necessary in order to deliver precise, consistent and well-founded solutions to the market. On the other hand, solutions to practical issues should be provided and not take too long to be produced in order not to be detached from the original real market needs. This paper proposed an ontological approach for logistics that balances the trade-off between precision and pragmatism, offering the best of both worlds to logistics professionals and organizations. This approach prescribes the development of a network of ontologies that is based on a core ontology, which explicitly specifies the main concepts adopted in the logistics domain. This core ontology can be further extended by creating new ontologies for the specific purpose of individual applications.

Current work in the iCargo and CASSANDRA projects focuses on the realization of prototypes for specific applications that facilitate interoperability among logistics organizations. These applications are based on the ontology proposed in this paper and their realization is used to validate the concepts described in this work and to extend our logistics core ontology with new modules that become relevant during the implementation process. One of the applications consists of an environment for service discovery and composition, in which logistics service providers that use different terminology and standards can specify their services, while potential customers can discover the (composition of) services that better suit to their needs. Further work needs to be done to define mappings of our ontology to specific standards in order to: (i) validate the logistics concepts and relations that we have identified in this work, and (ii) demonstrate that our ontology can be actually used as a shared model of consensus independently of specific standards.

9. Acknowledgements

The authors would like to thank Wout Hofman (TNO) and Ad Schrier (TNO) for their contribution in the development of the ontology presented in this paper.

10. References

Borst, W., "Construction of Engineering Ontologies". PhD Thesis, University of Twente, Enschede, The Netherlands (1997)

Doumeingts, G., Muller, J.P., Morel, G., Vallespir, B., Fox, M.S., Gruninger M., *Enterprise Interoperability-New Challenges and Approaches*. Springer Verlag (2007)

Fadel,F.G., Fox, M.S., Gruninger, M., "A Generic Enterprise Resource Ontology". In: Proceedings of the 3rd IEEE Workshop on Enabling Technologies: Infrastructure for Collaborative Enterprise, pp. 117-128 (1996)

Fox, M.S., Gruninger M., "Enterprise Modeling". In: *AI Magazine*, vol. 19 (3), pp. 109-121. American Association for Artificial Intelligence (AAAI) Press (1998)

Gruber, T. R., "A Translation Approach to Portable Ontology Specifications". In: *Knowledge Acquisition*, vol. 5(2), pp.199-220 (1993)

Gruber, T. R., "Ontology". In: *Encyclopedia of Database Systems*. Springer Verlag (2009)

Grubic, T., Fan, I.S.: "Supply chain ontology: Review, analysis and synthesis". In: *Computers in Industry*, vol. 61(8), pp. 776-786. Elsevier Science Press (2010)

Guarino, N., "Formal Ontology and Information Systems". In: Proceedings of the 1st International Conference on Formal Ontology in Information Systems (FOIS), pp. 3-15. IOS Press, Amsterdam (1998)

Guarino, N., Munsen, M.A., "Applied Ontology: Focusing on Content". In: *Applied Ontology*, vol.1, pp. 1-5. IOS Press (2005)

Guarino, N., Oberle, D., Staan, S., "What is an Ontology". In: *Handbook on Ontologies*, pp. 1-17. Springer Verlag (2009)

Guizzardi, G., "Ontological Foundations for Structural Conceptual Models". PhD Thesis, University of Twente, The Netherlands (2005)

Li, M.S., "Meeting the Grand Challenges of the Enterprise Interoperability Research Roadmap - A Business Perspective". In: *Expanding the Knowledge of Economy: Issues, Applications, Case studies*, pp. 5-13. IOS Press (2007)

Lin, H.K., Hardig, J.A., "A Manufacturing System Engineering Ontology Model on the Semantic Web for Inter-Enterprise Collaboration". In: *Computers in Industry*, vol. 58 (5), pp. 428-437. Elsevier Science Press (2007)

Madni, A.M., Lin, W., Madni, C.C., "IDEON™: an Extensible Ontology for Designing, Integrating and Managing Collaborative Distributed Enterprises". In: *System Engineering*, vol. 4 (1), pp. 35-48 (2001)

Mascardi, V., Cordi, V., Rosso, P., "A Comparison of Upper Ontologies". Technical Report DISI-TR-06-2, Genova, Italy (2007)

Scheuermann, A., Hoxha, J., "Ontologies for Intelligent Provision of Logistics Services". In: Proceedings of the 7th International Conference on Internet and Web Applications and Services (ICIW), pp. 106-111. IARIA (2012)

Studer, R. Benjamins, R., Fensel, D., "Knowledge engineering: Principles and methods". In: *Data & Knowledge Engineering*, vol. 25(1-2), pp.161-198 (1998)

Uschold, M., Gruninger, M., "Ontologies: Principles, Methods and Applications". In: *the Knowledge Engineering Review*, vol. 11(2), pp. 93-136. Cambridge University Press (1996)

Uschold, M., King, M., Moralee, S., Zorgios, Y., "The Enterprise Ontology". In: *the Knowledge Engineering Review*, vol. 13 (1), pp. 31-89. Cambridge University Press (1998)

Social Vision of Collaboration of Organizations on a Cloud Platform

Aurélie Montarnal — Wenxin Mu — Frédérick Bénaben — Anne-Marie Barthe-Delanoë — Jacques Lamothe

Université de Toulouse, Mines ALBI
Campus Jarlard
81000 Albi, France
Aurelie.montarnal@mines-albi.fr
Wenxin.mu@mines-albi.fr
Frederick.benaben@mines-albi.fr
Anne-marie.barthe@mines-albi.fr
Jacques.lamothe@mines-albi.fr

ABSTRACT: This article presents the French project OpenPaaS, a 'social' platform, which offers subscribing organizations a way to facilitate their collaboration. It exposes which kind of architecture has to be set up to support collaborative situations. On the one hand, a service is dedicated to the processes cartography deduction from collaborative objectives and from partners' functions. On the other hand, a Complex Event Processing allows finding new collaboration opportunities that are proposed to potential partners.

KEYWORDS: collaborative process deduction, complex event processing, platform as a service, information systems, service oriented architecture

1. Introduction

These last years, collaborative situations have been held between partners increasingly distant. Enterprises and more generally organizations need efficient and fast interactions. The French project OpenPaaS[1] (Open Platform As A Service) aims at implementing a way to facilitate these collaborations. The final aim of the platform is to enhance the coordination between several organizations during a collaborative situation in offering a way to orchestrate the process.

This is a 'social' platform, where each subscribing organization creates its own profile. This profile is a description of the organization: it must show its activities and informs of the organization business. In others words the aim of the profile is to have an exhaustive vision of the business services the organization can provide.

As a first tool, the OpenPaaS platform embeds a way for an organization to declare a collaboration opportunity. Opportunity could be defined as the proposal of a new collaborative situation that is set up to reach a specific goal, and that includes several organizations. As a consequence the proposal must explain the objectives to reach and also the context in which the collaboration will be led.

A Mediation Information System (MIS) is in charge of supporting the interoperability between the organizations. Interoperability has been defined as "the ability of two or more systems or components to exchange and use information" (IEEE Computer Society, 1998). Therefore the MIS receives the information (profiles, opportunities) and exploits it to obtain process cartography. After a transformation, the matching workflow is obtained and it is finally orchestrated by the MIS.

Furthermore the platform can receive events from organizations that have subscribed. It uses these events to deduce new potential collaboration opportunities.

The platform can be divided into two parts: the design time where the process cartography and the workflow are deduced and the run time, where the MIS supports partners' coordination.

This article will focus on the design time and more precisely on the process cartography deduction. Section 2 deals with an analysis of requirements to show research points on which to focus. Section 3 is a literature review that concerns the tools that have been implemented not only for collaborative processes deduction but also for events processing. Finally the adopted research approaches to answer the problematics are explained.

---

1. http://research.petalslink.org/display/openpaas/Open+PAAS+Overview

2. Requirements

The platform is designed to help organizations to create the collaboration opportunities, and to manage the collaborative situations. The

Figure 1 shows an overview of the information flow in the platform. To the left, an organization has three kinds of interactions with the platform. It can (i) suggest a collaborative opportunity, defining its context, objectives and if possible specific partners, (ii) complete a profile which characterizes its activities, and (iii) share events in an Events Market.

Consequently, there are two kinds of behavior:

– If an opportunity is suggested: Transformation 1 allows obtaining processes (e) from situation description (a) and partner descriptions (b).

– If an opportunity is deduced from events streams: Transformation 2 allows obtaining a collaborative opportunity (d) from a flow of events (c). Then Transformation 1 transforms this collaborative opportunity (d) and partner descriptions (b) into processes (e).

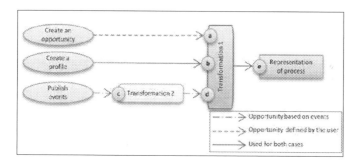

Figure 1. *Overview of the information flow*

The first consequence of these considerations is that (a) and (d) must have the same structure: the one that is accepted by Transformation 1.

Finally some questions emerge from this overview:

– Which structure is expected for an opportunity definition ((a) and (d))?

– How to obtain a process representation from an opportunity definition and profile business services (Transformation 1)?

– How to deduce an opportunity definition from events (Transformation 2)?

3. Foundations

In Section 2 three issues have been highlighted. The first part of the literature review that follows describes different types of organizations networks already existing and gives a global vision of the collaboration problematic. The second part deals with the two questions about the deduction of process cartography that are raised in the first Section. The last part brings information about events processing, for the third question.

3.1. *Organizations Networks*

Collaboration between several organizations is not a new research topic and many studies have already dealt with it. (Camarinha-Matos et al., 2005) depicts a historic of networks of organizations since 1970. Starting with collaborative situation in a Cell, networks have evolved into inter-enterprise networks in the 90'. First, Extended Enterprises (EE) is described as an organization surrounded by its suppliers. (Dyer, 2000) complements the definition of EE and adds set of collaboration processes that can be provided by each actor.

The Virtual Enterprise (VE) is another kind of collaborative coordination supported by computer networks and rather linked to supply chain (Wu et al., 2005). Based on a bidding approach which is near from the OpenPaaS' opportunity concept, "Virtual Enterprise is based on the ability to create temporary co-operations and to realize the value of a short business opportunity that the partners cannot [...] capture on their own" (Camarinha-Matos et al., 1999). Therefore the VE is a way for several organizations to temporary capitalizes every available business activity to reach a goal, in a more "democratic" coordination (Camarinha-Matos et al., 2006). Virtual Organizations are close from VE but also requires sharing of resources and expertise.

The last term: Collaborative Network defines a set of organizations working together and using a common information system as a support for their collaboration.

Henceforth the term collaboration is used as a generic term as commonly seen in the literature.

3.2. *Deduction of Process Cartography*

The Mediation Information System Engineering (MISE) project described in (Benaben et al., 2012) aims at providing an agile collaborative support. This system went through three iterations until the current MISE 3.0, which is structured according to three parts. The first step consists of gathering knowledge. As a second step the system deduces a process cartography, which is a BPMN-based modeling of the collaborative situation. Finally it is transformed into executable workflow that will allow orchestrating the collaboration.

MISE is based on the Service Oriented Architecture (SOA) whose goal is to help designing an interoperable platform. An Enterprise Service Bus (ESB) is used to implement the communication between the various web services that are deployed on it.

The point of this article is correlated with the first step of MISE (from the knowledge gathering to the processes cartography).

(Rajsiri et al., 2009) explains how to collect the knowledge to obtain a single collaborative process, which covers strategy, operation and support levels. (Mu et al., 2011) aims at providing a process cartography that divides the collaborative process into three types described in (AFNOR, 2000): strategy, operation and support processes levels. Each level concerns specific types of activity, and depends of the others in such a way that the three levels are nested together to form the whole process cartography. (Mu et al., 2011) explains how to deduce the BPMN-based collaborative process cartography by gathering collaboration objectives of partners and business activities. The modeling tool that has been implemented for the MISE 2.0 aims at helping the partners to create their collaborative process cartography by collecting basic knowledge.

First, the user provides two models. The first one is an objective model that defines the context by explaining the different goals (individual and common) and by showing partners' relationships. In parallel, each partner should give a function model that establishes his own functions, and for each one the partner must indicate its input/output messages.

Then a method allows obtaining three levels cartography to achieve the collaborative goals of the partners. This method is based on ontology, process of the MIT Process Handbook repository (Malone et al., 2003), and transformation rules.

(Wu et al., 2005) aims at finding a relevant way to select partners in the VE case. The assessment is based on two important criteria in the field of the supply chain: production costs and response time. The data about these two criteria come from the bidding responses. The selection process is divided into two parts. The first step is based on an algorithm that aims at finding the optimal partners selection considering manufacturing and transportation costs (Wu et al., 1999). The second step adds the time constraint and deals with an algorithm that calculates the earliest completion time. Therefore the two algorithms allow obtaining an optimal solution for the two selected criteria.

Finally the choice of both SOA and ESB provides loose coupling to the system, which is also more flexible. MISE 2.0 introduces a way to deduce three levels process cartography in an industrial context. Ontologies and transformation rules can be adapted to the main problematic about process cartography deduction. The partners' selection in the process cartography deduction is an important issue considering that the subscribing organizations can be competitors.

3.3. *Events Processing*

With the development of Internet 2.0 technologies, more and more events are published and accessible on the web. Therefore, the idea of Event-Driven Architecture (EDA) is to take advantage of this technology. In an EDA (Maréchaux, 2006) explains that there is a publish/subscribe mechanism which means that when a service publishes an event, only the services subscribing to this type of event receive it. (Maréchaux, 2006) also considers that this kind of architecture and SOA complement each other.

The French project SocEDA[2] aims at designing a new architecture based on an event management platform (Lauras et al., 2012). As it is an EDA based system, web services subscribe to certain event types. It allows them to sort the incoming events and to keep only those that are useful. A specific web service is dedicated to receive all events, to gather and to translate them. Then all translated events are stored on en event market place whose role is to distribute them to the web services that have subscribed to the event's type. Furthermore, the platform can use events to generate another events; therefore the system is constantly enriched. This enrichment allows the system to increase efficiency and reliability.

(Luckham et al., 2011) brings two different types of event processing agent: the Event Producer (sends the events) and the Event Consumer (receives the events). The Complex Event Processing (CEP) allows executing operations on events. For instance the CEP can read or transform events but also aggregate them together. Consequently, CEP is the device, through which the events are exploited.

The European PLAY[3] project deals with implementing a platform for event management (Barthe-Delanoë et al., 2012). As the SocEDA project, an event market place contains received events and CEP generated events. The defined queries are

---

2. http://research.petalslink.org/display/soceda/SocEDA+Overview
3. http://www.play-project.eu/

executed on the event market place and allow the correlation of events. (Rozsnyai et al., 2007) explains a way to correlate events through correlation sets. The events relationships are established according to their types, their attributes and finally their data. Therefore there are two models of events relationships: the first one is based on patterns comparison to deduce a situation and the second one aims at finding similarities.

The events market place allows storing events in a relevant manner and the previous service dedicated to receive, gather and translate events also allows having homogeneous information. When combined to a CEP, it enhances the system's reactivity during events correlation.

(Zhou et al., 2011) presents an inexact semantic complex event processing framework. Its aim is to enhance the flexibility of the complex event processing by detecting relevant inexact patterns. In a common CEP, the patterns comparison is based on identical attributes values. On the contrary, this framework is based on semantic comparisons between attributes. A specific number of mismatches given to the system allows detecting relevant inexact patterns. As a last point, the framework embeds a similarity function which evaluates the difference between the inexact matching patterns and the target.

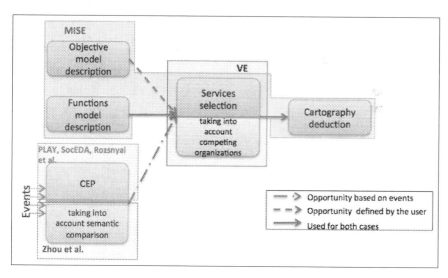

Figure 2. *Overview of information in the literature review*

Figure 2 gives an overview of the contributions of the literature review and how each piece of information takes place into the research.

4. Research Approach

Figure 3 below shows the global design of the OpenPaaS platform. It recalls the two ways to define the objectives and in parallel the business services given by organizations and brings a logical view.

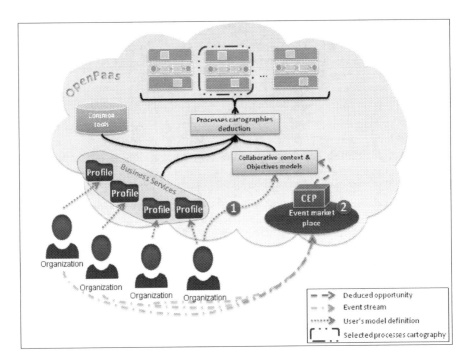

Figure 3. *Logic overview of the paas*

In parallel, Figure 4 conveys a technical vision of the paas and aims at providing an outline of the technical solution adopted to meet our issues. Firstly, organizations create their profiles on the platform using an editor like the function model described in (Mu et al., 2011).

A function model must be understandable by the MIS for the further deduction (cf. third indent). That is why the modeler should be based on a collaborative ontology based on a meta-model (MM) (functions modeler in Figure 4). In such a way the platform disposes of a set of understandable business services.

Concerning the opportunity creation, there are two cases:

– In case 1 (Figure 3), an organization proposes an opportunity. In this particular case a second editor helps the organization to create an objective model (e.g. by adapting the modeling tool presented in (Mu et al., 2011)). The conclusion for this case 1 is that the system disposes of the function model from the profiles, and the objective model from the proposed opportunity. This is why the work about processes cartography deduction that is cited in the literature review section can be adapted and reused. The opportunity structure is directly resulting since the already implemented deduction tool is adapted to further workflow transformation and orchestration. The context part of the MIS on Figure 4 is indeed composed of an objective modeler. To resolve the same issue as the functions modeler (understandable objective), the objective modeler has to be based on the collaborative ontology too. Moreover, the functions are stored as organizations capabilities, in a repository, in order to know each available capability when deducing the cartography.

– In case 2 (Figure 3), the platform disposes of events stored in an event market place. As said in the context section, case 1 and case 2 must have the same output structure since they undergo the same further transformation. Therefore a complex event processing (CEP) transforms stored events into objective model. Indeed this CEP allows comparing collaborative objectives patterns known by the system with the incoming events. When a set of organization's events fulfills the patterns the opportunity can be proposed to these organizations, and the objective model matches with this pattern.

Consequently, the CEP interacts with the event market place that stores the events but also with the objective modeler. Users interact only with the event market place, which they send events (Figure 4).

As a second point, it is interesting to focus on the CEP flexibility. There are two reasons: first, the system cannot judge if the organizations profiles are complete and exhaustive regarding to the activities of the organization. Secondly, the OpenPaaS platform aims to provide users business opportunities. It is possible that none of the subscribing organizations provides a service that is needed to complete a specific collaborative process. In such a situation it is interesting to detect if an organization has a relevant activity and is able to provide the missing service. The framework evoked in (Zhou et al., 2011) allows a semantic comparison between the incoming events attributes and the target. Once the adapted ontology has been set up this framework allows (i) selecting a service provided by an organization even if this service didn't appear in the profile of the organization and (ii) proposing a new activity easily feasible to an organization.

Finally the processes cartography is deduced from the objective and the function models. First, common tools are available on the OpenPaaS platform and can eventually be used as services in the deduced cartography. Then, Section 3 reports an already implemented service whose goal is to deduce processes cartography from collaborative objectives and from partners' functions (Mu et al., 2011). It can be reused and the ontology can eventually be adapted.

The main issue deals with the competitive partners' selection. On the one hand, Section 3 reported algorithms that allow assessing partners' response time and manufacturing and transportation costs. The two selected criteria are relevant and it is interesting to obtain an optimal answer. However this technique is applied to biddings that are often short time collaborations and consequently less complex collaborations than those coordinated by the OpenPaaS.

On the other hand, Key Performance Indicators (KPI) generally allow assessing a business activity for an enterprise. They are commonly periodically assessed measurable indicators and allow knowing the performance of a system. Influenced by the KPI, another system is proposed. The aim is to provide the user a selected number of different evaluated cartographies. For example the user could focus on specific indicators: costs and response time of the services. The system assesses each service's capacity in terms of cost and response times, and the two corresponding scores, for each indicator, are deduced. After having deduced several scenarios and having added each service's scores, the system proposes the selected number of the best scored processes cartographies. Then the user can choose the final processes cartography regarding the different scores. As the KPI concept, this assessment is executed to assess each service of the cartography and finally allows having a global vision of the proposed process performances. Moreover, this is adapted to a complex cartography and allows the user to adapt the final cartography to his needs.

The two methods have advantages and must be adapted: the first one is deeply efficient but must be adapted to other eventual criteria and to more complex process cartographies; the second one offers the user a good global vision of the process cartography's performances but the calculation does not provide an optimal final solution.

However both partners' selection systems impose two things. First, a relevant set of criteria has to be selected before implementing the system. Secondly, each subscribing organization must inform of its performance regarding each criterion. This last point refers to a new issue that is resource management and the way to know in near real time an organization's capabilities.

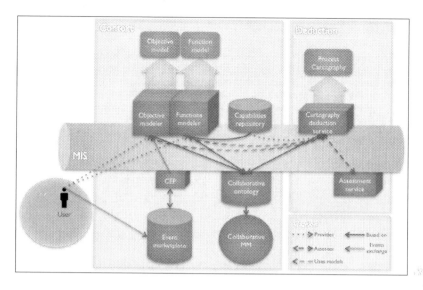

Figure 4. *Technical overview of the paas*

5. Conclusion

This paper presented a part of the French project OpenPaaS and its design time's specifications. The proposed platform follows up an Event Driven Architecture and is mainly the object of an improvement of the MISE 2.0 project. On the one hand, it deals with moving the current system on a platform. On the other hand the current deduction service must be adapted: ontologies and transformation rules have to be extended to fit many kinds of organizations wishes. A particular importance should be given to the partners' selection system. The CEP must be implemented to obtain most relevant and feasible opportunities. Thus further researches will deal with partners' selection systems and real time organizations' capabilities monitoring, events correlation and ontologies to use.

6. References

AFNOR. ISO : ISO 9001 Version 2000, Système De Management De La Qualité - Exigences, 2000.

Barthe-Delanoë A.-M., Truptil S., Stühmer R., Benaben F., "Definition of a Nuclear Crisis Use-case Management to s (t) Imulate an Event Management Platform.", 7th International Workshop on Semantic Business Process Management (sBPM), 2012.

Benaben F., Lauras M., Truptil S., Lamothe J., "MISE 3.0: An Agile Support for Collaborative Situation.", 13th IFIP WG 5.5 Working Conference on Virtual Enterprises, PRO-VE, Bournemouth, UK, October 1-3 2012, Springer Berlin Heidelberg, p. 645-654.

Camarinha-Matos L., Afsarmanesh H., "The Virtual Enterprise Concept.", Proceedings of the IFIP TC5 WG5.3 / PRODNET Working Conference on Infrastructures for Virtual Enterprises: Networking Industrial Enterprises, Deventer, The Netherlands , 1999, Kluwer, B.V., p. 3–14.

Camarinha-Matos L., Afsarmanesh H., "Virtual Enterprise Modeling and Support Infrastructures: Applying Multi-agent System Approaches." Multi-agent Systems and Applications, 2006, p. 335–364.

Dyer J. H., *Collaborative Advantage : Winning Through Extended Enterprise Supplier Networks*, Oxford University Press, 2000.

Event Processing Technical Society, Event Processing Glossary – Version 2.0, Event Processing Technical Society (EPTS), 2011.

IEEE Computer Society, IEEE Standard Glossary of Software Engineering Terminology, IEEE Computer Society, 1990.

Lauras M., Charles A., Truptil S., Bénaben F., "Towards an Interoperable IT Platform for Better Coordination of Crisis Response.", Enterprise Interoperability I-ESA'12 Proceedings, 2012, ISTE London, John Wiley & Sons, p. 75–81.

Malone T. W., Crowston K., Herman G. A., *Organizing Business Knowledge: The MIT Process Handbook*, MIT press, 2003.

Maréchaux J.-L., "Combining Service-oriented Architecture and Event-driven Architecture Using an Enterprise Service Bus.", IBM Developer Works, 2006, p. 1269–1275.

Mu W., Bénaben F., Pingaud H., Boissel-Dallier N., Lorré J.-P., "A Model-Driven BPM Approach for SOA Mediation Information System Design in a Collaborative Context.", IEEE International Conference on Services Computing (SCC), Washington DC, 4-9 July 2011, IEEE Computer Society, p. 747–748.

Rajsiri V., Lorre J.-P., Benaben F., Pingaud H., "Prototype of an Ontology-Based Approach for Collaborative Process Specification.", International Conference on Interoperability for Enterprise Software and Applications, China, 2009, IEEE Computer Society, p. 53–59.

Rozsnyai, S., R. Vecera, J. Schiefer, and A. Schatten. "Event Cloud - Searching for Correlated Business Events", 9th IEEE International Conference on E-Commerce Technology and the 4th IEEE International Conference on Enterprise Computing, E-Commerce, and E-Services (CEC/EEE), Tokyo, 23-26 July 2007, IEEE Computer Society, p. 409–420.

Wu N., Mao N., Qian Y., "An Approach to Partner Selection in Agile Manufacturing.", Journal of Intelligent Manufacturing, vol. 10 no. 6, 1999, p. 519–529.

Wu N., Su P., "Selection of Partners in Virtual Enterprise Paradigm.", *Robotics and Computer-Integrated Manufacturing*, vol. 21 no. 2, 2005, p. 119–131.

Zhou Q., Simmhan Y., Prasanna V., "Poster: Towards an Inexact Semantic Complex Event Processing Framework.", Proceedings of the 5th ACM international conference on Distributed event-based system, New York, 11-15 July 2011, p. 401–402.

Semantic Standards Quality Measured for Achieving Enterprise Interoperability: The Case of the SETU Standard for Flexible Staffing

Erwin Folmer * — Harris Wu *

University of Twente & TNO, The Netherlands
erwin.folmer@tno.nl

** *Old Dominion University, USA*
hwu@odu.edu

ABSTRACT: *Semantic standards should play an important role in achieving inter-organizational interoperability. Millions are spent on development and adoption of these standards, but does it lead to interoperability? This important question is often not addressed. In this study data interoperability in the Dutch temporary staffing industry is studied by focusing on the quality of the SETU standard and its implementations in practice. The Stichting Elektronische Transacties Uitzendbranche (foundation for electronic transactions in the staffing industry,) or SETU, develops and maintains standards for exchange of electronic data in the staffing industry. Our results show that although the SETU standard is equipped for achieving interoperability, this in practice has not been achieved due to low quality implementations. We raise the question why these studies are not being performed on every standard. Another result is that localizations (profiles) may be needed for high quality standards; without localizations interoperability is limited in the SETU case.*

KEYWORDS: *semantic standards, standardization, interoperability, quality*

1. Introduction

Achieving interoperability in many industries is challenging but has great impact. Studies of the US automobile sector, for example, estimate that insufficient interoperability in the supply chain adds at least one billion dollars to operating costs, of which 86% is attributable to data exchange problems (Brunnermeier and Martin 2002). Later studies mention5 billion dollars for the US automotive industry and 3.9 billion dollars for the electro technical industry, both representing an impressive 1.2% of the value of shipments in each industry (Steinfield et al. 2011). The adoption of standards to improve interoperability in the automotive, aerospace, shipbuilding and other sectors could save billions (Gallaher et al. 2002).

The already huge importance of standards and interoperability will continue to grow. Networked business models are becoming indisputable reality in today's economy (Legner and Lebreton 2007). A recent Capgemini study concludes that to be ready for 2020 companies need to "significantly increase their degree of collaboration as well as their networking capability" (Falge et al. 2012).

Standards are important for ensuring interoperability (Rada 1993). "Standards are necessary both for integration and for interoperability" (Dogac et al. 2008). "Adopting standards-based integration solutions is the most promising way to reduce the long-term costs of integration and facilitate a flexible infrastructure" (Chari and Seshadri 2004). Some go even further: "Inter-organizational collaboration requires systems interoperability which is not possible in the absence of common standards" (Gerst et al. 2005). And the potential of standards, in relation to the problematic introduction of proprietary solutions, is shown in a case study from the automotive industry (Steinfield et al. 2011).

There is hardly any research on the achievements of semantic standards in achieving interoperability. A survey among semantic standards organizations shows that the vast majority believe that their standards can be improved, and that improvements will lead to more interoperable systems. However, standard developers need statistical support to find the needed improvements (Folmer et al. 2011).

2. Background

2.1. *Semantic Standards Defined*

Semantic standards reside at the presentation and application layer of the OSI model (Steinfield et al. 2007). They include business transaction standards, inter-organizational information system (IOS) standards, ontologies, vocabularies, messaging standards, document-based, e-business, horizontal (cross-industry) and vertical industry standards. The often used examples are RosettaNet for the electro technical industry, HealthLevel7 for the health care domain, HR-XML for the human resources industry and Universal Business Language (UBL) for procurement. Semantic standards are designed to promote communication and coordination among organizations; these standards may address product identification, data definitions, business document layout, and/or business process sequences (adapted from (Steinfield et al. 2007)).

2.2. *Quality Measured in Application: Relevance and Completeness*

Zhu & Wu have introduced how relevance and completeness can be measured in standards' implementations (Zhu and Fu 2009; Zhu and Wu 2010; Zhu and Wu 2011). The completeness and relevancy of the same data standard can be different to different users. Further, they can be different between an individual user and the user community. To formalize the metrics, let the S be the set of data elements specified in the data standard, U_i be the data elements required by the user i. From the user i's perspective, the metrics can be defined as (Zhu & Wu 2010)

$$Completeness_i = \frac{|U_i \cap S|}{|U_i|}, \text{ and } Relevancy_i = \frac{|U_i \cap S|}{|S|}$$

From the user community's perspective, the metrics can be defined as

$$Completeness_c = \frac{\left|\left(\bigcup_i U_i\right) \cap S\right|}{\left|\bigcup_i U_i\right|}, \text{ and } Relevancy_c = \frac{\left|\left(\bigcup_i U_i\right) \cap S\right|}{|S|}$$

Although the concept of completeness and relevancy is a limited, incomplete view on standard quality, it is an important contribution since it is the only notion of quality in practice that can be objectively measured using a large number of data instances.

Zhu and Wu focused on the standard of public financial reporting in US based on US-GAAP (United States Generally Accepted Accounting Principles). This reporting standard is one of the most important standards based on XBRL (Extensible Business Reporting Language). Thousands of companies are mandated to report quarterly and annual financial reports to US Stock and Exchange Commission, using the US-GAAP XBRL standard. Applying automated tools to thousands of public financial reports, Zhu and Wu were able to perform a series of analyses on the quality of US-GAAP XBRL standard and interoperability of public financial reports, including trend and industry-based analyses. Most importantly, Zhu and Wu's studies produced a number of practical suggestions to both the standard defining body and standard users/implementers (i.e. the individual reporting companies), which may substantially improve standard compliance and data interoperability.

The XBRL standard in Zhu and Wu's studies are used in financial reports, which are relatively static information. No researchers have yet studied the quality of electronic standards used for dynamic business processes, using similar implementation-based metrics.

3. The SETU Standard

SETU stands for the Stichting Elektronische Transacties Uitzendbranche (foundation for electronic transactions in the staffing industry). The SETU standard is a semantic standard trying to achieve interoperability among different actors in the business processes related to flexible staffing. The staffing industry consists of a large number of customers and suppliers, and increasingly relies on electronic transactions.

The SETU standard has been acclaimed by the Dutch government for achieving interoperability within the process of hiring temporary staffers through staffing organizations. Since May 2009, SETU is listed on the "comply or explain" list, which means that every (semi) public organization in the Netherlands has to comply with using the SETU standard when ordering temporary staffing is executed electronically. Achieving this status implies that SETU passed the process of the Dutch government, suggesting that SETU is expected to be of high quality.

SETU is a set of specifications, including XML Schemas, for amongst others assignments, timecards, and invoices related to temporary staffing. It is a Dutch localization of the international HR-XML standard (Van Hillegersberg & Minnecre, 2009). SETU standardizes additional rules on top of HR-XML, and thereby limits the options within HR-XML. An instance that validates correctly with HR-XML does not necessarily comply with SETU. However the other way around is always true: Each instance that is SETU compliant is compliant to HR-XML as well.

Since SETU uses the same XML Schema files as HR-XML, the additional rules are captured within text (the SETU specifications) and the business rules in Schematron. The SETU standard comprises of different sub-standards. Our focus is on SETU standard for invoicing version 1.1, which is freely available at www.setu.nl.

4. Research Approach

On a high level we want to know if we can assess the quality of the standard by assessing the implementations of the standard. We study this question by performing a case study on the SETU standard. We selected this standard because it is important to workforce mobility and integration, and is highly acclaimed for its quality, adoption success and business savings. Our main research question is: What is the quality of the SETU *standard and its implementations*?

To be able to answer this question we have to analyze the implementations of the SETU standard and search for (avoidable) errors that negatively affect the quality of both standard and implementations. The SETU standard has to be compared with other standards in terms of quality but so far only quality results from XBRL are available for comparison.

Our second research aim is to study whether this implementation measuring approach is useful in identifying improvement suggestions for semantic standards. In this specific case we will identify improvement suggestions for the SETU standard. In other words, can our approach be used as quality assessment instruments requested by standard developers (Folmer et al. 2011)?

4.1. *Data Collection*

For our research approach we need to collect data of SETU implementations. One of the authors contacted the main staffing organizations and system providers that together have the vast majority in market share of temporary staffing in the Netherlands.

Data of four large staffing organizations has been gathered, just as the data from 3 system providers, which have been anonymized. In total 54 "messages" have been gathered including 32 timecards and 22 invoices. These messages are instantiations based on the SETU standards: For instance a specific invoice for worker X, week Y, sent by staffing organization A to staffing customer B. The data then contains invoices from staffing organizations to staffing customers.

There is some overlap in data, since the staffing customer may overlap for different instantiations of staffing organizations. Also, some staffing organizations make extensively use of system providers. Therefore the data gathered from the system providers may include the same data as received from a staffing organization.

4.2. *Validation Process*

As first step we decided to take one set of message: the invoices. From our data set 22 are invoices, of which 2 have the same system-staffing organization – staffing customer configuration and will therefore have the same characteristics.

These two have been removed from the data set. Our approach consisted then of 3 steps:

- Validate the messages in the SETU eValidator. This Validation Service is available at www.setu.nl and validates the instances three way: a. XML well-formedness, b. XML Schema validation and c. Business Rules validation. The latter is a set of Schematron expressions that has been set up by the SETU organization that encapsulates additional rules described in the SETU specification that cannot be validated with XML Schema.

- Count the usage of elements within the implementations; by doing that we find frequently used or totally unused elements.

- Analyze and calculate metrics. Within this step we analyze the previous results and calculate error percentages and the completeness and relevance metrics.

5. SETU Measurement Results for the Invoice standard

This section contains the results of the measurement of the SETU invoice implementations. We will start by explaining the validation results, followed by looking at more details into the data elements. Finally we will discuss the results on relevance and completeness metrics.

5.1. *Validation Errors*

Table 1 contains the validation results. For each usage scenario (such as StaffinOrg1 invoicing StaffingCustomer1), the numbers of XML structure errors, HR-XML schema validation errors and SETU business rules errors are counted. Although most errors are counted by occurrences, when structure errors occur the tool may exit immediately and therefore a yes/no is used for scoring.

#	Usage scenario (invoice type)	Structure Errors	Schema Errors	Rule Errors	Total Errors
1	StafOrg1-StafCust1	No	0	2	2
2	StafOrg1-StafCust2	No	0	2	2
3	StafOrg1-StafCust3	No	0	2	2
4	StafOrg1-StafCust4	No	0	2	2
5	StafOrg1-StafCust5	No	0	2	2
6	StafOrg1-StafCust6	No	0	2	2
7	StafOrg2-StafCust1	No	0	3	3
8	StafOrg2-StafCust2	No	0	1	1
9	StafOrg2-StafCust3	No	0	3	3
10	StafOrg2-StafCust4	No	0	3	3
11	StafOrg3-StafCust3	No	1	2	3
12	StafOrg3-StafCust4	No	11	14	25
13	StafOrg4-StafCust1	No	0	4	4
14	StafOrg4-StafCust2	No	0	4	4
15	StafOrg4-StafCust3	No	16	4	20
16	System1-StafOrg1-StafCust1	No	0	2	2
17	System1-StafOrg1-StafCust2	No	0	2	2
18	System1-StafOrg2-StafCust3	No	0	2	2
19	System1-StafOrg3-StafCust4	No	1	-*	1*
20	System3-StafOrg1-StafCust1	Yes	7	3	10
	Invoice Errors		36	59	95

Table 1. *Validation results for SETU invoices*

5.2. Validation Data Explanation

The * denotes the fact that due to the schema errors the business rules validation was cancelled. We received more invoices of the system implementations, but since they have the same errors we excluded them from the data set. This is logical since when the invoice standard is implemented in the system of the staffing organizations, even if we collect 1, 10 or 1000 instances of the invoice, they will all have the same errors. System2 is excluded from this set because it has only timecards implemented and no invoices.

The implementations gathered from an organization often contain the same characteristics and errors. For example Staffing Organization 1 succeeded in their implementation to avoid schema errors. Some staffing organizations have their own ICT implementation, while others use a system from a software vendor.

StaffingOrg 4 has 16 schema errors which are in fact the same error that returns in many places. It shows that the number of errors in itself is not always useful. For instance if the amount is missing on an invoice line, and there are 20 invoice Lines, than it will count as 20 rule errors.

These explanations show that the analysis is valuable; however, carefulness is needed when quantifying measurements.

5.3. *Validation Data Analysis*

It is valuable to summarize the numbers of implementations that have or have not errors. Below are some statistics:

- 1 out of 20 is not well-formed, and has basic structure errors

- 5 out of 20 have basic XML Schema error and do not validate against schema

- 19 out of 19 (100%) have Business Rules error and do not comply to the SETU standard

The first two statistics can be easily manipulated by changing the data set, but still it is remarkable that these errors exist in practice. The fact that 100% contain business rules errors and no instance is SETU compliant is even more remarkable. If we look in detail into the errors:

– XML Schema errors:

A wide range of "clumsy" errors. For instance incorrect use of date notation within DocumentDateTime element, a missing element, or usage of a non-existent value from the code list. All these errors can be easily avoidable.

– Business Rules:

In contrast to the XML Schema errors, the Business Rules errors have a lot of similarities in all implementations. We found two groups of errors:

Group 1: The usage of "SupplierParty", "BillToParty" and "RemitToParty" leads to many errors.

Group 2: The usage of "Invoice Lines" without "Amount" or "Price per Quantity".

It seems like implementers have difficulties with using these elements correctly. This might indicate that the specification is not clear about how to use these elements.

5.4. Data Elements

Our analysis shows that several data elements from the standard are never used within our data set. These unused elements are: DiscountAmount, DiscountPercentage, DepartmentCode, and CostCenterName. On the other hand there are several data elements that are used in every instance: DocumentDateTime, Header, Id, IdValue, Invoice, Line, LineNumber, PercentQuantity, TaxBaseAmount, Total, TotalAmount, TotalTax, Type. The customer reporting requirement module is a set of optional elements that allow flexible usage for specific needs of staffing customers. The most used items of the customer reporting requirements are listed in table 2.

Element	Count
PurchaseOrderLineItem	14
AdditionalRequirement	12
CostCenterCode	10
PurchaseOrderNumber	8
CustomerReferenceNumber	6
CostCenterName	2
ProjectCode	1

Table 2. *Most used items from Customer Reporting Requirements*

The list of frequencies of these optional elements provides many insights. For instance since PurchaseOrderLineItem is used that often, it might be questioned whether the element should be mandatory. Additional to the optional elements within the Customer Reporting Requirements, the SETU standard allows users to define custom fields in the "AdditionalRequirement" element. Out the 22 invoices, 16 of them have defined AdditionalRequirement with the list of custom fields below. Several organizations independently developed same or similarly-titled custom fields, which may suggest a need for these elements to be included in the SETU standard.

```
requirementTitle="TotalHours"
requirementTitle="geboortedatum"
requirementTitle="Postcode"
requirementTitle="werkweeknummer"
requirementTitle="plaatsingsnummer"
requirementTitle="TotalHours"
requirementTitle="Weeknr."
requirementTitle="Uitzendkracht"
requirementTitle="Jaar"
requirementTitle="MP_Omschrijving_Factuur"
requirementTitle="Correctietekst"
```

5.5. *Completeness and Relevance*

HR-XML standard contains 385 elements. SETU invoicing standard defined 78 elements, 55 of which are from the HR-XML standard. Considering SETU as the user of the HR-XML standard, the relevancy of HR-XML is 14.29%, while the completeness is 70.51%.

Standard User	Standard	Completeness	Relevancy
SETU	HR-XML	55/78 = 70.51%	55/385 = 14.29%
SETU community	SETU Invoicing Standard	1	74/78 = 94.87%
SETU community considering AdditionalRequirement as custom elements	SETU Invoicing Standard	74/85 = 87.06%	74/78 = 94.87%

Table 3. *SETU results on completeness and relevance*

All invoices in our data collection are specified using elements specified in SETU. For SETU community, most of the 78 SETU elements have been used in invoices. The relevancy of SETU invoicing standard is 94.87%. All elements used in invoices are defined in SETU invoicing standard, therefore its completeness is 1. However, if the custom fields in AdditionalRequirement are considered as custom elements, the completeness of SETU standard in the context of our data collection is 87.06%.

6. Discussion

Most remarkable is the outcome that no single instance is a correct implementation of the standard. The SETU workgroup should analysis these results. But based on these results we suggest:

–To clarify the use of SupplierParty, RemitToParty and BillToParty

–To clarify the use of Invoice Lines that requires amounts and price per quantity.

–To remove the unused elements: this makes implementations easier

–To change the cardinality to mandatory of the always used elements: again, this makes implementations easier

–Analyze the results of the usage of the customer reporting module

Remarkable is that we used the eValidator in our study, which is accessible through the SETU.NL website. Our results make it questionable if this validation tool is currently used by the SETU implementers. We guess that the quality of the implementations would have been better if the implementers had used the validation service freely available to them.

6.1. *Comparison of SETU and XBRL Results*

Zhu and Wu (2011)'s study finds that for the US-GAAP XBRL user community, the completeness of US-GAAP standard is 32.12% and the relevancy is 19.29%. Their study is based on all annual financial reports that have been submitted to US Stock and Exchange Commission as of 2010. SETU invoicing standard seems to have a better fitness for use by the staffing community. As measured by our data collection, SETU invoicing standard's completeness is 87.06%, and relevancy is 94.87%. However, note that if the data collection is larger, such as if we were able to collect all invoices from the staffing community in Netherlands, the completeness of SETU invoicing standard would have been somewhat lower (considering custom fields in AdditionalRequirement as custom elements). Also, financial reports are much more complex than timesheets and invoices. The US-GAAP standard has more than 12000 elements and is much more complex than the SETU invoicing standard. The lower fitness for use of US-GAAP XBRL standard, as measured by completeness and relevancy, can be partly attributed to its complexity.

The results show the value of having localizations on top of broader semantic standards (such as HR-XML), in line with earlier findings that localizations are essential for interoperability (Brutti et al. 2011).

6.2. *Discussion on Potential Reasons of Outcome*

The results are highly remarkable and definitely not expected for SETU. Therefore we discussed the outcome with both developers of the SETU standard, and its users. Based on these discussions we defined the following potential reasons for the low quality of the implementations:

1. Early stage of SETU standard in life cycle. The SETU standard is relatively new, and implementations have mainly started from 2009 onwards. So the tested implementations are probably from the first batch of implementations. It might be expected that during the years both the standards and its implementations have been improved. Follow-up research in which this validation is repeated is required to test this assumption.

2. Plug-and-play interoperability, the goal of standards such as SETU, is not desired on business level. This might be surprising since plug-and-play interoperability is seen as some kind of holy grail since the uprise of e-business, and in particular the ebXML years. However in discussion with business people from the staffing companies they state that 90% interoperability is better than 100%. Simply because they would like to have contact with the customer about the final 10%. Plug and play would reduce that customer contact and will reduce the feeling the customer will have with the staffing company. So far academia is convinced that 100% plug and play should be the goal, but this research might question that. Validation of the suspected 100% plug and play requirement from business perspective is needed.

3. SETU is used as a marketing term. Nobody cares about the correctness of the implementations. For especially the staffing companies and system providers it is essential to state that they are SETU compliant. Even during the early years most companies said they had implemented SETU although these statements were highly questionable. Customers are asking for SETU, especially in large government tenders, and failing to state SETU compliancy might cost contracts. However since implementations are never tested, and there is no official SETU compliance organized, it might lead to issues regarding implementations as shown in this study.

4. Knowledge problem of implementers, both on semantics (business) level and technical level. On semantic level, it is hard to understand the real meaning of the semantics if the implementer did not participate in the SETU workgroup. However our study is not focused on semantic errors, but on technical errors. There might even be more errors on semantic level, but these are hard to find. Second there might be a mismatch between the technology used within the SETU standard and the technical knowledge of the implementers. Although this is hard to imagine since SETU is using very traditional XML technology. On the other side the IT maturity of the temporary staffing industry is expected to be low.

For this, and the previous reason, certification might be a potential solution to improve the implementations.

5. The flexibility of the standard, especially during early stages of life cycle. There is always a debate on how flexible a standard should be and how many changes and version updates are needed to accommodate the community. This is not much likely to be a real reason since not many of the errors are related to issues that later on have been accommodated within the standard.

6. Standard is being used in situations that are not foreseen or explicitly mentioned as use case. Within the SETU case the standard is explicitly designed for a situation in which staffing customer and staffing company directly exchange the messages. However in practice the standard is also being used in situations with an

intermediary system provider in the middle. The requirements of that situation might not be taken into account during the SETU standards development and might lead to implementation issues.

Although we searched and discussed the reasons in particular related to the SETU implementations, these reasons might as well be valid for other semantic standards.

7. Conclusions

This paper has shown an analysis of the implementations of a semantic standard. The quality of SETU implementations is highly questionable since no single instance proved to be a correct implementation. The quality of SETU standard seems to be ok compared to other electronic standards such as the US-GAAP XBRL standard in financial reporting.

We have provided valuable results to the SETU standards organization, in two ways:

1. The low quality of implementations raises the question what the SETU organization can do to improve the implementations. Education, mandatory validation, or even certification might be solutions.

2. This analysis has been used for an improvement project within SETU. The analysis of element usage frequency and the two groups of frequent errors might lead to changes in new version of the standard.

We have provided supporting evidence to earlier claims that localizations (profiles) are needed for achieving interoperability. But our study also shows that it is not enough to have a single view on standard quality, especially when studying the interoperability effect of standards. SETU scored almost perfectly on completeness and relevance, but still interoperability was questionable due to low quality of implementations. The other way around could be said for other standards. At minimum an interoperability achievement study should include a study of:

– Completeness and Relevance of the standard

– Validity of standard implementations

It is remarkable that no semantic standardization organizations are using above measures to improve their standards, or other quality measurement approaches (Folmer, 2012). Based on our research we strongly advise all semantic standardization workgroups to perform such an analysis and improve the standards or set up policies to improve implementations.

8. References

Brunnermeier, S.B., and Martin, S.A. "Interoperability Costs in the Us Automotive Supply Chain," *Supply Chain Management,* vol. 7 no. 2, 2002, p. 71-82.

Brutti, A., De Sabbata, P., Frascella, A., Novelli, C., and Gessa, N. "Standard for Ebusiness in Smes Networks: The Increasing Role of Customization Rules and Conformance Testing Tools to Achieve Interoperability," in *Enterprise Interoperability, Proceedings of the Workshops of the Third International Ifip Working Conference Iwei 2011,* M. Zelm, M. Van Sinderen, G. Doumeingts and P. Johnson (eds.). Stockholm: Wiley.

Chari, K., and Seshadri, S. "Demystifying Integration," *Communications of the ACM ,*vol 47 no 7,2004, p. 58-63.

Dogac, A., Kabak, Y., Namli, T., and Okcan, A. 2008. "Collaborative Business Process Support in Ehealth: Integrating Ihe Profiles through Ebxml Business Process Specification Language," *IEEE Transactions on Information Technology in Biomedicine ,*vol 12 no 6,2008, p. 754-762.

Falge, C., Otto, B., and Österle, H. "Data Quality Requirements of Collaborative Business Processes," *45th Hawaii International Conference on System Sciences (HICSS),*2012, Hawaii.

Folmer, E., Oude Luttighuis, P., and van Hillegersberg, J. "Do Semantic Standards Lack Quality? A Survey among 34 Semantic Standards," *Electronic Markets ,*vol 21 no 2, 2011, p. 99-111.

Gallaher, M.P., O'Conner, A.C., and Phelps, T. "Economic Impact Assessment of the International Standard for the Exchange of Product Model Data (Step) in Transportation Equipment Industries," 2002, RTI Project Number 07007.016.

Gerst, M., Bunduchi, R., and Williams, R. "Social Shaping & Standardization: A Case Study from Auto Industry," *38th Hawaii International Conference on System Sciences (HICSS),* J.R.H. Spraque (ed.), 2005, Hawaii.

Legner, C., and Lebreton, B. 2007. "Preface to the Focus Theme Section: 'Business Interoperability' Business Interoperability Research: Present Achievements and Upcoming Challenges," *Electronic Markets ,*vol 17 no 3 ,2007, p. 176-186.

Rada, R. 1993. "Standards: The Language for Success," *Communications of the ACM ,*vol 36 no 12,1993, p. 17-23.

Steinfield, C.W., Markus, M.L., and Wigand, R.T. "Cooperative Advantage and Vertical Information System Standards: An Automotive Supply Chain Case Study," *44th Hawaii International Conference on System Sciences (HICSS),* 2011, Hawaii.

Steinfield, C.W., Wigand, R.T., Markus, M.L., and Minton, G. "Promoting E-Business through Vertical Is Standards: Lessons from the Us Home Mortgage Industry," in *Standards and Public Policy,* S. Greenstein and V. Stango (eds.). Cambridge: Cambridge University Press, 2007, p. 160-207.

Zhu, H., and Fu, L. "Towards Quality of Data Standards: Empirical Findings from Xbrl," *International Conference on Information Systems (ICIS),* 2009, Phoenix.

Zhu, H., and Wu, H. "Quality of Data Standards: Framework and Illustration Using Xbrl Taxonomy and Instances," *Electronic Markets* ,vol 21 no 2,2011 , p. 129-139.

Zhu, H., and Wu, H. "Quality of Xbrl Us Gaap Taxonomy: Empirical Evaluation Using Sec Filings," *Americas Conference on Information Systems (AMCIS)*, 2010, Lima, Peru.

Requirements Formalization for Systems Engineering: An Approach for Interoperability Analysis in Collaborative Process Model

Sihem Mallek* — Nicolas Daclin* — Vincent Chapurlat* — Bruno Vallespir **

* LGI2P - Laboratoire de Génie Informatique et d'Ingénierie de Production
site de l'Ecole des Mines d'Alès, Parc Scientifique Georges Besse,
F30035 Nîmes Cedex 5, France
Sihem.Mallek@mines-ales.fr
Nicolas.Daclin@mines-ales.fr
Vincent.Chapurlat@mines-ales.fr

** Université Bordeaux, IMS, UMR 5218, F – 33400 Talence, France
Bruno.Vallespir@ims-bordeaux.fr

ABSTRACT: In the field of requirement's engineering, writing requirements is a fundamental stage. Indeed, requirements must be (1) written correctly by the user, (2) relevant to the studied domain and (3), verifiable. In this research work, the studied domain is related to the verification of interoperability requirements on a collaborative process model by formal verification techniques. In this case, it is necessary to offer to a user the mean to write its own interoperability requirements easily, correctly and human readable in order to be re-writing into properties and to allow their verification. Precisely, this communication presents the mapping between interoperability requirements expressed in SBVR into properties expressed in TCTL.

KEYWORDS: interoperability requirements, formalization, rules mapping, SBVR, UPPAAL

1. Introduction

In Systems Engineering domain (SE)1 as in any more specific engineering domain (mechanical, information systems, mechatronic…), requirements description, analysis and verification are crucial activities. On the one hand, a requirement results from stakeholders' expectations and prescriptions *i.e.* from stakeholders' needs analysis. It can be also induced by technical, technological or organizational choices made by designers. So, a requirement fixes without ambiguities, in a coherent way, and even constraints, what designers have to respect when designing a solution. First, in order to describe a requirement, these designers can be helped by standards *e.g.* (ANS/EIA-632 1998) and (ISO/IEC 2008) that propose reference models and reference vocabularies. In the same way, they promote splitting up requirements into various categories. There are based classically on the distinction between functional requirements (what a system S has to do?) and non-functional requirements (how this must be done?). However, the resulting vocabularies and requirements check lists commonly adopted in the SE domain are more or less perfectible when taking into account interoperability problematic. On the other hand, a requirement can evolve, being refined or decomposed all along the System Engineering project. These refinements or decompositions are requested, and then done by designers from various domains having different points of view about the system under design. So, they require various domains vocabularies having to be coherent for describing a requirement. Last, design activities are considered generally as model based or model guided activities (Estefan 2007). Indeed, designers' work is oriented on modelling and analysis activities of the obtained models. However, verification, and even partial validation, activities of these models are required for two reasons. First, it is necessary to assume the quality of any model of a system S under design before performing any analysis. For instance, analysis can consist to simulate the behaviour of S in order to evaluate the performance and the relevance of a given communication protocol between S and another system. Second, when verified, a model has to be used in order to check if a given part of the requirements is really respected (Grady 2007).

This is classically the aim of verification and validation activities. The goal is to prove and to justify that the system meets these requirements based only on models of this system we have. There is obviously no magic bullet to ensure completeness of modeling and then of the requested proofs. However, it should help designers to ensure that at least some of these requirements are met. The research work herein presented focuses on writing, verifying, partially validating and justifying

---

1 Guide to the Systems Engineering Body of Knowledge (SEBoK), version 1.0, see http://www.sebokwiki.org/ (last visited 16/11/2012)

requirements in a model based design environment by using various formal techniques *e.g.* those promoted by (Dasgupta 2010).

This communication applies and illustrates a research work in order to help designers for writing and proving interoperability requirements on a sociotechnical system. This one is a collaborative process aiming to involve various partners from various business domains, to share activities, data and time. By assumption, in this case, interoperability requirements allow us to focus precisely on issues dreaded but often implied a non-interoperable partner involved in a collaborative process will sooner or later lead to malfunctions and interfacing problems both from technical, organizational or also human points of view. As a consequence, this paper is organized as follow. Section 2 presents the problematic of writing interoperability requirements and related state of the art. Section 3 presents our proposed approach to write correctly and easily interoperability requirements and its re-writing to make their verification possible. Section 4 gives a case study in order to illustrate the re-writing of interoperability requirements.

2. State of the Art and Problematic

From (Mallek *et al.*, 2012), four categories of interoperability requirements have to be considered (compatibility, interoperation, autonomy and reversibility). In this study, an interoperability requirement can be qualified as a-temporal *i.e.* it is independent of time and has to be verified in all steps of system behavior. Conversely, it can be qualified as temporal *i.e.* it is dependent of temporal hypotheses and has to be verified only at some stages of the system life cycle. The problem addressed in this article is triple that means it is necessary to ensure that:

1. *Interoperability requirements are well written i.e. written correctly.* Natural language is usually used for writing them and often preferred rather than using formal language (*e.g.* logic) which can be difficult to understand by end users. This induces, however, classical rewording problems and ambiguities. As a consequence, various business vocabularies exist to overcome natural language. These vocabularies help end user not only to write the requirement itself, but also to decompose or refine it from a more relevant and formal manner into a set of sub-requirements. It exist several approaches such as KAOS method (Van lamsweerde *et al.*, 1991), Boiler plates approaches (Fanmuy *et al.*, 2011), Use Case Map notation2, standardized requirements check lists (ISO/IEC 2008) or the REGAL approach (REGAL 2008) which are now recognized as good methodologies. Last, it seems more adequate here to use standards and implanted tools which remain conform to these standards. We propose then to use Semantic Business Vocabulary Rules

---

2 Use Case Map (UCM) notation, available at (last visited 16/11/2012) : http://jucmnav.softwareengineering.ca/ucm/bin/view/UCM/AboutUseCaseMaps

(SBVR) (OMG 2008) but let's mention also URN (Itu-T Z.151 2008) or GRL3 as potential candidates.

2. *These requirements are good and relevant* when regarding the system to be designed. In this way, requirements have to be expressed according to all concepts used to describe the system to analyze. Thus, it is necessary to ensure that the used language to write requirements is sufficient, complete and correctly built to guide the user in the writing process of its requirements.

3. *The system model can allow us to check all or part of these requirements* taking into account their nature (functional or non-functional) and other characteristics. It is proposed here to make a mapping between the used language to describe requirements and the used verification technique to analyze them.

This approach is applied, in order to guide designer in the definition and the expression of interoperability requirements. Precisely, the final goal is to allow verification of interoperability requirements in a collaborative process model using formal verification techniques. In this case, the collaborative process is modelled using the BPMN 2.0 language (OMG 2011) and has to be translated - using model transformation rules (not presented here) - into an equivalent model upon which the formal verification techniques can be applied as presented in (Mallek *et al.*, 2012). In this way, one of the used formal verification techniques is based on model checking (Edmund *et al.*, 1999) using the model checker UPPAAL (Behrmann *et al.*, 2004) to verify temporal interoperability requirements. As a consequence, it is necessary to write these interoperability requirements into properties with TCTL (temporal logic used by UPPAAL). However, it is difficult to ensure compliance and quality of expression of a property. In addition, the user must have the mastery explicit representation languages properties. As a consequence, it is proposed in this research work to focus on good writing requirements with a structured vocabulary and their automatic rewriting into formal language. Although requirements writing is a well know problematic, few studies focus on this aspect.

It is proposed in this paper

(1) to allow the user to express correctly its requirements in a readable language (*i.e.* closest to natural language),

(2) to establish mapping rules to re-write correctly these interoperability requirements into TCTL properties and facilitate the use of our tool for the end user as presented in the following figure.

---

3 Goal-oriented Requirement Language, available at (last visited 16/11/2012) : http://www.cs.toronto.edu/km/GRL/

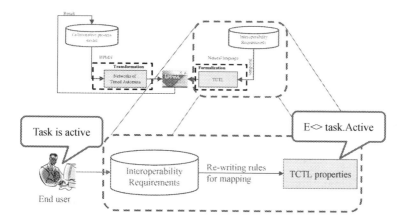

Figure 1. *From the expression of an interoperability requirement to the corresponding TCTL property to verify*

Based on these hypotheses, next sections present the proposed approach of re-writing interoperability requirements expressed in structural language into TCTL based on the use of mapping rules.

3. Interoperability Requirements Writing

As mentioned previously, it is necessary to help stakeholders to write their interoperability requirements with a simplified language such as natural language. So, it is important to offer a language readily understandable and easily accessible for each stakeholder. This research work is based on the use of SBVR (Semantic of Business Vocabulary and Rule) (OMG 2008). In fact, SBVR *"defines the vocabulary and rules for documenting the semantics vocabularies, business facts and business rules for the interchange of business vocabularies and business rules among organizations and between software tools"*. SBVR is based on natural language allowing to write requirements easier rather than with a more formal language – such as temporal logic as presented in (Mallek *et al.*, 2011). The SBVR language allows to define a limited but sufficient vocabulary to write rules and to ensure, further, their verification supported by a verification technique. Thus, this vocabulary has to be made in accordance with the studied domain. In our case the vocabulary is based on:

- The modelling language used to model the collaborative process, *i.e.* BPMN (OMG 2011). Thus, the proposed vocabulary has to allow considering all concepts included in BPMN (e.g. task, resource, event…). For instance, each BPMN object and its attributes are well considered in the *BPMNVocabulary* as *"terms"*.

- The verification technique *i.e.* UPPAAL language (Behrmann *et al.*, 2004) used to model the process behaviour as well as properties. Thus, the vocabulary has to allow to consider all the automaton and their states that corresponds to the behaviour of each BPMN object (*e.g.* task is in state "Working", resource is in state "Active"...). As an example, states of an automaton are described as in *UPPAALVocabulary* as "*verbs*".

- Interoperability concepts that represent all concepts that are not proposed in the previous defined vocabularies but that allow to write an interoperability requirement (Chen *et al.*, 2007) (aptitude, is_less_than, authorization...). Depending of the nature of the interoperability concepts, they can be either a "*term*" or a "*verb*". For instance, the interoperability concept "aptitude" is an attribute added to enrich the BPMN language, thus, it is *de facto* a "*term*". Furthermore, the interoperability concept "*is_less_than*" represents an operator and so a "*verb*" in *InteroperabilityVocabulary*.

As a consequence the proposed vocabulary can be formalized as shown in the following formula:

InteroperabilityRequirementVocabulary = {BPMNVocabulary,   [1]
UPPAALVocabulary, InteroperabiltyVocabulary}

Based on this vocabulary, a user (*e.g.* stakeholder) can write an interoperability requirement which can be verified on a collaborative process model. For instance, the simplified interoperability requirement "*it is possible that a task is working and a resource is active*" is built based on *BPMNVocabulary* (task, resource) and *UPPAALVocabulary* (working, active). Once the vocabulary is defined, and the SBVR rule is written, it is necessary to re-write the rule into a property expressed in the target property verification language (TCTL in our case). In order to perform this step, it is mandatory to dispose of the SBVR syntax to write an SBVR rule, to dispose of the TCTL syntax to write TCTL property, and finally to establish mapping rule between SBVR rule and TCTL property. In this way, the following sections describes (1) the syntax of SBVR rules, (2) the syntax of TCTL property and (3) the mapping rules of re-writing at the current stage of our research work.

3.1. *SBVR Rules Syntax*

SBVR defines an SBVR rule such as "*a rule always tends to remove some degree of* freedom" (OMG 2008). The advantage to write a rule with SBVR is that it allows to write a requirement that follow good practices such as SMART (Mannion *et al.*, 1995). Therefore, SBVR rules are based on "*facts*", and "*facts*" are based on "*terms*". The syntax of an SBVR rule is described in this section, without going into details (for more details, reader may wish to refer to (OMG 2008)). Formally, an SBVR rule can be written such as:

Rule ::= modality? p   [2]

Where:
Modality = {alethic, deontic}   [3]

With:
alethic = {necessity, possibility, contingency}   [4]
deontic = {obligation, permission, optionally}   [5]

and:

$p=\{fact_i, quantifiers_j, logicalOperation_k, keyword_l\}, i \in [1, n], j, k, l \in [0, m],$ [6]
$n, m \in N^+$

with:
- *fact ∈ Fact, Fact ⊂ InteroperabilityRequirementVocabulary*
- *quantifier ∈ Quantifier, Quantifier = {each, some, at least, at most, exactly, at least n and at most n, more than one}*
- *logicalOperation ∈ LogicaOperation, LogicalOperation = {it is not the case that, and, or, but not both, if p then q, if and only if, neither, nor, whether or not}*
- *keyword ∈ Keywords, Keywords= {the, a, an, another, a given, that, who, of, what}*

Following the previous defined SBVR rule syntax, the Figure 2 describes a given rule that is conforming to the SBVR syntax.

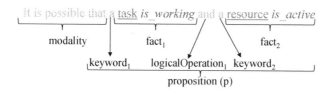

Figure 2. *Syntax of SBVR*

3.2. *TCTL Property Syntax*

A property in UPPAAL is written using a fragment of the TCTL logic (Behrmann *et al.*, 2004). Therefore, the TCTL syntax is presented in this section without going into details (for more details, reader may wish to refer to (Behrmann *et al.*, 2004)). Formally, a TCTL property can be written respecting the following syntax.

Property ::= quantifier p | p → q   [7]

Where:
Quantifier = (pathQuantifier, temporalOperator)   [8]
With:
- *pathQuantifier ={[](all states in a path), <>(some state in a path)}*
- *temporalOperator = {A (for all paths),E (exists a path)}*
- *leadTo = {→}*

and
p, q = expression   [9]

An expression (p) is written according to existing automaton and their states and variables such as presented in the following figure with the automaton of a task which has 4 states (Waiting, Start, Working and Stop) and two variables (timeMin and timeMax) used in a clock T.

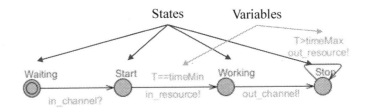

Figure 3. *Task automaton in UPPAAL*

Following the previous defined TCTL property syntax, the Figure 4 describes a given property using TCTL logic.

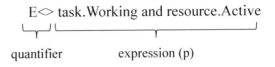

Figure 4. *Syntax of TCTL property in UPPAAL*

3.3. *Mapping Rules from SBVR Rule to TCTL Property*

According to the syntax previously defined (SBVR rule syntax and TCTL property syntax), it is possible to observe that an SBVR rule and a TCTL property have both a proposition/expression which can be precede by a modality in the case of an SBVR rule and by a quantifier in the case of TCTL property. In this way, it is proposed to develop two mappings to re-write SBVR rules into TCTL property. Thus, the first mapping allows to re-write modality into quantifier if this one exists or if it is possible. Then, the second mapping allows to re-write SBVR rule proposition into TCTL property expression. For the first mapping, it is possible to highlight that the modality and the quantifier are issued from the modal logic (Zalta 1995). From this consideration and the definitions of modalities from SBVR rules and quantifiers from TCTL properties, it is proposed to develop the following mapping as presented in the Table 1.

SBVR modality	Definition	TCTL quantifier	Definition
It is necessary that	Necessity. The meaning of its embedded logical formulation is true in all possible worlds	A<>	Inevitable. The proposition will inevitably become true.
It is possible that	Possibility. The meaning of its embedded logical formulation is true in some possible worlds.	E<>	Reachability. It is possible to reach a state in which the proposition is satisfied
It is obligatory that	Obligation. The meaning of its embedded logical formulation is true in all acceptable worlds	A[]	Invariantly. The proposition is true in all reachable states.
It is permitted that	Permission. The meaning of its embedded logical formulation is true in some acceptable worlds.	E[]	Potentially. The proposition is potentially always true.

Table 1. *Mapping between SBVR modality and TCTL quantifier*

This mapping considers, first, the nature of the modality such as alethic or deontic. Alethic modalities determine the fundamental conditions of possible worlds. In the case of a NTA, this type of modalities can indicates that a property is true in some state in a path ($<>$) according to the conditions. At the opposite, deontic modalities determine acceptable worlds. In this way, according to NTA verification, this type of modalities can indicates that a property is true in all states in a path ([]). Second, this mapping considers the nature of the alethic or deontic modality according to the consideration of some or all worlds. In this case, the proposed mapping determines the used temporal operator such as the use of temporal operator "A" in the case of the consideration of all worlds. Furthermore, an SBVR proposition can be written using *keywords*, *logicalOperations* and *facts* that are based on *terms* and *verbs*. As presented previously, *interoperabilityRequirementVocabulary* was defined according to (1) BPMN language, (2) the used verification technique

(UPPAAL) and (3), the interoperability concepts. In this way, in order to perform the second mapping, a given *term* corresponds to an automaton or variable. Furthermore, a *verb* corresponds to a state of an automaton or an operator. The reason of this mapping is related to the transformation from BPMN to a Network of Timed Automata where all concepts from BPMN related to the behaviour of the process are transformed into automaton such as (resource, task…) with several states representing the evolution of the process. Finally, we define that a *logicalOperator* corresponds to a logical operator into TCTL as presented Table 2. It is to note that *keywords* are not considered in the following mapping.

SBVR proposition	TCTL proposition
term	automaton or variable
verb	state or operator
logicalOperator	logical operator

Table 2. *Mapping between SBVR proposition and TCTL proposition*

For instance, according to the presented syntaxes of SBVR rule and TCTL property, a mapping can be done to re-write the following interoperability requirements "*It is possible that a task is_working and a resource is_active and a clock is_less_than timeMax and clock is_greater_than timeMin*". This requirement is expressed as an SBVR rule based on a defined vocabulary and can be re-written into TCTL such as "*E<> task.Working ans resource.Active and T<timeMax and T>timeMin* ". Indeed, considering and respecting the proposed mapping the modality is re-written into a quantifier and the SBVR rule proposition is re-written into a TCTL property expression as presented in the following figure.

	SBVR rule decomposition (source)	TCTL property decomposition (target)	
modality	It is possible that	E<>	quantifier
	task (term)	task. (automata)	
	is_working (verb)	Working (state)	
	and	and	
	resource (term)	resource. (automata)	
proposition (p)	is_active (verb)	Active (state)	expression (q)
	clock (term)	T (variable)	
	is_less_than (verb)	< (operator)	
	time_max (term)	timeMax (variable)	
	is_greater_than (verb)	> (operator)	
	time_min (term)	timeMin (variable)	

Figure 5. *Mapping between an SBVR rule and a TCTL property*

The proposed mapping, in its current stage, is limited to re-write an SBVR rule into a TCTL property. In the case of another expression of an SBVR rule, this one can be verified with another verification tool such as, for example, COGITANT4 based on Conceptual Graphs (Sowa 1976) in the case of a-temporal requirements or with the expertise for requirements that cannot be verified using formal verification techniques. In fact, the objective of this research work, in a first time, is to ensure the verification of 15-20% of interoperability requirements thanks to formal verification techniques. To illustrate the proposed approach, an application case is given in next section to re-write interoperability requirements expressed in SBVR rules into TCTL to make their verification possible using model checker UPPAAL.

4. Application Case: Drug Circuit Process

The drug circuit is a critical process (*e.g.* it is mandatory to provide the right drug to the right patient in time and in right measure) inside a hospital. Although this process seems simple, its good execution depends primarily on good interactions among its participants and precisely interactions between resources used by the process. Thus, this process has to closely involve stakeholders in enhancing pharmacy practices and strengthening the role of the Medicine Committee (care unit). A drug circuit is typically composed of three main steps such as prescription, dispensation, and administration performed by both the care unit and the pharmacy following several tasks. These tasks and their interactions on the drug circuit are modelled thanks to a BPMN 2.0 modeller, as represented in the following figure.

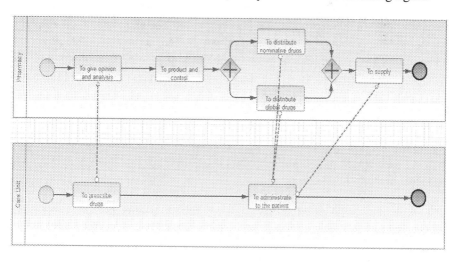

Figure 6. *Drug circuit process modelled with BPMN 2.0*

---

4 Cogitant, *CoGITaNT Version 5.2.0*, Reference Manual (http://cogitant.sourceforge.net), 2009.

To demonstrate the usability of this approach, it is proposed here to verify the following temporal interoperability requirements expressed by the user into natural language.

- "Medical practitioner is available to write a medical prescription when it is required."

- "Nurses confirm to the pharmacy the administration of drugs to the patient."

To make verification of these requirements possible, it is proposed, (1) to write them into SBVR rules in order to (2) re-write these ones into TCTL properties respecting the presented mapping rules. Let us consider the first interoperability requirement. This requirement considers the task "To prescribe drugs" and the resource "Medical practitioner". As a consequence, the end user can easily write or choose (into an interoperability requirement repository) an SBVR rule which corresponds to its initial requirement. Thus, the corresponding SBVR rule is expressed such as: "It is possible that a task is_starting and a resource is_available". Furthermore, the proposed approach offers the possibility to instantiate a rule with the consideration of elements that are present in the process. This one is then instantiated with the considered task and resource. For instance, it can be instantiated such as "*It is possible that a **To prescribe drugs** is_starting and a **MedicalPractitioner** is_available*". In the same way, the second requirement is expressed with the following SBVR rule: "It is possible that if a task is_stop then a task is_starting". Then, it is instantiated with the corresponding tasks: "To administrate to the patient" and "To supply". After the instantiation, the mapping can be done to get TCTL properties that can be verified using UPPAAL on the equivalent behaviour model as a Network of Timed Automata. For information, the previous SBVR rules are written into TCTL properties such as:

- "E<> Topresicibedrugs_.Start and Medicalpractitioner.Available"

- "E<> Toadministratetothepatient_.Stop imply Tosupply_.Start"

The different steps of the approach supported by an application tool are presented in the following figure.

Finally, the verification (checking task) of both requirements can be done and gives the result that the two properties are satisfied by the collaborative process model as presented on the following figure. Finally, it is to note that the mapping and the verification steps are not visible to the end user.

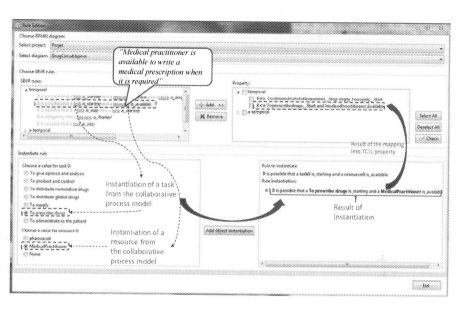

Figure 7. *From the instantiation of SBVR rules to the equivalent TCTL properties to verify*

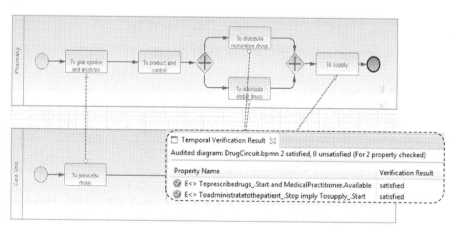

Figure 8. *Results of TCTL properties verification*

5. Conclusion

In Systems Engineering domain, requirements engineering is one of the most important step and precisely in writing requirements. Indeed, before any conception of a system, it is necessary to dispose of requirements that are (1) well written, (2) good and relevant to the studied domain and (3) verifiable. In our research work, these characteristics are applied in the field of collaborative process analysis to verify interoperability requirements. One of the most challenges is to allow the users - who do not necessarily have knowledge about the language used by the formal verification techniques - to write interoperability requirements correctly. The use of a language such as SBVR should help and guide these users in writing their requirements and overcome the problems of ambiguity, redundancy and inconsistency ... The presented approach, in its present development, provides a set of interoperability rules that are consistent with a vocabulary which currently includes approximately one hundred *"terms"* and *"verbs"*. This approach also allows (1) to instantiate the interoperability rules according to the studied collaborative process model and (2) to re-write them - using mapping rules established and demonstrated in this communication - into properties in order to make their verification possible using UPPAAL. Currently the audit coverage of verification using formal verification techniques is 20% of all identified interoperability requirements. Although the proposition of a set of interoperability rules (with SBVR), that the user can choose, facilitates the expression of a requirement and its verification, in the future, the goal is to enable the user to write directly its own interoperability rules with SBVR using the defined vocabulary. Furthermore, future works are related to the proposition of mapping rules to re-write interoperability requirements expressed with SBVR into Conceptual Graphs to make the verification of a-temporal requirements possible using the tool COGITANT.

6. References

All links in references are accessible on February 2012.

ANS/EIA 632, Standard: Processes for Engineering a System, 1998.

Behrmann G., David A., Larsen K. G., A tutorial on Uppaal. Department of Computer Science, Aalborg University, Denmark 2004

Chen D., Dassisti M., Elveaeter B., Enterprise interoperability framework and knowledge corpus – final report, Interop deliverable DI.3, may 2007.

Dasgupta P., A roadmap for formal property verification, Springer, 2010.

Edmund M., Clarke Jr., Grumbereg O., Doron A.P., *Model checking*. The MIT Press, 1999.

Estefan J. A., Survey of model-based systems engineering (MBSE) methodologies. Incose MBSE Focus Group, 25, p 1-70, 2007.

Fanmuy G., Llorens J., Fraga A., Requirements verification in the industry, CSDM 2011.

Grady J.O., *System Verification: proving the design solutions satisfies the requirements*, Academic Press, Elsevier editor, 2007.

ISO/IEC 15288:2008(E) / IEEE Standards 15288.2008 – Systems engineering – System life cycle processes (2nd edition), February 2008.

Itu-T Z.151, Telecommunication Standardization Sector Of Itu: Series Z: Languages And General Software Aspects For Telecommunication Systems - Formal description techniques (FDT) – User Requirements Notation (URN), Language, Definition Recommendation, 2008.

Mallek S., Daclin N., Chapurlat V., Formalisation and Verification of Interoperation Requirements on Collaborative Processes. 18th IFAC World Congress (IFAC'11), Milano, Italy, 2011.

Mallek S., Daclin N., Chapurlat V., The application of interoperability requirement specification and verification to collaborative processes in industry. International Journal Computers in Industry, COMIND, May 2012.

Mannion M., Keepence B., SMART Requirements. Software Engineering Notes Vol 20 N2. April 1995.

Open Management Group (OMG), Business Process Model and Notation (BPMN) - version 2.0, available online at: http://www.omg.org/spec/BPMN/2.0/, January 3rd 2011.

Open Management Group (OMG), Semantics of Business Vocabulary and Business Rules (SBVR) – version 1.0, available online at http://www.omg.org/spec/SBVR/1.0/PDF, January 2008.

REGAL, Requirements Engineering Guide for All, but applicable to Systems Engineering, 2008

Sowa J.F., Conceptual Graphs. IBM Journal of Research and Development, 1976.

Van lamsweerde A., Dardenne A., Delcourt B., Dubisy F., The KAOS Project : Knowledge Acquisition in Automated Specification of Software, AAAI Spring Symposium Series, American Association for Artificial Intelligence, 1991.

Zalta E. N., Basic Concepts in Modal Logic, Center for the Study of Language and Information, Stanford University 1995.

Index of Authors